A new book in
THE JOSSEY-BASS
HIGHER EDUCATION SERIES

MASTERING THE TECHNIQUES OF TEACHING

Students often complain of boring lectures, grim discussion sections, and unapproachable professors—with good reason. Few teachers receive instruction in how to present intellectually exciting lectures, lead engaging discussions, or relate to students in ways that promote motivation and independent learning. This new book by Joseph Lowman provides that instruction.

Drawing on direct observation of teaching, the useful literature on college instruction, and student accounts of outstanding professors, Lowman examines what constitutes good teaching and shows how to master effective teaching techniques. He covers the major activities (such as setting objectives and planning course work) as well as the fine details of teaching (such as opening a lecture in an interesting way, encouraging comments from the quiet student, and promoting rapport with individual students).

Lowman offers detailed advice on how to improve key communication skills such as speaking in front of groups and interacting well with students. He also provides tips on ways to structure classes and assignments toward specific aims, such as creating a stimulating lecture or thought provoking discussion. He reviews how teaching ability and the learning environment each contribute to the quality of teaching, details ways student ratings of instruction can be used

Mastering the Techniques of Teaching

to guide improvements, and recommends types of preparation and training needed to help graduate instructors and junior faculty improve their performance. Beginning instructors will benefit from reviewing what constitutes effective teaching.

THE AUTHOR

JOSEPH LOWMAN is associate professor of psychology, University of North Carolina at Chapel Hill. He received an award for his model of teaching (outlined in Chapter One) at the Sixth National Institute on the Teaching of Psychology to Undergraduates.

Joseph Lowman

Mastering the Techniques of Teaching

 Jossey-Bass Publishers

San Francisco • Washington • London • 1984

MASTERING THE TECHNIQUES OF TEACHING
by Joseph Lowman

Library of Congress Cataloging in Publication Data

Lowman, Joseph
  Mastering the techniques of teaching.

  Bibliography: p. 229
  Includes index.
  1. College teaching—United States.   I. Title.
LB2331.L68   1984   378'.125   83.49265
ISBN 0-87589-598-0

Manufactured in the United States of America

The paper in this book meets the guidelines for
permanence and durability of the Committee on
Production Guidelines for Book Longevity of the
Council on Library Resources.

JACKET DESIGN BY WILLI BAUM

FIRST EDITION
  First printing: March 1984
  Second printing: August 1984

Code 8413

The Jossey-Bass
Higher Education Series

To my parents,
Everett H. Lowman, minister
Eunice Drum Lowman, teacher

Preface

Few college teachers receive instruction in how to present intellectually exciting lectures, to lead engaging discussions, or to relate to students in ways that promote motivation and independent learning. This book is designed to fill that gap. The systematic course of instruction outlined here stresses fundamental teaching skills rather than the use of technological innovations such as individual or computer-assisted methods. While this book is primarily for less-experienced instructors of college undergraduates, such as graduate students and junior faculty, seasoned professors and the faculties of graduate, professional, and secondary schools will find much that is useful here. The text deals with the elements of teaching common to all academic disciplines — from anthropology to zoology — and is designed to help any college teacher acquire the skills necessary for outstanding classroom instruction.

This book is more than a collection of isolated techniques for good teaching. A model of effective college instruction is proposed in the first chapter that organizes the specific skills and suggestions presented later on. The model, which includes nine unique styles of classroom instruction, is based on two assumptions: The college classroom is a *dramatic arena* first and a setting for intellectual discourse second; and it is also a *human arena*, wherein the interpersonal dealings of students and instructors — many of them emotional, subtle, and symbolic — strongly affect student morale, motivation, and learning. Consequently, specific instruction is offered on how to speak well before groups and how to understand

and interpret the interpersonal behavior of college students and teachers. Speaking skills and classroom dynamics are examined before more traditional topics (lecturing, leading discussions, planning, evaluating) are discussed. The dramatic and interpersonal aspects of teaching are themes that reappear throughout the book; they serve both to suggest and to justify recommendations offered on specific matters.

Another theme also runs throughout: the college instructor as *skilled artist*. The aim of this volume is not to promote "adequate" or "competent" instruction but to start college teachers on the road to becoming masters of this long-standing art. Excellent teaching captivates and stimulates students' imaginations with exciting ideas and rational discourse. Student satisfaction and enjoyment are stressed here as important criteria for successful teaching. Outstanding instructors select and organize intellectually challenging content *and* present it in an involving and memorable way. They are also interpersonally sophisticated and promote student satisfaction and motivation. Though considerable relevant research is cited, teaching and learning are not thought of here as cold and technological but warm, exciting, and personal — decidedly *human processes* in which emotion and magic abound.

This book's perspective on effective college teaching is consistent with published research, but its origins are experiential and observational. It evolved over my thirteen years' experience as a college teacher of psychology and supervisor of graduate instructors. My approach has been sharpened during the past two years by observing and interviewing twenty-five college professors reputed to be masters at schools in the Southeast and New England. Those studied were nominated by faculty or administrators who were asked which faculty members were thought to be "superb classroom instructors." Two or three inquiries usually produced a common list of four or five top instructors at each college or university. All but a few of those I contacted agreed to being observed and interviewed. Almost without exception, I found the teaching they demonstrated to be of the highest quality: It was intellectually stimulating, clear, engaging, at times inspiring. The students of these instructors obviously held them in high regard. Having seen them in action, I would be eager to have my children in their classes and believe them worthy of emulation.

The purpose of observing these instructors was not to recognize teaching excellence but to identify a sample of highly skilled practitioners of the teaching art representing a variety of academic subjects to assess philosophies and collect specific teaching practices. My aim was not to write a generalized essay about the contemporary master teacher (as did Axelrod, 1973) or a position paper on faculty development. My goal was to seek practical information. A number of tricks of the trade and attitudes about students and teaching were generously shared by the men and women I interviewed, and I present them here for the benefit of all teachers who aspire to improve their classroom presentation.

The first four chapters are fundamental. In Chapter One, descriptions of notable college teachers and contemporary empirical research on college teaching are examined to answer the question "What constitutes masterful college teaching?" The two-dimensional model of effective teaching is described here in detail. Chapter Two examines the classroom as an interpersonal arena in which students and instructors attempt to meet basic psychological needs and reveal their underlying personalities in the process. Richard Mann's research on classroom dynamics (1970) receives special emphasis. Specific teaching techniques and suggestions for dealing with students based on these ideas are presented in Chapter Three. Chapter Four discusses speech, movement, and suspense in the classroom — including traditional stage techniques, exercises for analyzing and improving one's speaking skill, and ways of seeing classrooms and teaching through the eyes of a stage director.

The next two chapters are of central importance. Chapter Five concerns the lecture and discusses how to select, organize, and present content to promote understanding and retention. Chapter Six describes techniques for leading discussions in ways that involve students and foster independent thinking. Careful attention to the language college teachers use in discussion sessions is examined in light of the interpersonal psychology of classroom groups. Suggestions are offered for using discussion to promote rapport as well as to stimulate thought. Because most college teaching involves a combination of lectures and discussion, these chapters should interest experienced as well as novice instructors.

The next three chapters offer insights into traditional aspects of teaching: planning courses and individual class meetings (Chapter Seven); using reading, writing, and observational assignments (Chapter Eight); and evaluating students (Chapter Nine). The specific suggestions contained in these three chapters reflect this book's premise that the classroom functions as a dramatic and interpersonal arena as well as an intellectual one.

Chapter Ten sums up and extends the discussion in Chapter One by asking what combination of factors (individual talent, motivation, and supportive teaching environment) is associated with superior teaching. Chapter Ten also discusses ways evaluative student ratings can be used to help instructors improve and describes a comprehensive method for training college teachers. The chapter ends by addressing the question of why, given competing demands for scholarship and administrative labor, a college teacher should strive to excel in the classroom, especially teaching undergraduates.

The perspective of this book is fundamentally conservative. My aim is to teach instructors how to excel at traditional college teaching using group meetings in the lecture/discussion format. Instead of heralding technological innovation as the salvation of contemporary higher education, college teachers are encouraged to view teaching as an art and to rediscover and master the ancient skills that pertain to it.

Acknowledgments

I completed this book while on leave from the University of North Carolina at Chapel Hill, and I am thus grateful to the university administrators for being relieved of my duties to devote more time to scholarly activity. I am also indebted to Williams College, where I taught part-time during my leave. Williams stresses teaching excellence. Mark Hopkins "on a log" presided there during the nineteenth century. By coming to Williams to write a book on college teaching, I did not presume to bring coals to Newcastle, though this "Newcastle" proved an ideal place to write a book about "coal."

I am especially grateful to the outstanding teachers who allowed me to observe their classes and who shared their ideas freely. Because several asked that I not acknowledge them publicly, and since my search was never intended as a formal identification of the country's best instructors, I thank them here collectively. Meeting and watching these outstanding men and women was truly inspiring, one of the genuine pleasures of writing this book.

My wife, Betsy Caudle Lowman, deserves special thanks. Though I received my share of support and encouragement (the traditional laurels assigned spouses), Betsy's library research and sharp editing contributed much to the finished product. Betsy is an educational psychologist, and though she does not agree with all of the views on teaching and learning presented here, she contributed greatly to their communication. David Galinsky and John Schopler, colleagues at the University of North Carolina, also provided encouragement and specific guidance.

Chapel Hill, North Carolina   Joseph Lowman
February 1984

Contents

Contents

The Author

Joseph Lowman is associate professor of psychology at the University of North Carolina at Chapel Hill, where he has taught since 1971. He received his A.B. degree (1966) in psychology from Greensboro College and his Ph.D. degree in clinical psychology (1971) from the University of North Carolina at Chapel Hill. He was visiting associate professor at Williams College during the 1982–83 academic year.

Lowman's research interests have been in the area of family processes applied to the preventive goals of community mental health. He has published articles on measurement of family affective structure and grief intervention with parents of victims of sudden infant death syndrome. He is author of *Predicting Achievement: A Ten-Year Followup of Black and White Adolescents* (with David Galinsky and Bernadette Gray-Little, 1980).

Lowman is a practicing clinician specializing in marital therapy and has been heavily involved in training graduate students in teaching and clinical skills. He is director of Psychological Services, a community-oriented program of consultation and clinical services sponsored by the Department of Psychology at the University of North Carolina for the Chapel Hill community.

In January 1984, Lowman received the Frank Costin Award for Excellence at the Sixth National Institute on the Teaching of Psychology to Undergraduates, held in Clearwater Beach, Florida. The award was given for a presentation Lowman made based on Chapter One of this book.

Mastering
the Techniques
of Teaching

CHAPTER 1

❧❧❧❧❧❧❧❧❧❧❧❧❧❧❧❧❧❧❧❧❧❧

What Constitutes
Masterful Teaching?

> What all the great teachers appear to have in common is love of their subject, an obvious satisfaction in arousing this love in their students, and an ability to convince them that what they are being taught is deadly serious. *Epstein (1981, p. xii)*

If I were to ask you to picture a masterful college teacher, any of a number of images could come to mind. One image might be that of an awe-inspiring scholar lecturing from the stage of an amphitheater to an audience of students who are leaning forward to catch every word. Another might be that of a warm, approachable person seated at a seminar table among a group of students, facilitating an animated discussion, firmly but gently guiding the students to insight, awareness, self-confidence, and a heightened ability to think critically. Still another image might be that of an instructor engaged with one or two students in freewheeling sessions in the professor's study, over a glass of beer in the students' haunt, or in the laboratory — sessions in which each student has the opportunity to see at close range the way the teacher thinks and perhaps to glimpse an older person attempting to live a life committed to ideas and knowledge.

Varied as these images are, they are alike in fundamental ways. In each of them the instructor is pictured not while studying

1

alone or presenting a paper to learned colleagues but while interacting with students. The images all convey a sense of impact, of
an instructor having a potentially profound effect on the students.
In each, the students are emotionally as well as intellectually stimulated by the proceedings, whether as members of an audience or
in one-to-one relationships.

    If instruction is first rate, we can expect that several kinds
of learning will occur. The learning of facts, theories, and methods
will take place, to be sure. Beyond that, students will have the
chance to gain an understanding of relationships among varied
kinds of knowledge, sharpen their thinking and communication
skills, and receive a perspective from which to evaluate information critically. This learning meets the broad goals of liberal education.

    The three imaginary scenes illustrate and circumscribe the
subject of this book: masterful college teaching. The view of outstanding college teaching presented here emphasizes the traditional skills of lecturing and leading discussions. In contrast to
approaches that focus on detailed planning or rely on technological innovations, my perspective rests squarely on the assumption
that college teaching is and should be interpersonal, that it is
above all an enterprise involving human beings and their personalities, and that it is incapable of being reduced to mechanical
cause-and-effect relationships. This book provides detailed, practical instruction that a graduate instructor or professor can use to
fully master the art of college teaching.

    The premise of this book is that superior college teaching
involves two distinct sets of skills. The first is speaking ability.
This includes skill not only in giving clear, intellectually exciting
lectures but also in leading discussions. The second is interpersonal
skills. Such skills allow one to create the sort of warm, close relationships with one's students that motivate them to work independently. To become an excellent instructor, one must be outstanding in one of these sets of skills and at least competent in the other.
This first chapter considers the nature of the necessary and sufficient characteristics of masterful college teaching and presents the
two-dimensional model of effective college instruction upon which
the specific suggestions offered in this book are based.

Is Knowledge Taught or Learned?

If the members of an academic community are polled on ways to improve the quality of education, the students are likely to suggest hiring and promoting faculty who are better teachers, while the faculty probably will suggest admitting brighter, better prepared, and more motivated students. Whose opinion is the more valid? How responsible, in fact, are the faculty for how much students learn and for how insightful they become? How responsible are faculty members for students' proficiencies in fundamental skills — reading, thinking, writing, and speaking — or for students' attitudes toward learning? Who is most to blame when students pursue college merely for vocational rewards or social distractions? Conversely, who deserves credit for those rare students who not only master basic content and skills but understand a discipline in fresh and original ways and are somehow able to integrate the knowledge they have gleaned in various areas into a single, personal vision?

In *College Professoring,* O. P. Kolstoe answers these questions by asserting that "nobody can't teach nobody nothing" (1975, p. 61). He is correct. No instructor can *make* students learn. Consequently, college teachers cannot claim full credit when a student learns something well, nor must they carry all the blame when students fail to learn. Given students' freedom to take or leave what we instructors have to offer, it is crucial that we take pains to see that they become involved in learning. The importance of this motivational function is immense.

What differences among students require different teaching methods? Individual differences in students' abilities to do academic work are foremost. Students learn a subject at different rates and with strikingly different levels of completeness. College teachers are often amazed at the brilliance of some students and the shallowness of others. Regardless of the amount of work some students put into their studies, the complexity of their thinking fails to match that of others. Our society's contemporary social ethic tends to deny the importance of differences in fundamental academic ability, but psychological research (Guilford, 1968; Scarr, 1981) and the experience of college teachers support the influence of intelligence on the quality of student learning. How fully students apply themselves also affects how much they learn, but motivation can go only so far in compensating for differences in ability.

We as instructors cannot be held responsible for the differences in ability students bring with them, but we *are* responsible for motivating all students, from the gifted to the barely adequate, to do their best work and to love the learning experience. College teachers have as much power to dampen students' enthusiasm for learning as to excite it.

Student Memories of Excellent Instructors

Everyone can remember a few college teachers who stood out from the rest. If we were lucky, we had several who were superb; however, each of us likely had more poor teachers than outstanding ones. We can all remember classes that were boring and frustrating, when we dreaded going to class or meeting the professor in the hallway, when we ritualistically counted off the number of classes remaining in the term. But we also had classes we attended eagerly and finished with regret. Remembering notable positive and negative examples from our past is useful in choosing ideals to emulate.

There are also written descriptions of highly esteemed instructors to consider. A particularly interesting collection is Joseph Epstein's *Masters: Portraits of Great Teachers* (1981), which contains essays that originally appeared in *The American Scholar.* Professors such as Christian Gauss of Princeton, Ruth Benedict of Columbia, Morris Cohen of City College, Alfred North Whitehead of Harvard, John William Miller of Williams, Frederick Teggart of Berkeley, F. O. Mathiessen of Harvard, and Hannah Arendt of the New School are included. Subjects taught by these masters included philosophy, political thought, literature, theoretical physics, history, and anthropology.

Epstein's contributors remember their instructors as particularly skilled in specific teaching settings. The specialty for some was lecturing to large introductory classes attended primarily by freshmen and sophomores. For others it was leading senior or graduate seminars. In all cases, however, the writers remark on the instructors' influence and skill in tutorials or informal one-to-one interactions.

The most striking thing about these portraits of twentieth-century college teachers is the importance of their lecture or seminar performance to the level of personal and intellectual impact they had on their students. Not only did these men and women have a great deal to offer their students; they were also highly skilled at getting it across. As Epstein relates in his introduction to the collection, they had individual styles, using "socratic teasing, sonorous lecturing, sympathetic discussion; passionate argument, witty exposition, dramatics and other sorts of derring-do; plain power of personal example, main force of intellect, and sometimes even bullying" (p. xii).

Finally, it is clear that all of these outstanding instructors took their teaching responsibilities very seriously. They put a great deal of themselves into their classes and expected a similar level of commitment from their students. The tremendous personal satisfaction they received from their teaching was evident to their students.

Outstanding Teaching as Portrayed by Contemporary Research

The large body of findings from empirical research on college teaching presents a consistent picture of the outstanding teacher. Studying questionnaires that assess students' satisfaction with professors' teaching skills has been very fruitful for educational research, although the routine use of such student ratings to give instructors personal feedback, to provide public information for course selection, and to aid in faculty personnel decisions has become an increasingly controversial topic (Chandler, 1978; Marg, 1979; Raskin and Plante, 1979; Ryan and others, 1980).

Faculty ambivalence about student ratings of instruction probably stems from a number of concerns, some noble (preserving academic freedom and faculty power, promoting excellent scholarship), some petty (jealousy of others, excuses for receiving low ratings). Beyond this ambivalence about student ratings may lie a deeper ambivalence about the importance of quality teaching. Colleges and academic departments differ in the amount of actual encouragement and reinforcement (as opposed to ritualistic lip service) they give to quality undergraduate teaching. It is a sad commentary on contemporary higher education that among the varied arenas for achievement open to faculty (scholarship, grant-getting, consulting, or administration), classroom teaching ranks in importance near the bottom for many.

In contrast to this controversy among faculty, students very much favor evaluating their professors' teaching and consider it quite legitimate to do so (Gmelch and Glasman, 1978). Some teachers claim that student raters are not competent to evaluate instructors' command of subject or research expertise, and several studies indicate that students do not consider themselves able to evaluate professors in this way either (Kroman, 1978). Students do not generally believe they have sufficient knowledge to evaluate the depth of their instructors' understanding or the long-range importance of the instructors' contribution to a field. However, students *do* believe themselves capable of evaluating how well a college teacher taught them a subject and how much they were excited by the process of learning it. Regardless of individual attitudes toward the ways student evaluations are used, data from such instruments are highly relevant to the question of what constitutes outstanding teaching—especially in the eyes of instructional "consumers," the students themselves.

What does the research on student ratings of teaching effectiveness show about outstanding college instruction? Two types of research need to be discussed. One is studies relating overall teaching ratings to other kinds of information known about the classes, teachers, and students; this line of inquiry examines the external validity of the evaluation questionnaires. The other type of relevant research is studies focusing on relationships among the evaluation questions, with the aim of condensing the numerous items into the fundamental dimensions being measured.

In a number of studies the overall level of student ratings was found to have little if any relationship to the time of day courses were taught, the subject under consideration, the extent of the instructor's experience, or the size of the class. Though a number of studies have attempted to show that factors other than the instructor's teaching ability influence such ratings, on the whole it is clear that such variables have much less effect on ratings than the qualities students see in the individual college teachers (Braskamp, Ory, and Pieper, 1981; Freedman, Stumpf, and Aquano, 1979; Hoffman, 1978; Korth, 1979; Marsh, 1980; Marsh and Overall, 1981; Meredith, 1980).

A common notion among faculty is that ratings merely reflect instructor popularity, attractiveness, or grading stringency and have little to do with competence as a teacher. Arguing against this position are the results of studies showing that students consider the quality of teacher-student relationships to be second in importance to an instructor's ability to present material clearly (Abbott and Perkins, 1978; Reardon and Waters, 1979). The contention that students' ratings of teaching are functions of the amount of work an instructor assigns and the severity with which he or she evaluates it also is little supported by research (Abrami and others, 1980; Frey, 1978; Howard and Maxwell, 1980; Palmer, Carliner, and Romer, 1978; Peterson and Cooper, 1980). Difficult, demanding professors are just as likely to be given outstanding student evaluations as are less demanding ones. Teachers of "slide" courses (available in quantity at most schools) frequently receive poor or mediocre student ratings, even though seats in their classes may be in demand. It is not accurate to say that most students are so concerned about grades that their satisfaction with a teacher is related mainly to the difficulty of the course. Grading practices and the attitude with which work is assigned can adversely affect class morale, but satisfaction with an instructor's teaching comes more from positive emotions (excitement, enthusiasm, respect) than from the absence of negative ones.

A variation of this misconception about difficulty is the belief that if students enjoy or are excited by an instructor, the quality of that teacher's material must be second rate. The source of this puritanical attitude toward learning and teaching is difficult to pin down, but there is nothing compelling about arguments for its validity. Great teachers demonstrate a pleasure in learning and create a love of learning in their students. The best protection against being seen as a modern-day sophist is to aim for substance as well as enjoyment. Stiff, businesslike, or aversive behavior in a teacher is no assurance of quality instruction.

Professors who believe that high student ratings must reflect sweetened or watered-down knowledge often have the covert hope that students who rate them poorly will one day value them more than the instructors they found satisfying at the time. In a growing number of studies, however, evaluations of faculty made several years after graduation (up to ten years in one case) have been found to be remarkably consistent with the students' original opinions (Firth, 1979; Marsh and Overall, 1979; Overall and Marsh, 1980). Student ratings thus cannot be dismissed as reflecting merely the poor judgment of youth.

Even if student ratings are consistent over time and classes (professors typically receive similar ratings across different semesters and courses), some will argue that they have no relationship to the way the teachers' peers would evaluate their effectiveness. Available evidence runs contrary to this notion as well (Aleamoni, 1978; Ballard, Rearden, and Nelson, 1976). One study compared student ratings, professors' evaluations of their own teaching, and expert judges' ratings of videotape recordings of the professors' classroom presentations. A similar pattern for each teacher was found with each of the three types of measures. Those college teachers seen as excellent by their students were also rated highly by the judges and by themselves; weaker instructors also were rated similarly by all three groups. The only notable difference among the ratings was that students tended to rate the faculty members lower than did the instructors or their peers (Marsh, Overall, and Kesler, 1979). If anything, students may be tougher judges of teaching than faculty.

But what, some may ask, do student ratings of teaching have to do with student learning, regardless of whether the ratings are valid? Is not student demonstration of what they have learned the only outcome of importance in education? The fact that some studies have found student achievement to have little correlation with student ratings (Braskamp, Caulley, and Costin, 1979; Costin, 1978; Hoffman, 1979; Moody, 1976; Palmer, Carliner, and Romer, 1978) is sometimes interpreted as support for this argument against the importance of student ratings. More research indicates that teacher ratings *are* positively associated with student learning, however (see Cohen's 1981 meta-analysis).

The overall level of student ratings, then, is mostly a function of the degree of students' satisfaction with the instruction they receive. Internal analysis of the various questions on student rating questionnaires tells us what students find satisfying and dissatisfying about teaching. In factor analytic studies of ratings, as many as six or seven mathematically distinct factors and as few as two or three have been reported (Feldman, 1976; Mannan and Traicoff, 1976; Marques, Lane, and Dorfman, 1979; Tennyson, Boutwell, and Frey, 1978). It is instructive to examine the different types of factors (or fundamental dimensions) that have been described in published studies.

The most prominent factors concern clarity of presentation. Specific items in this category usually deal with whether an instructor presents material clearly and in a logically organized way that is easy for students who know little about the subject to understand. Some studies suggest that frequent use of concrete examples is associated with the ability to present material understandably. Another strong factor is the instructor's ability to stimulate students' thinking about the material rather than simply encouraging them to absorb it. A factor found prominent in most studies is the instructor's ability to stimulate enthusiasm for the subject, a skill frequently related to the teacher's personal enthusiasm.

Secondarily, student ratings have been shown to reflect the quality of interpersonal relationships between instructor and students. Some studies refer to this factor as student-teacher rapport; others discuss the degree to which students perceive an instructor as being concerned about them as individuals. Questionnaire items contributing to this category ask how warm students perceive an instructor as being and how much the instructor seems to enjoy sharing knowledge with them. Students may learn something important from a class in which the instructor shows a lack of respect or a negative and cynical attitude toward them, but it will be in spite of the teacher's attitude rather than because of it.

Thus, studies of student ratings of instruction present a consistent picture of outstanding and, by contrast, undesirable teaching. Fundamentally, such ratings reflect how well the instructor presents material and fosters positive interpersonal relationships with students. These two categories closely resemble Bales's classic definition of "task" and "maintenance" functions of group leadership (Bales, 1950; Bales and Slater, 1955). The two-dimensional model of effective college teaching discussed in the next section has been built around them.

A Two-Dimensional Model of Effective College Teaching

The specific lessons in this book are based on a two-dimensional model of teaching effectiveness in which the quality of instruction results from a college teacher's skill at creating both intellectual excitement and positive rapport in students, the kinds of emotions and relationships that motivate them to do their best work. These two kinds of skills are relatively independent, and excellence at either can ensure effective teaching with some students and in certain kinds of classes. A teacher who is accomplished at both is most likely to be outstanding for all students and in any setting.

Dimension I: Intellectual Excitement. Skill at creating intellectual excitement has two components: the clarity of an instructor's communications and their positive emotional impact on students. Clarity is related to *what* one presents, and positive emotional impact results from the *way* in which material is presented.

Clarity can be no better than the accuracy of content, of course, but it is assumed that most instructors have mastered their content adequately. Knowing material well is quite different from being able to present it clearly, however.

Knowledge is far more than the accumulation of isolated facts and figures. It involves a deeper understanding, an ability to "walk around" facts and see them from different angles. As Bloom argues in his classic taxonomy of educational goals (Bloom, Madaus, and Hastings, 1981), knowledge includes the ability to analyze and integrate facts, to apply them to new situations, and to evaluate them critically within the broad context available to the educated person. For a teacher to do an excellent job, he or she must be able to do far more than simply present the details of a subject — and students seem to know this. They like to receive an overall perspective and love to compare and contrast different concepts in addition to learning individual facts.

To be able to present material clearly, instructors must approach and organize their subject matter as if they too know little about it. They must focus on the early observations, essential milestones, key assumptions, and critical insights in a subject and not be distracted by the qualifications and limitations that most concern them as scholars. Being able to do this leads to the ability to explain a complex subject simply.

Outstanding teachers share this facility for clear exposition. Ernest Rutherford, the nineteenth-century British physicist, believed that he had not completed a scientific discovery until he was able to translate it into readily understandable language (Highet, 1950). Similarly, the ancient Greek and Hebrew teachers were masters of metaphor, making complex points by using simple language and concrete images. It is false snobbery to claim that one's knowledge is too grand to be understandable by a reasonably intelligent outsider. Outstanding college teachers are able to explain ideas and the connections between them in ways that make eminently good sense to the uninitiated.

Most students who receive consistently clear presentations will be able to correctly define, illustrate, and compare and contrast concepts. However, understanding material is not the same thing as being intellectually excited about it — being, for example, so highly engaged in a presentation as to be free from distracting thoughts and fantasies, surprised when the class period is over, or compelled to talk about the class to others during the day. To have this kind of impact on students, an instructor must do far more than present material clearly. In other words, for maximum effectiveness on this first dimension, clarity is necessary but not sufficient. It must be accompanied by virtuosity at speaking in front of groups. Why is this believed to be the case?

College classrooms are fundamentally dramatic arenas in which the teacher is the focal point, just as the actor or orator is on a stage. The students are subject to the same influences — both satisfactions and distractions — as any audience. As Epstein's portraits demonstrate, teaching is undeniably a performing art. Excellent teachers use their voices, gestures, and movements to elicit and maintain attention and to stimulate students' emotions. Like other performers, teachers must convey a strong sense of presence, of highly focused energy. Some teachers do this by being overtly enthusiastic, animated, or witty, while others accomplish the same effect with a quieter, more serious and intense style. The ability to stimulate strong positive emotions in students separates the competent from the outstanding college teacher.

Table 1 describes instructors at the high, middle, and lower ranges of this dimension of intellectual excitement as seen by an outside observer and as experienced by students. A teacher at the upper end of this dimension is an unusually skilled individual. To master college teaching to this degree, an instructor must be able to do more than prepare an accurate, well-organized synopsis of a content area. He or she must also be able to organize and deliver the material with the skill of a seasoned speaker. Such teaching is not simply showmanship or gratuitous attention-getting, as is assumed by disparagers who refer to it as "hamming it up," "showing off," or "faking it." As followup research on the famous Dr. Fox experiment has demonstrated, exciting teaching is not merely acting or entertaining (Kaplan, 1974; Meier and Feldhusen, 1979; Naftulin, Ware, and Donnelly, 1973; Perry, Abrami, and Leventhal, 1979; Williams and Ware, 1977). Entertainment involves the stimulation of emotions and the creation of pleasure for their own sakes. Outstanding teaching is characterized by stimulation of emotions associated with intellectual activity: the excitement of considering ideas, understanding abstract concepts and seeing their relevance to one's life, and participating in the process of discovery.

Dimension II: Interpersonal Rapport. In theory, the college classroom is strictly an intellectual and rational arena. In reality, a classroom is a highly emotional interpersonal arena in which a wide range of psychological phenomena occur. For example, students' motivation to work will be reduced if they feel that they are disliked by their instructor or controlled in heavy-handed or autocratic ways. All students are vulnerable to such disrupting emotions, and some students are especially sensitive to them. Also, like anyone else, students have a potential to react emotionally when they are being challenged and evaluated in group settings.

Table 1. Dimension I: Intellectual Excitement.

Level of Student Response	Observer's Description of Teaching	Impact on Students
High: Extremely clear and exciting	All content is extremely well organized and presented in clear language	Students know where the teacher is going and can distinguish important from unimportant material
	Relationships among specific concepts and applications to new situations are stressed	Students see connections among concepts and can apply them to new situations
	Content is presented in an engaging way, with high energy and strong sense of dramatic tension	Students have little confusion about material or about what the teacher has said
	Teacher appears to love presenting material	Students have a good sense of why concepts are defined as they are
		Ideas seem simple and reasonable, almost obvious, and are easily remembered
		It is very easy to pay attention to teacher (almost impossible to daydream)
		Class time seems to pass very quickly, and students may get so caught up in the ideas that they forget to take notes
		Stude ; experience a sense of excitement about the ideas under study and generally hate to miss class
		Course and teacher are likely to be described as "great" or "fantastic"
Moderate: Reasonably clear and interesting	Facts and theories are presented clearly within an organized framework	Students' understanding of most concepts is accurate and complete; they find it easy to take good notes
	Material is presented in an interesting manner, with a	Students can see connections between most

Table 1. Dimension I: Intellectual Excitement, Cont'd.

Level of Student Response	Observer's Description of Teaching	Impact on Students
Moderate	moderate level of energy	concepts and understand examples offered in class or in the text
	Teacher seems moderately enthusiastic and involved in teaching the class	Class is moderately interesting and enjoyable for most students
		Course and teacher are likely to be described as "good" or "solid"
Low: Vague and dull	Some material is organized well and presented clearly, but much is vague and confusing	Students have little idea of where the teacher is going or why material is presented as it is or even at all
	Most material is presented with little energy or enthusiasm	Students experience confusion or uncertainty frequently
	Teacher may seem to hate teaching the class and to be as bored with it as the students	Most students find taking notes difficult
		Students see few relationships among concepts and little relevance of content to their own experience
		Students find it difficult to pay attention, and class time may seem to pass very slowly
		Students frequently experience a sense of frustration or anger and may dread coming to class and welcome excuses not to go
		Course and teacher are likely to be described as "boring" and "awful"

Even students whose work is superior will become angry if testing and grading practices seem unfair.

Instructors are not immune to what happens in the classroom, either; many events can interfere with their enjoyment of teaching and lessen their motivation to teach well. Most professors have strong needs for achievement and success. The common desire to be at least average makes instructors' professional self-esteem vulnerable to their students' achievement and end-of-term ratings. This is especially true of those teaching for the first few times and for junior faculty facing tenure and promotion decisions. If students are not learning as much as expected, a teacher is only human in feeling threatened and being tempted to show anger by criticizing student efforts. Also, because they are human, instructors want to be liked and respected as individuals, and walking into a room of 50 to 100 strangers is guaranteed to raise interpersonal anxiety in anyone.

Psychologically, classes of students behave like other groups. The study of group phenomena has demonstrated convincingly that people in almost any kind of group situation, from digging a ditch to designing a research program, show predictable emotional reactions to their interactions with one another (Cartwright and Zander, 1960; Shaffer and Galinsky, 1974). Issues of *leadership* (or control) and *affection* (or the degree to which individuals feel respected and liked by others) will always be present.

College classrooms are no different. They are complex interpersonal arenas in which a variety of emotional reactions can influence how much is learned and how the participants feel about it. Richard Mann and his colleagues at the University of Michigan (1970) convincingly illustrated these college classroom phenomena by coding and analyzing individual comments of students and teachers in four introductory psychology classes. They offer a rich and insightful portrayal of this emotional substratum of college classrooms, detailing teacher roles, student types, and predictable changes over a semester (see Chapters Two and Three of this book).

Dimension II deals with an instructor's awareness of these interpersonal phenomena and with his or her skill at communicating with students in ways that increase motivation, enjoyment, and independent learning. This is done in essentially two ways. The first is to avoid stimulation of negative emotions, notably excessive anxiety and anger toward the teacher. The second is to promote positive emotions, such as the feeling that the instructor respects the students as individuals and sees them as capable of performing well. These sets of emotions strongly affect students' motivation to complete their assignments and learn material, whether their motivation is a desire for approval from the teacher or an attempt to meet their own personal standards.

Dimension II is especially critical to success in one-to-one teaching situations. For most settings, however, Dimension II is not as critical to outstanding teaching as Dimension I, although it does contribute significantly to class atmosphere and the conditions under which students are motivated to learn. It should also be noted that Dimension I refers almost totally to what an instructor does in the classroom, while Dimension II is significantly influenced by teacher-student interactions outside as well as inside class. Table 2 contains descriptions of teaching at three levels within this second dimension of teaching effectiveness.

Dimension II is admittedly more controversial than Dimension I. No one is likely to advocate that teachers be vague and dull, though some professors may believe that clarity is all that is required for good teaching and see attempts to be exciting or inspiring as demeaning. However, less consensus would be found among college faculties about the place on Dimension II where an outstanding instructor should fall—whether he or she should be autocratic and aloof or democratic and approachable. Some professors sincerely believe that recognizing students' personal reactions not only is irrelevant to teaching content but also impedes students' growth into mature and responsible adults because it indulges or coddles them. Other instructors are just as certain that a distant, autocratic style of teaching is a cruel vestige of the past and does not promote independent learning that is likely to continue when the class is over. Faculty holding this more humanistic position emphasize two-way interaction between teachers and students. Socrates is their ideal teacher, not the irascible "Herr Professor" of the nineteenth-century German lecture hall.

In contrast to faculty disagreement about Dimension II,

Table 2. Dimension II: Interpersonal Rapport.

Level of Interpersonal Rapport	Observer's Description of Teaching	Impact on Students
High: Extremely warm and open; highly student-centered; predictable	Teacher appears to have strong interest in the students as individuals and high sensitivity to subtle messages from them about the way they feel about the material or its presentation	Students feel that the teacher knows who they are and cares about them and their learning a great deal
	Teacher acknowledges students' feelings about matters of class assignments or policy and encourages them to express such feelings; may poll their preferences on some matters	Students have positive, perhaps even affectionate, thoughts about the teacher; some may identify with him or her strongly
	Teacher encourages students to ask questions and seems eager for them to express personal viewpoints	Students believe teacher has confidence that they can learn and think independently about the subject
	Teacher communicates both openly and subtly that each student's understanding of the material is important to him or her	Students are highly motivated to do their best, in part so as not to disappoint the teacher's high expectation of them
	Teacher encourages students to be creative and independent in dealing with the material, to formulate their own views	Students are likely to describe teacher as a "fantastic person"
Moderate: Relatively warm, approachable, and democratic; predictable	Teacher is friendly and personable to students but makes no great effort to get to know most of them	Students have little fear or anxiety about the teacher or their ability to perform successfully in the class
	Teacher announces policies and discusses student reactions to them if the students complain	Students know what the teacher expects of them but feel little responsibility to go beyond that level of performance
	Teacher responds to student questions and personal	Students are reasonably well motivated to complete

Table 2. Dimension II: Interpersonal Rapport, Cont'd.

Level of Interpersonal Rapport	Observer's Description of Teaching	Impact on Students
Moderate	comments politely and without apparent irritation	assigned work and to perform well
	Teacher is relatively consistent and predictable in behavior toward students; gives ample notice before announcing requirements or changes in schedule	Students are likely to describe teacher as a "nice person" or a "good guy" or "nice woman"
Low: Cold, distant, highly controlling; may also be unpredictable	Teacher shows little interest in students as persons; knows few of their names and may fail to recognize many of them out of class	Students feel teacher has no personal interest in them or their learning; some students may believe teacher actively dislikes them or is "out to get them"
	Teacher is occasionally sarcastic or openly disdainful about students, their level of performance in the course, or their nonacademic interests	Students believe teacher has a low opinion of their ability or motivation to learn course content
	Teacher seems irritated or rushed when students ask questions or drop by, sometimes even during office hours	Students generally are afraid to ask questions, and only the boldest will voice a personal opinion
	Teacher simply announces requirements and policies and seems defensive or angry if they are questioned	Students are motivated to work primarily by a fear of failure or ridicule by the teacher and see assignments as something the teacher imposes on them
	Teacher may be inconsistent and unpredictable, for example, by smiling when saying insulting things about students, by giving backhanded compliments, or by announcing assignments or requirements at the last minute	Even if students are interested in the content, they may dread studying it or may rethink their previous desire to major in the subject
		Students feel uneasy in class or around the teacher and may sometimes experience significant anxiety or anger
		Students are likely to describe teacher as a "bitch" or "bastard"

the summary of research on student ratings shows that there is little question about which end of this continuum most students prefer. They prefer more democratic and approachable teachers (Uranowitz and Doyle, 1978) — provided first that the teachers are clear and interesting. Research indicates that students give relatively more weight to Dimension I than Dimension II (Keaveny and McGann, 1978; Marques, Lane, and Dorfman, 1979).

Combining Dimensions I and II. Table 3 presents the full model in which Dimensions I and II form nine combinations or cells, each representing a unique style of instruction associated with different probabilities that students will learn to their fullest potential from instructors following that style. The nine styles are numbered in ascending order of overall effectiveness, with cell 1 the least effective and cell 9 the most effective.

Keep in mind that the nine styles of teaching are generalizations and will not describe every college teacher exactly; individual instructors may show elements of more than one type. Instructors in cells 1, 2, and 3 are less than fully competent. The "Adequates" will be minimally successful in lecture classes and with relatively compliant students but need increased interpersonal skill to expand the range of students and situations in which they will be effective. Similarly, the "Marginals" need to improve their ability to present material. Teachers in cells 4 and 6 represent the most unusual combinations of skills. The "Socratics" excel at promoting independent work and will be ideal for students and subjects well suited to seminars. Their approach will be inadequate in larger classes requiring lecturing, however. Conversely, the "Intellectual Authorities" will be able to create intellectual excitement and promote achievement in students who are confident in their own abilities and comfortable with these instructors' distant manner, but younger or less able students are likely to experience anxiety under such instruction. An "Intellectual Authority" is more likely to be respected than loved by most students.

All instructors in cells 7, 8, and 9 are outstanding individuals who have unquestionably attained excellence at college teaching. Students are likely to describe "Masterful Lecturers" as those who captivate them by sheer intellectual force and motivate them to learn material because it seems a terribly important and excit-

Table 3. Two-Dimensional Model of Effective College Teaching.

Dimension I: Intellectual Excitement	Dimension II: Interpersonal Rapport		
	Low: Cold, distant, highly controlling, unpredictable	*Moderate:* Relatively warm, approachable, and democratic; predictable	*High:* Warm, open, predictable, and highly student-centered
High: Extremely clear and exciting	*Cell 6: Intellectual Authorities* — Outstanding for some students and classes but not for others	*Cell 8: Masterful Lecturers* — Especially skilled at large introductory classes	*Cell 9: Complete Masters* — Excellent for any student and situation
Moderate: Reasonably clear and interesting	*Cell 3: Adequates* — Minimally adequate for many students in lecture classes	*Cell 5: Competents* — Effective for most students and classes	*Cell 7: Masterful Facilitators* — Especially skilled at smaller, more advanced classes
Low: vague and dull	*Cell 1: Inadequates* — Unable to present material or motivate students well	*Cell 2: Marginals* — Unable to present material well but will be liked by some students	*Cell 4: Socratics* — Outstanding for some students and situations but not for most

ing thing to do. Students might also describe these cell 8 instructors as a bit mysterious — persons they would like to know better. Many students do their best work under such a teacher. However, younger students or those with limited academic skills and confidence are less likely to benefit maximally from what this instructor has to offer.

In contrast, students of "Masterful Facilitators" feel close to their instructors. Such instructors are likely to be able to stimulate independent work of high quality. They are sought out by students after class and are particularly effective in smaller, more advanced classes characterized by considerable discussion. "Masterful Facilitators" are also likely to become important in their students' personal lives; students may come to them for advice or attempt to model their lives or careers after them. Both "Masterful Lecturers" and "Masterful Facilitators" have their fortes, but each is capable of providing competent instruction in all situations.

The rare "Complete Masters" of cell 9 are able to perform superbly in both lecture hall and seminar room and to modify their approach so as to motivate all students, from the brilliant to the mediocre. Few if any of Epstein's portraits reach this degree of flexibility; of teachers I interviewed, I can classify in this cell only one or two.

Most students will do well under any cell 7, 8, or 9 instructor, and are likely to rate all these masterful types highly, but they may prefer one type or the other. Some will be more comfortable with the impersonality of "Masterful Lecturers," preferring to learn someone else's view of the content. On the other hand, students desiring to express their creativity, to tackle learning more independently, or to have more personal relationships and individualized instruction will prefer "Masterful Facilitators."

Outstanding instructors, then, are those who excel at one or both of these two dimensions of teaching effectiveness. Every competent teacher must have at least moderate skill in each dimension, but there is considerable room for variation. My model assumes that some students will learn more under one style of instruction than another but that all students will learn more and prefer college teachers in the masterful cells. It also assumes that instructor skill on Dimensions I and II is distributed normally;

that is, that most teachers are competent, falling at the midrange of each dimension, and relatively few are above or below the norm. The lessons in the following chapters are designed to help those with less than adequate skills to improve and those already in the midrange to attain excellence.

CHAPTER 2

Understanding
Classroom Dynamics

> The proper goal of the college classroom is 'work,'
> and only by understanding the obstacles to work that
> flow from the complexity of the teacher's task, the
> students' diversity, and the nature of group develop-
> ment can the teacher make his optimal contribution
> to this goal. *Mann (1970, p. vi)*

We human beings are more capable of reason and logical, non-
emotional thinking than other mammals, but we are also capable
of emotional and irrational thinking. Emotions are a universal
part of our lives. In the process of evolution, the emotional
responsiveness so essential in the fight-or-flight situations of pre-
history has not entirely disappeared as new behaviors have been
developed. Nothing from the past is lost as species evolve; new
adaptations are selected and added on (Alcock, 1979). It is no surprise, then, that our uniquely human ability to think rationally,
with little emotion, coexists with a highly emotional heritage.

Human emotion in college education is a theme running
throughout this book, but two chapters, this chapter and Chapter
Four, deal with it especially. This chapter explores the many ways
that emotions influence interpersonal rapport in the classroom. It
discusses the positive emotions that encourage maximum effort
and confidence and the negative emotions that sap both. The

relevance of instructor and student emotional needs to teaching and learning, and the strategies teachers and students show for handling emotions, are discussed in detail. Chapter Four deals with the role of emotions in creating intellectual excitement and the dramatic techniques available to college teachers for stimulating their students.

Even though college classrooms are dramatic arenas with intellectual purposes, faculty members and students have far more important relationships than that of performer and spectator. College courses are settings in which myriad interpersonal encounters, some fleeting and others involved, unavoidably occur between the participants. As in all interpersonal encounters, college teachers and students use strategies to maximize positive and minimize negative feelings about themselves. Though the groups have different interpersonal concerns, largely resulting from the different amounts of power they have in the classroom context, both seek to satisfy basic needs for affection and control. The ways in which instructors and students meet these needs produce predictable interpersonal phenomena that influence the degree to which and the conditions under which students are motivated to master the content placed before them.

Attitudes That Influence Classroom Interpersonal Phenomena

Student Attitudes. Students vary greatly in the way they approach the work assigned and the degree to which they apply their intellectual talents. Some will do anything asked of them, dutifully reading every assignment on time and memorizing every definition written on the board. Such students may be frustrating to a teacher, however, because of their excessive dependency. Dutiful and compliant students are often unduly anxious about the way their work will be evaluated.

In contrast, some students are contentious and distrustful. This attitude is evident in their tone of voice when they object to instructor comments or in the fatalistic little jokes they make about grades or the value of an education. Such a student might say, for example, "What good is psychology, anyway? What can you really prove about the reasons people behave as they do?" The consistently cutting edge of class comments, openly critical questions about content (often delivered with quick glances that seek support from fellow students), and the avoidance of eye contact and one-to-one encounters with the professor reveal such students as fundamentally angry and distrustful of instructors as authority figures.

Fortunately, most students expect college teachers to be warm and friendly, and they are friendly in return. They smile frequently during class and talk warmly and informally after class. Friendly students are much more likely than their more fearful or angry peers to elicit from a teacher the positive behaviors they seek.

There is an important psychological principle at work here. Both students and instructors generally will be treated by others as they expect to be treated. Research on interpersonal perceptions and behavior has clearly demonstrated an interactive effect: Personal attitudes tend to produce reciprocal attitudes in others (Jones, 1972; Altman and Taylor, 1973). For example, if a clerk in a store believes that customers are rude and inconsiderate, this attitude is likely to be evident, however subtly, and customers can be expected to be less friendly and considerate toward this employee than they might be in general. This principle of human interaction has been demonstrated in most interpersonal relationships, and college teachers and students are no exceptions.

Teacher Attitudes. Just as students vary in what they expect from instructors, so instructors vary in what they expect from students. From the beginning of a course, some teachers trust students to be able, motivated, and enthusiastic about course content. On the other hand, some college teachers have little initial faith in most students' intellectual ability, commitment, or honesty. Fortunately, most instructors are not so bound by initial expectations that their attitudes toward particular students cannot change as the term progresses.

Instructors also have quite understandable emotional reactions to the ways students behave in and out of class. Anyone is likely to become angry at a student who calls at 11 P.M. to beg off from the next day's exam and then fails to report for a scheduled make-up. It is also the unusual person who is immune to the urge to give a little extra attention or grading consideration to a student whom he or she finds attractive.

Class Morale. On occasion the class as a group appears to become caught up in common emotional concerns. This is most frequently seen as overall class morale — how eager the students' faces appear on a given day, how responsive they are to questions and discussion. Class meetings just before and after exams are especially likely to demonstrate low morale, even an undercurrent of hostility toward the instructor. Many classes show a gradual decline in student enthusiasm and involvement over the course of the term, often with few cues as to why a good beginning turned sour. Group morale may even deteriorate so much that an overt rebellion occurs, with a few brave leaders petitioning the instructor, dean, or department chairman on behalf of the entire class to protest some assignment or grading practice that the class considers unreasonable or unfair. Fortunately, such occurrences are rare.

College teacher morale may also vary over time. For many it wanes as the semester progresses, and, if an overt rebellion of the kind described above occurs, it may drop painfully low. Some teachers grow increasingly disappointed with student performance and mark time in the hope of a better class next term. But for others, the opposite pattern may emerge: Their satisfaction with a class grows steadily, and they find themselves bragging about what fine students they have this term. The last meeting of such classes can bring a genuine sense of loss to the instructor, of sadness that the course is ending. This change in morale, like the others previously described, is both predictable and understandable.

These, then, are some of the attitudes and interpersonal phenomena likely to appear in college classes. Some are a direct result of the individual psychology and social roles of students and teachers. Others result from the interaction of student and instructor concerns, the group dynamics that produce overall class morale or atmosphere.

The remainder of this chapter discusses, in greater detail, the major predictable interpersonal phenomena seen in college classes. The psychology of college teachers is discussed first, then the psychology of students, and finally their collective or group interactions over time. The interpersonal dimension of college classrooms surveyed here will be referred to repeatedly in subsequent chapters. For example, Chapter Three builds on these ideas to suggest specific teacher strategies for creating an engaging and satisfying group atmosphere that is likely to motivate students to work independently.

The Psychology of College Teachers

Some college teachers gain little satisfaction from meeting their classes and welcome the opportunity to spend their time at other academic pursuits, especially the scholarly research on which reputation, promotion, and salary depend. But many — in fact, I suspect, the majority — *do* receive considerable personal satisfaction from classroom teaching, though the culture in many schools and departments does not encourage them to express such satisfaction openly. Other than the mixed blessing of hearing parents brag to their friends about "my child, the college professor," what are the common satisfactions that instructors gain from classroom teaching?

Sources of Satisfaction. Student recognition of an instructor's accumulated knowledge about a subject is certainly important to all teachers. Teaching classes provides an opportunity to display knowledge and to validate implicitly the time and effort spent in acquiring it. Discussing one's area of expertise with colleagues and presenting papers at national meetings provide similar arenas, but having a fresh audience, one not yet aware of how much the instructor knows about a subject, offers more certain acknowledgement of subject mastery.

Teaching students what one knows also provides the warm satisfaction that comes whenever one gives away something one values, as when one purchases a present or composes a poem for a special occasion. Teaching is giving knowledge away, and many college teachers are compulsive sharers of what they know, eager to pass on insights or facts to willing listeners. Teaching at any level is pleasurable for such individuals. People who find little joy in giving to others are likely to find less personal satisfaction in teaching than those who are intrinsically generous.

For some college teachers, the opportunity to be in charge is attractive. In the classroom, instructors are absolute monarchs with considerable power to reward, punish, and control. Some find it satisfying to give students freedom to direct their own learning; for them, pleasure comes from subtly controlling (or motivating) students to behave autonomously. Others attempt to satisfy needs for power by controlling students directly. They try to preserve as much power for themselves as possible, lest students slip beyond their influence.

Though classroom instruction inevitably requires public performance, being front and center is not universally exhilarating. Many instructors find teaching pleasurable *in spite of* the fact it must be done standing alone in front of a group. Others, however, clearly relish the chance to captivate, to entertain, to astonish the audience that appears regularly to hear them. A frequently heard homily about college teaching is that "all great teachers are hams at heart." It is not essential for teachers to be "hams" to be outstanding. Instructors who do enjoy performing are more likely to find college teaching rewarding, however.

Many instructors take genuine delight in identifying, recruiting, and guiding talented students into their field. Satisfaction from this source usually increases as a teacher matures, but even graduate instructors are pleased when an able student decides to major in their subject. It is not surprising that such gatekeeping activities can be rewarding: Who would not be flattered by having a student aspire to follow in his or her footsteps?

Some college teachers derive satisfaction from forming personal relationships with their students as a group. To help create such intimacy, they may make disclosures in class about their careers, their families, or even their pets. No doubt some instructors dwell on themselves to excess in class ("Let's talk about my favorite subject — me"), but a judicious number of personal disclosures can make an instructor seem more human and less forbidding to students as well as contributing to satisfaction for the teacher.

Other instructors encourage individual relationships with particular students by offering them teaching or research assistantships. Many students will eagerly take advantage of an opportunity to get to know the professor well. Students encourage such relationships on occasion by inviting professors to meals, parties, or artistic or athletic events. Developing personal relationships, many of them lasting, with students is one of the most pleasant fringe benefits of an academic career.

College teaching offers many potential satisfactions. However, these satisfactions can easily be tainted or even totally destroyed by negative feelings about students and teaching.

Sources of Dissatisfaction. Perhaps the most common way in which students reduce a teacher's satisfaction is by failing to master course content sufficiently. At some time every instructor is likely to react with anger when reading student work that woefully misses the mark. Setting high standards can motivate students to do their best work, but an instructor who takes these goals too seriously is often doomed to disappointment. Even in the best of schools and classes, the quality of performance will vary from student to student, and the teacher who takes too much responsibility for what his or her students learn is likely to find teaching frustrating. Having high but realistic expectations for student achievement will help to preserve an instructor's enthusiasm for teaching.

College teachers' needs to control students also are frequently frustrated. They put considerable demands on busy students and are legitimately fearful that the students will not do what they ask. Course management fears nag any instructor, but such fears may be especially strong in teachers who are inexperienced or are planning a new semester after an unsuccessful one: "What if the students do not do the reading? What if their papers are superficial or turned in late (or not at all)? What if other faculty see me as weak and indulgent?" Questions relating to student classroom behavior also crop up: "What if they do not pay attention in class? What if they do not even come to class? What if they do not respond to my attempts to elicit questions or discussion?" College teachers inescapably are authorities within the school or university organization, and they are responsible for enforcing rules and maintaining order. If the methods of controlling students used by an instructor are ineffective, teaching will not be satisfying.

Dissatisfaction resulting from student failure to learn adequately or submit sufficiently to an instructor's control is related to the formal role of the college teacher, to the duties that teachers are paid for and are clearly expected to perform. Students also have tremendous potential to sour the pleasures of teaching by rejecting an instructor in other ways, both personally and professionally.

It is easier to illustrate professional rejection and for an instructor to acknowledge disliking it. Because every college teacher has spent considerable time and energy mastering and promoting a subject, it is difficult to find pleasure at sharing this knowledge if students state or imply that the subject is boring or irrelevant.

When students reject course content, it is easy to dismiss their scorn as reflecting their superficiality, but it is more difficult for an instructor to protect feelings of professional and personal esteem when students evaluate his or her teaching or intellectual competence negatively. Even a successful researcher who acknowledges to trusted colleagues his mediocre teaching skills will find it painful to be rated poorly by students. Though students are much more likely to attack course content or teaching skill than personal academic abilities, teachers are also vulnerable to classroom innuendos, overheard remarks between students, or anonymous direct attacks (such as insulting notes slid under office doors) that denigrate the instructor's content mastery or intelligence.

Instructor satisfaction and dissatisfaction affect the quality of teaching and learning in several ways. First, satisfaction and dissatisfaction interact with each other. Dissatisfaction obviously reduces the satisfaction a teacher receives. The reverse is also true: The more satisfaction instructors gain from students and teaching, the less vulnerable they are to occasional negative evaluations.

The kinds of activities that teachers find satisfying also tend to change over time. Initially, joy at having expertise and control confirmed when students respond enthusiastically to a given lecture or discussion is rewarding. These simple pleasures become less satisfying once the novelty and initial challenge of teaching wears off. Individuals who continue to gain personal and professional satisfaction from classroom teaching are those who realize the widest possible range of satisfactions from it. Understanding the individual and group psychology of classrooms also increases a college teacher's resistance to the kinds of perplexing, even troubling, behavior that students sometimes show.

Types of Behavior Toward Students. Educators have long tried to define teaching styles and to measure how much learning each produces. In an excellent study of college classrooms, Richard Mann and his colleagues at the University of Michigan (1970) applied a system created for coding implied emotional and relationship messages of members of psychotherapy and self-analytic groups to four small (twenty-five students) introductory psychology classes. Each graduate instructor had taught the course only once previously. Data consisted of tape recordings of all class meetings over the semester and questionnaires given to instructors and students. Observers also attended all classes and took notes on nonverbal behavior. Those interested in a technical description of the Mann group's methods and results should consult their book, *The College Classroom: Conflict, Change, and Learning.*

In one of their studies, the Mann group used cluster analysis to concentrate the thousands of ratings of comments from all four instructors into seven independent clusters or dimensions, each of which describes a common type of behavior toward students. For our purposes, their seven dimensions can be further reduced to three categories: the amount of control used, the quality of affect shown, and the instructor's degree of satisfaction with the class.

The first of two clusters in the control category describes how actively the teachers directed classroom proceedings (lectured versus reacted to student questions or discussion). The second control cluster reflects the interpersonal distance the instructors tried to maintain between themselves and students; some chose to maximize the distance by being formal, while others minimized it by treating students almost as equals. When the size of these clusters in Mann's analyses is considered, it is clear that the way college teachers control students is the most prominent feature of their interpersonal behavior in classrooms.

How instructors felt about students was also of considerable importance, since three of the seven clusters are related to quality of affect. Teacher punitiveness — being openly critical of students or trying to make them feel guilty ("Your exams show that you are not taking this course seriously") — was an important dimension. Positive instructor affect appeared as two independent clusters, teacher warmth and teacher enthusiasm.

The third category of teacher behaviors identified by Mann reflects the way the instructors felt about themselves and their teaching. The two specific clusters associated with this category are expressed satisfaction (or dissatisfaction) with teaching ("I am pleased that we are only two classes behind schedule") and apprehension about the future ("I am afraid we will not have time to finish the syllabus if we do not move on").

Mann's analyses demonstrate that there is significant variation in the quality of affect that teachers show toward students, the type of control they attempt to use, and the degree of satisfaction they express. How do these teacher behaviors affect students and learning?

Affective and Control Messages. Studies of human communication demonstrate that all of us communicate far more than we say — or think we say — in words (Watzlawick, Beavin, and Jackson, 1967). The tone of voice, the degree of inflection or emphasis, the expression on our faces, and the gestures we make communicate as much or more than our words. The context of particular statements also can affect, or even change completely, the way those statements are received by others. For example, an instructor who remarks to a class, "I am glad you took the time to read the assignment — this time," offends by adding "this time" to the compliment. If the class had been chided at its last meeting for failing to read the assignment, some students would find today's comment sarcastic even if the qualifier were omitted. A college teacher's history of comments, then, influences the way given words or gestures may be taken by students.

Added to this complexity are the affective (relating to the way the instructor feels about students) and control messages that verbal statements can carry. The following illustration will help to clarify this point. Suppose an instructor wishes to have his or her students review the literature relevant to a topic of their choosing and write a term paper presenting what they have learned. The most emotionally neutral way to announce this requirement would be "I want you to write a paper covering the major approaches to any topic in the course you wish." No affective attitudes toward the students or their likelihood of success and no controlling messages are implied by this statement.

If the instructor adds affective messages such as "I think you will enjoy selecting your own topics and thinking independently about them. I will look forward to reading your papers," he or she conveys the expectation that the students will both enjoy and succeed at writing their term papers. In contrast, if the instructor adds, "I want you to show some independent thinking for a change and not just give me ideas you have copied out of books," students could accurately surmise that the instructor has little faith in their ability to think independently or conduct themselves honorably and is not looking forward to reading the papers. Though these examples are more obvious than those commonly occurring in college classes, they illustrate how the little addenda to instructor communications can determine their emotional impact on students.

The same assignment could also have been announced in a much more controlling way. More dominating but emotionally neutral instructions might be, "I expect you to write a paper covering the major approaches to any important topic in the course. Be sure to do a thorough literature search and identify major themes or issues — see the reference desk at the library if you do not know how to do this — and use the last half of your paper to compare and contrast the major points." By giving so many specific instructions on the way to proceed with the assignment, the instructor assumes a more dominant position with the students and consequently makes them more dependent.

This announcement is also more directive than the original one because of two subtle changes in wording. The substitutions of "I expect" for "I want" and "any important topic" for "any topic. . . you wish," though apparently trivial, emphasize the teacher's role as a controlling and evaluative authority. It is more controlling to "expect" than to "want" and to imply that the students should pick a topic that *the instructor* thinks is important.

Teacher messages that are overtly controlling or emphasize the hierarchical power relationship between teacher and student encourage students to be less independent. Whether a student finds such remarks positive or negative depends on how much the student likes having things structured by someone else; but extensive directions are more likely to be appreciated by anyone when associated with affection than when coupled with rejection.

The Psychology of Students

Though college students are not children, some college-age students *are* immature — more adolescent than adult. Some may be acutely sensitive to a teacher's criticism or control. Mature or not, all students want to be regarded positively and controlled democratically and will bristle if these needs are unduly frustrated. This section focuses on the emotional needs of college students, the typical classroom conflicts engendered by these needs, and individual differences in the ways students attempt to meet them. As with the section on the psychology of college teachers, the goal of this section is to increase instructor awareness of the emotional interactions of the classroom so that this knowledge can be used to enhance motivation and learning.

Sources of Satisfaction. Every faculty member is aware that students differ in their interest in academics and motivation to achieve in school. A few students are so narrowly invested in the world of ideas that they completely disdain nonintellectual activities such as athletic contests and social events. Other students find little pleasure in reading, writing, thinking, or attending class, though their academic performance may be adequate. However, most students at any school have at least a modicum of intellectual curiosity and find learning pleasurable for its own sake. They feel satisfaction from discovering answers, excitement at seeing how their minds work, appreciation of the arts, and confirmation of their ideas through discovery that others have interpreted human experience in ways similar to their own.

College study also provides opportunities to meet the need for mastery, for meeting and successfully overcoming challenges.

This need also can be satisfied through nonacademic pursuits such as athletics or student politics, of course, and many students, unfortunately, have never learned to satisfy it through schoolwork.

A related source of satisfaction is bettering one's peers in competition. Competition for high grades and academic honors is the form of competition most apparent in the classroom. Experienced teachers appreciate the effort and high achievement that competitive needs can produce, but they also know that learning primarily to surpass other students does not lead to lasting satisfaction and can cause selfish or harmful behavior toward others. Skillful instructors are able to channel student needs for competition into activities that promote learning rather than encouraging students to study just for marks.

The three kinds of student satisfaction discussed thus far are all associated with the general human need to control events around us (White, 1963). By seeking information, mastering problems, and besting our fellows, we control our environment. Students also desire to have control in the classroom. Most do not attempt to direct the proceedings overtly, however, although a few are habitual rebels.

It is easier for both compliant and rebellious students to feel in control with a predictable teacher than with a capricious one. Research on parental attitudes (Martin, 1975) and on leadership styles (Cartwright and Zander, 1960; Gibbard, Hartman, and Mann, 1973) has shown that inconsistency creates almost as much anxiety as rejection. Most students are likely to find a class satisfying if they believe that they can successfully meet the demands of a challenging but predictable instructor.

Primarily because they are human but secondarily because they are late adolescents, college students need affection and approval from others, especially authority figures. These needs are potent sources of satisfaction in the classroom, as shown by the importance of items related to such needs in the factor analyses of student evaluation forms. Foremost among these affectional needs is the desire for a personal relationship with a college teacher. Students' often-expressed preferences for smaller classes may reflect this wish. As Kirkpatrick Sale argues so well in

Human Scale (1980), largeness in human institutions, whether neighborhoods, businesses, or governments, breeds an impersonality that few people find satisfying. College classrooms are no different.

In addition to a personal relationship, students desire to have their instructor think well of them. Students need affection from college teachers, not as parents or lovers, but as adults who approve of them as learners and persons. Students find learning much more satisfying when they believe that their instructor likes and trusts them.

Students also need the approval of classmates, and not only as friends or dates. Students wish to be seen by their classmates as academically able and also, interestingly, as keeping an appropriate distance from the teacher. Most students fear making comments in class that their classmates may view as foolish or as "sucking up to the teacher." Though most classroom satisfaction of students' affectional needs comes from teachers, a significant portion comes from other students, especially as individuals become emotionally invested in the class over time.

Sources of Dissatisfaction. Like college teachers, students are vulnerable to a number of potential dissatisfactions in their academic lives. The mildest dissatisfaction students are likely to experience in the classroom is the absence of a personal relationship with their instructor. Physical barriers such as size of hall and number of other students can prevent even the most rudimentary relationship from forming. Smaller classes alone do not guarantee that students will experience a satisfying relationship, however. Many instructors do not remember students' names, and a few may not recognize students who drop by their office or greet them when coming out of a movie. Most students will allow the teacher several encounters in which to learn to recognize them and be able to recall their names, but almost all will be disappointed if the teacher does not remember them once the school term is well under way.

Frustration of student need for control is more likely to create significant dissatisfaction than is the absence of a personal relationship with the instructor. Poorly organized or unpredictable classes are especially frustrating. When students are unsure what topics will be covered, what the assignments are, or what the teacher's objectives are, they miss the sense of control that comes from knowing why the challenges that await them were selected and what rules will govern their evaluation.

Student needs for mastery can be frustrated in several ways. Uninteresting or confusing presentations can dampen almost any student's curiosity and desire to seek challenges. Though some students relish overcoming obstacles more than others, all expect to be challenged, and classes that move too slowly, focus on obvious points excessively, or are devoid of even occasional references to critical questions are likely to be dissatisfying.

Some students' need for mastery is indistinguishable from their need to surpass their classmates by receiving higher grades. Unfortunately, it is difficult to design a course that satisfies some students' competitive needs without frustrating others' needs for success. Teachers share with athletic coaches the dilemma of handling students emotionally to avoid complacency among those who "win" and hopelessness among those who "lose." Grades are exceedingly important to most students, especially those who are accustomed to receiving high or low ones. Like good coaches, skillful instructors are able to motivate all students to improve their performance and not become discouraged when they are less successful than they might wish.

Because professors must evaluate students' work, they assume a role as symbolic parent figures, which makes students vulnerable to the belief—correct or not—that the teacher who gives a negative evaluation is rejecting or disapproving of them personally. Though less frequent than frustration of needs for control and mastery, the feeling of being personally rejected by a teacher can profoundly reduce motivation and satisfaction.

Students may be fully aware that they are not intellectual giants or especially hard working, but they do not appreciate it when their teachers remind them of these defects openly. Neither do they need to be reminded that they have only a beginner's grasp of a discipline and are not yet professional artists, scientists, musicians, or writers. Students do, however, need accurate evaluations of the quality of their work. How can an instructor give accurate feedback without dampening students' self-confidence and motivation? The key is in the way criticism is given and the overall quality of the relationship within which it is given. Almost any student can benefit from an accurate evaluation of academic performance that is given with tact and affirmation of his or her basic worth as student and person.

Complimenting students' effort and enthusiasm before offering criticism reassures them that the instructor does not think them hopeless and helps them to hear specific suggestions for improvement without becoming upset. Criticism also is more likely to be well received if it is specific rather than general ("These two paragraphs are not connected" instead of "Your paper is disorganized") and if it criticizes the product rather than the producer ("This paper is poorly written" instead of "You can't write"). Carefully constructed criticism in which emotional support and specific feedback are combined will show a student how to improve without destroying his or her motivation to do so. Because most students consider teachers' critical judgments indisputably valid, they may be devastated by negative comments untempered by tact. These considerations all point to the special need for teachers to actively seek interpersonal rapport with students so that students will be able to use the criticism certain to come later on. Even when positive interpersonal relationships are present, however, diplomatic skill is needed in order for teacher criticism to have a constructive effect.

Evaluative comments by teachers are further complicated if such comments are made in the presence of other students. An instructor who openly criticises any student—even if others can see clearly that the student deserves the criticism—risks decreasing the quality of his or her relationships with everyone in the class; by rejecting one student, the teacher introduces the possibility that all may one day receive similar treatment. Excessive praise can also backfire by creating resentment or jealousy among those not praised and by emphasizing the teacher's evaluative role. Thus, college teachers must be skillful in the way they praise and criticize students, whether individually or collectively.

Instructors at times make evaluative statements about characteristics of students other than the quality of their work. Teachers who imply or state explicitly that individual students or the class as a whole are poorly motivated ("You are not applying yourselves fully to your studies!"), superficial in their interests ("I find it hard to understand how you can get so excited about a mere basketball game!"), or morally culpable ("It is elitist and insensitive of you to support that position!") are more likely to produce guilt and dissatisfaction in students than to change their attitudes. Even a clergyman, who has a clear mandate to question others' values and behavior, risks preaching to empty pews if he does not temper his moral criticism with assurances to the congregation that he cares about them and does not consider them despicable. College teachers who desire to improve their students' character in addition to teaching them face a similar challenge.

Types of Behavior Toward Teachers. Students are in no way passive pawns in the classroom game, doing just as instructed and keeping their emotions to themselves. Students communicate their personal feelings and expectations toward college teachers by their classroom behavior—the kinds of questions they pose, the ways they respond to an instructor's questions, and the readiness with which they smile or meet the teacher's eyes. Students also communicate a great deal in one-to-one encounters before and after class or during office hours. Much student communication is subtle, however, and college teachers must be perceptive and a bit speculative to read the messages fully. Instructors skilled at creating high interpersonal rapport with students are able to do this, whether their understanding is intuitive or acquired from deliberate study of the complexity of interpersonal communications.

The Mann studies (1970) described in the section on instructors present a rich portrait of the varieties of student feelings and behavior toward classroom instructors. Mann and his colleagues performed a cluster analysis of student comments to identify eight different types of students in terms of the emotional messages that the students expressed over a semester. Some students were compliant, some anxious, some oppositional, and a few independent. Because the classes were small and characterized by considerable discussion, most students (80 percent) made enough comments to be classified. Other data available on each student—SAT scores, overall GPA, and questionnaires about

family background, personal feelings about the teacher, and preferences for different styles of instruction — showed other ways in
which the students in each cluster were similar. Though few students will fit any of these types exactly, students resembling them
can be found in every college class. Mann's student types and
some techniques for motivating each are discussed in detail in the
next chapter.

Predictable Changes in Class Rapport over Time

Studies of group behavior have demonstrated that the ways
in which people attempt to meet needs for control and affection in
small groups are predictable. The kinds of groups studied have
varied from work groups with highly structured tasks to unstructured sensitivity or self-analytic groups. A predictable sequence of
phenomena occurs in the life of every group, structured or
unstructured (Cartwright and Zander, 1960; Shaffer and Galinsky, 1974).

Regardless of who is officially in charge, all groups initially
show great concern about leadership — about who is going to control whom and whether the methods used will be mindful of the
followers' opinions and feelings. Once an initial solution to the
problem of leadership is made, group members then become concerned about how close they will let themselves become to each
other. Though the issue of leadership may appear to have been
settled, after a few meetings a minor revolt of the members almost
always occurs, during which the initial solution is called into
question. When an implicit system of leadership is worked out
and accepted once again (even if the original solution is
readopted, it will now have more genuine support), group
members will be less distracted by emotional concerns and can
devote more of their energies to the purpose of the group. For
groups having a limited life, such as college classes, a period of
heightened emotionality always occurs at the end. Sadness is
common as members withdraw their emotional investment in the
leader and each other.

A fundamental observation about the way groups function
over time is that little stays the same for very long. One of the

clearest explanations of the reason why small groups change so regularly is Robert Bales's differentiation between *task* needs and *maintenance* needs in groups (Bales, 1950; Bales and Slater, 1955). Task needs relate to the work of the group, its external purpose. Learning course content would be the task of a college class. Maintenance needs are the personal needs of the members, primarily needs for control and affection. Bales's critical points are that both types of needs must be met and that groups vacillate over time between meeting primarily task or primarily maintenance needs, each type always being met at the expense of the other. For example, a group that works exceedingly hard to meet a production deadline (focuses most of its energies into meeting its task needs) will necessarily create a relative deprivation of the members' needs for relationships with each other (their maintenance needs). After a long stint of heavy investment in the task, dissatisfaction will increase to the point that work effectiveness decreases greatly. (Employee slowdowns or strikes are extreme examples of maintenance deprivation.) At this point, the group must hear grievances or reconsider its operating procedures (systems of leadership and division of labor) to right the balance. When the group spends time on enhancing personal relationships, pressure for meeting its task needs increases, and the focus must swing back to the work at hand. . . and so forth.

The implication of this theory for group and organizational leaders (including college teachers) is that the best way to avoid large swings back and forth, the kind of swings that wreck production schedules and lead to employee unrest, is to attend to the maintenance needs of groups at the outset rather than waiting until members force the leader to show concern for them. This book's emphasis on personal teaching is based on this well-accepted principle of organizational leadership: Recognizing and attempting to meet the emotional needs of group members from the outset leads to greater work (or learning) in the long run.

Mann's group applied these group dynamics principles to time trends in their classroom data. They found remarkable similarity in the patterns of students' and instructors' feelings and control strategies over the semester, even though the four classes differed in overall teacher effectiveness and student satisfaction.

Mann's description of "the natural history of the college classroom" rings true for most experienced college teachers. Newer instructors can benefit greatly from being aware of the predictable stages Mann describes. The following discussion of the typical emotional progression of a college class over a semester has been adapted from Mann's empirically-derived stages.

Regardless of whatever underlying fears students and instructors may hold, college courses almost always start with an air of optimism and positive anticipation in everyone. Students usually arrive early for the first class meeting, and many hope that this course and their own performance will somehow be different from their past experience. Instructors commonly hope that they will teach effectively and be well received by students. Those teaching for the first time have an even richer array of initial expectations, many unfortunately based on unrealistic ideas about being a college instructor.

Underlying this surface excitement and anticipation are a number of fears. Students fear that the instructor will be authoritarian and rejecting and that they will fail to perform as well as they would like. Concern over success on exams and papers is felt by all students, both by the consistently outstanding who must once again enter the fray and emerge with a high mark and by those who have not performed up to their own or their parents' expectations. College teachers know they must win their laurels with still another group of strangers, no matter how highly their previous classes regarded them. Even with these fears, however, the overall mood at the beginning of a class tends to be positive for everyone.

The first few classes build on these initial positive expectations. Teachers are typically relatively controlling at first, and students are comfortably compliant. Students suggest by their initial comments what impression they wish to make on the instructor and their fellow students — whether they expect the teacher to structure their learning or give them their head, for example. The initial positive expectations of students and instructors lead to a brief honeymoon period of good feelings: The college teacher is not as controlling as the students had feared, nor are the students as dependent or dull as the instructor had feared. These early positive attitudes arise from initial expectations more than actual experience, however, and so they must eventually be questioned.

The "era of good feeling" ends with a relatively sharp drop in satisfaction and rise in anxiety among students and instructors. In Mann's four classes, this occurred after six to eight meetings (about four weeks). Even the class that has been working well must now swing back to address emotional needs. This drop in morale occurs at four to six weeks even in classes without an exam, though first exams often are given about that time and are frequently the focus of student dissatisfaction. Giving an exam or graded assignment speeds up the revolt by dramatizing the teacher's evaluative role. Grading students' work reminds instructors that student mastery of content is never as complete as they had hoped and that their relationship with students is unavoidably an evaluative one; thus, college teachers' morale drops too.

Fortunately, college teachers can be assured that the drop in morale is usually brief and ushers in a more realistic period of satisfaction and independent work. The optimal work atmosphere, in which students more readily participate in discussion and show independent thinking and work outside class, falls in most classes in the middle third and last half and, according to Mann's thinking, could not occur without the emotional crisis that precedes it. This optimal work atmosphere can be extended by fostering positive interpersonal relationships, but it cannot be gained too quickly or by simple gimmicks such as class picnics.

The end of a class is emotional for everyone. During the last few class meetings, students often become anxious about the final exam and course grades, but this anxiety rarely reaches the height attained just before the first exam. Students now are commonly dissatisfied that the course is ending, even if it has not been particularly satisfying to them. College teachers may be disappointed that they were not able to present more material or to help students master it more fully. Though dissatisfaction expressed in the last few class meetings (especially the final meeting) usually concerns course content, students and instructors are also sorry to have their personal relationships come to an end. They shared an important common experience, the class, and are sad to say good bye. In classes in which student morale has been high, it is not uncommon for students to ask the instructor personal questions during the last class, as if to make a final attempt to be intimate.

Some students in every course, to be sure, are happy to have the class end, to move on to a vacation or a new course. In highly unsatisfactory classes, the last few meetings are occasions for such students to express dissatisfaction openly. Teachers as well frequently feel the need to share negative feelings they hold about the class. Regardless of the specific kinds of feelings expressed, students and instructors need at this time to communicate the way they feel about one another, and these needs will take precedence over the course content.

Emotional needs during the last class meeting are so important that I strongly recommend against the common practice of covering one last topic or scheduling an exam at this time. Students need a time to reflect emotionally as well as intellectually on the semester coming to an end (Eble, 1976). Because students' ratings of instruction are a major vehicle through which to communicate their feelings about the course and instructor, the last meeting is a particularly apt time to administer rating questionnaires.

In conclusion, college classrooms are rich laboratories of human psychology. Though students and instructors show characteristic behavior as each seeks to satisfy the same fundamental human needs, considerable diversity in individual patterns is possible. Chapter Three applies what has been presented here to the practical demands of the classroom and suggests specific techniques for interpersonally skillful teaching.

CHAPTER 3

෧෦෭෩ඁ෭෩ඁ෭෩ඁ෭෩ඁ෭෩ඁ෭෩ඁ෭෩ඁ෭෩ඁ෭෩ඁ෭෩ඁ෭෩ඁ෭෩ඁ෭෩ඁ෧

Developing Interpersonal Skills and Teaching Style

> Social events early in the term do not harm the development of rapport but have limited power to produce it, are not likely to be attended by the students who most need rapport, and cannot offset distancing or rejecting remarks by the teacher in class.

Some college teachers try to promote rapport and reduce their classroom image as authority figures by dressing casually, encouraging students to call them by their first names, or giving students considerable freedom to select the work they do. Others encourage informal interaction with students outside classrooms by scheduling conferences, sponsoring parties or picnics, inviting students to lunch, or holding class meetings outside on the grass or in their homes. Unfortunately, none of these strategies ensures satisfied students. Furthermore, none are necessary for interpersonal rapport to develop and for students to be highly motivated.

The students most likely to call the instructor by his or her first name or to accept social invitations are the ones who already feel relatively comfortable, not those who are most in need of special attention. Many students find the novelty of calling their instructor "Bill" or "Betsy" refreshing for a while, but, like the honeymoon period near the beginning of a course, this comfort is superficial and is no quick substitute for a real relationship developed over time. As Kenneth Eble observes in *The Craft of Teaching* (1976, p. 73), the best strategy for developing rapport "may be no more formal than providing excuses and opportunities for easy talk." One-to-one interactions with students in the second half of a course are likely to be more meaningful than those that occur earlier. The subtleties of a college teacher's behavior toward a class throughout the term do more to produce an optimal class atmosphere than sweeping structural changes at the beginning ("Let's move the chairs back and sit on the floor").

This chapter suggests specific ways in which college teachers can foster relationships with students that promote motivation and satisfaction. The techniques presented here were collected from books on college teaching and observations of outstanding teachers. They are organized into groups of techniques dealing with (1) fostering personal relationships with students, (2) obtaining regular feedback from them, (3) motivating students to work through effective classroom leadership, (4) showing special attention to certain types of students, and (5) handling miscellaneous interpersonal issues.

Fostering Personal Relationships with Students

The easiest way to begin forming personal relationships with students is to learn their names. Nothing so impresses students as a college teacher who makes a serious effort to get to know them as individuals. Any instructor can learn to match up to 50 student names with faces in the first few classes if he or she approaches the task with a positive attitude and commitment. With practice, some may be able to learn up to 100. Learning each student's name is so effective at promoting rapport because it begins personal contact immediately but does not seem forced, rushed, or intrusive. When we meet a new colleague, we learn his or her name as the first step in forming a working relationship; so it should be between college teacher and student.

The following paragraphs describe a name-learning strategy

that has been successful for many instructors. Other general techniques for improving memory can be used (Cermak, 1976) but, like the system advocated here, any method will require effort to be effective.

Begin by introducing yourself on the first day of class. Then hand out index cards and ask the students to write the usual information about themselves (plus whatever else you would like to know) on the cards. Be sure to ask them to indicate what they would like to be called. Then, ask them to add anything else they wish you, the instructor, to know. This asks the students to reply to your personal introduction to all of them by making individual introductions of themselves. The instruction "Add whatever you wish," politely pressures them to divulge a bit of themselves. Most students will add nothing, but a few will dutifully list other courses they have had in the subject or their extracurricular activities; a few will attempt to show off their wit or political attitudes, demonstrating what interesting persons they are.

It helps to have reviewed the names on a preregistration list beforehand, even though these lists are never completely accurate. Certain first names are common, so make a mental note of how many Jims, Bobs, Kathys, Kims, Lisas, and so forth are in the class. Consulting "face books" (annuals or other directories with student pictures) beforehand will make learning the names a little easier, but it is ineffective to attempt to learn all the names in this way before the first group meeting. Learning them in class requires a large amount of eye contact, and this may contribute as much to the growth of the individual relationships as your permanent association of face and name.

After asking students to pass in their cards (grouping them by rows makes things a bit easier), read off each student's name and move near enough to the appropriate row to be able to see that student's face distinctly. You need make no effort to learn last names at this time; first names will suffice for calling on students in class and beginning a personal relationship. You will learn last names almost automatically when you grade and record the first exams or papers.

Note on the card other information about each student if needed, but concentrate on looking directly at the students' faces, forming a visual image of each face while silently saying the matching first name over and over. Then go on to the next card, and so forth. After every three or four students, make a quick mental note of the first names you have just learned, and ask again for any that you cannot recall. Practice the whole row once more before moving on to the next one. The key to doing this activity well is to control any anxiety or embarrassment you may have at taking class time for it. If you find yourself going too fast, starting to get tense, or immediately forgetting names, make a little joke or ask a casual question of an occasional student ("How far is Lake Forest from the Loop?").

When you have gone through the whole class, set the cards aside, begin at the first row, and attempt to call each student's first name. Students do not expect an instructor to be able to do this immediately, so you have nothing to lose. Even if you have forgotten over half the names, continue on through the entire class. Tell the students that learning their names is difficult but important and that you are going to keep practicing for a while during each class until you learn them all. Students are more likely to believe that you really do want to get to know them if you put this statement into practice. At the end of the first class, practice calling names by looking at faces one last time.

As soon after the first class meeting as you can, go through the cards again, saying each first name silently and attempting to picture the face that goes with it. Repeat this process once more later in the day and once each day thereafter until the class meets next. Give yourself a final refresher just before going to the second class, but do not be disconcerted if you can remember only a few of the faces with confidence.

At the beginning of the second class, look at each face and try to call each student's first name. Though this is easier than trying to imagine the faces from the names, no more than 50 percent accuracy is normal. Once again, try to remain calm when you must ask for a student's name. In dismissing the second class, call each student's name again. Most likely you will do better now than at the beginning of class.

Continue going through the students' names at the beginning and end of each class and picturing the faces from the cards each day until you can say every name correctly the first time. By the third or fourth class meeting it is usually no longer necessary to call every student's name; you can scan the room before class and call only those about which you are not completely confident. In addition to these steps, use students' names as much as possible when calling on them in class, answering questions after class, or meeting them on campus. This helps to solidify initial learning, and you will rarely forget the names during the rest of the semester.

This no doubt seems like a lot of time to spend on such a modest goal—and instructors who pursue it report that it does require effort and commitment, especially at first. Most find that their memory for names improves over successive semesters, however, and that the resulting rapport is well worth the investment. Learning names is the most important single thing a college teacher can do to communicate to students that he or she values them as individuals. It also satisfies the instructor's need for personal contact with students and opens up other channels to personal relationships with them.

Another way to develop rapport with students is to come to class five to ten minutes early, especially before the initial class meetings. This conditions students to expect to start on time and also provides opportunities to chat informally with them before class or for them to approach you about their concerns. Similarly, staying after class accomplishes educational as well as interpersonal objectives by allowing in-depth discussions of the content just presented. Most students will not come up after class, however, whereas before class you have a chance to contact the students who are unlikely to approach you afterward.

Announced office hours are a traditional way of communicating accessibility to students, though only a minority will use them, and it is rare for a student to come by during the early weeks of the term. Because students expect college teachers to post office hours and want to know that they *can* come by without an appointment, it is very important to do this. Being available over a large number of hours does not increase the personal interest that students perceive, however; two or three hours per week is usually sufficient. The last section of this chapter offers specific suggestions on ways to achieve maximum interpersonal and educational value from individual conferences with students.

In addition to being available during regular office hours, offer to schedule meetings at other times as well. Students will take your interest in being accessible to them for questions or discussions more seriously if your home telephone number is listed on the course syllabus and you encourage them to call you in the evening and on weekends ("But never after 10:30 at night!"). Few students will call, but all will view the invitation as a serious indication of your commitment to communicate with them. The accessibility you offer will take little time in actuality and will be more than repaid by the positive attitudes you will create in the class as a whole.

Anything you can do to show interest in students as individuals will help to promote rapport. For example, one outstanding teacher I interviewed reported that he regularly scans the student newspaper (especially the letters to the editor and sports news) for the names of any of his students so that he can congratulate (or console) them or merely acknowledge seeing their name or letter. Other teachers make a special effort to attend athletic and artistic events in which their students are involved. For these techniques to be effective, however, a teacher's interest must be genuine.

Soliciting Feedback from Students

Giving students many opportunities to communicate and listening carefully to them can be valuable for a number of reasons (Barnes-McConnell, 1978). Interpersonal relationships require a dialogue, a two-way communication, so any teaching method that encourages students to communicate will help to form personal bonds. Instructors are more likely to know when to clarify content or give emotional support if students feel free to raise their concerns. Some students need little encouragement, but active solicitation of feedback from all students will help to form and improve relationships with those who are less comfortable or who avoid contact.

One effective method of encouraging student communication is to begin the third week of class by handing out index cards and asking students to ask a question about you or the content or make a personal comment — anything they want to say about you, the course, or the subject. Stress that they are free to question or comment anonymously but that you will write a personal reply if they sign their names. Circulate more cards than students, and point out they can send in two cards (signed and unsigned) if they wish. Offering this opportunity for personal communication with great latitude in the ways that students may choose to comply (including not at all) says implicitly that you care what they think but respect their privacy. This method makes it very easy for students to say what is on their minds. By writing personal notes in reply you will complete the communication circle, strengthening the personal relationship. Some college teachers who use this method hand out cards as frequently as every third class meeting, but students become less interested in filling them out as the semester progresses. Using the technique after about two weeks of class and once again after seven or eight weeks (or whenever class morale seems low) is usually sufficient.

Student questions and comments are commonly divided about equally between substantive topics and personal subjects. When you answer their content questions, you obviously aid their learning. When a student comments on your style of presentation ("You mumble at the end of phrases" or "You jingle your keys in your pocket and it's distracting"), paying attention to the comment may improve your teaching. Even if students write "I can't think of anything at this time," they are still relating to you. Most will ask important questions and will greatly appreciate the notes you write in reply. Using this technique to actively solicit comments from each student (including the quieter ones) in a nondemanding way provides useful feedback on your teaching and establishes the personal relationships with a class from which satisfaction and motivation spring.

As important as fostering personal relationships and seeking feedback from students are, these goals are insufficient for teaching success. College teachers must also be able to control classroom proceedings and motivate students to work. Students will be more motivated to please those whom they believe care about them, but instructors also need effective methods of classroom leadership. The following section outlines some ways for classroom instructors to control students subtly through careful attention to the language chosen when trying to influence them.

Indirect Classroom Leadership

Some instructors believe that being liked by students and being firmly in charge are mutually exclusive — that students do not like teachers who control them, assign them challenging work, and evaluate it rigorously. Not only is it possible for college teachers to demand a great deal from students and still have positive interpersonal relationships with them, it is *necessary* for students to view teachers as being in control for the students to be maximally satisfied with their leadership (Kinichi and Schriesheim, 1978). The key here is the choice of methods. As we shall see, indirect methods are almost always superior to direct or autocratic ones.

Does indirect control mean indicating that students should not worry about grades or exams and should learn only what they see as relevant? Not at all. Such a laissez-faire policy of classroom management fails to recognize that all students need to master challenges and compete with peers and that students differ in the style of leadership to which they respond best. The section after this one details ways in which students with different emotional needs and styles of dealing with authority can be optimally motivated by varying the teacher's interpersonal approach. Indirect methods are ideal for such individualization.

The key to using indirect methods is to select words carefully when attempting to control students, suggesting and implying rather than ordering or directing openly. Indirect control is similar to the covert control exercised by the hypnotist or Zen master in that a college teacher lays verbal traps that control students' choices of behavior while giving the illusion of personal freedom (Bandler and Grinder, 1975). This sort of control is advantageous because it leads students to take responsibility for their own behavior — become controlled from within — rather than expecting others to exercise control.

How is indirect control accomplished? In Chapter Two the

example of the complex messages an instructor can give when announcing a term paper illustrated the importance of the way an assignment is presented. When announcing a course assignment, college teachers emphasize the formal dimension of their relationship with students when they say "I require," "I expect," or "You must." In contrast, saying "I would like," "It is my hope," or "You will probably want" emphasizes the instructor as person rather than as authority. Using these words implies that the students will choose to do something because it is what they, or someone they like, wants rather than because they have been coerced. Word choice may seem trivial, but research in human communication has demonstrated that subtleties of language strongly influence the leadership relationships that develop in a group over time, chiefly how much persons with less power resent those in charge (Watzlawick, Beavin, and Jackson, 1967). College teachers who use more egalitarian language promote independence among students and are at least as likely to have assignments completed as those who are more authoritarian.

Another way to control students indirectly is to give a rational justification for assignments. If students see the work asked of them as consistent with their own goals, they are less likely to respond to it simply as a frustrating task imposed by an educational authority. There are many sound reasons for a college teacher to formulate course objectives (see Chapter Seven), not the least of which is that sharing objectives with students makes them more likely to see requirements as something they want to do rather than as something the instructor says they must do.

Giving students choices whenever possible also increases their feeling of freedom in the classroom. This does not mean taking the first few class meetings to formulate course objectives or agree on assignments in order to enhance the group's ownership of the course. It means giving students choices about a few decisions of much smaller consequence, such as whether to have an exam on a Monday or a Friday or whether to schedule a film during class or in the evening. Giving students choices between options that are consistent with the instructor's objectives and the available time tells them that their preferences are recognized and will be considered whenever possible; thus, interpersonal rapport is also enhanced. At the same time, the fact that the instructor exempts important decisions about requirements from a class vote communicates to students that he or she is firmly in charge.

A final principle of indirect classroom leadership is making sure the students can walk before expecting them to run. As Mann has demonstrated, students need more structure at the beginning of a course and are more capable of independent learning in the later portions. Requiring mastery of instructor-defined content at the beginning and more independent thinking and choice of topics at the end is a traditional academic arrangement consistent with what has been learned recently about the "natural history" of college classes.

Treating Students Individually

There are certain students with whom instructors should make a special effort to establish positive interpersonal relationships. The following suggestions about ways to do this should not be taken as sure formulas for achieving rapport and optimal motivation. Rather, they are illustrations of techniques that a college teacher can use to individualize his or her approach to certain students. Such individualization, far from being unfair or producing negative effects by "unequal" treatment, helps all students work up to their academic potential in a course.

Mann's Student Types. The student categories described below are based on Mann's research (1970) and expanded by my own informal observations. Though some of Mann's labels ("hero" or "sniper," for example) may seem disparaging, they are retained and used here because they are easily remembered and aptly capture the key emotional concerns of each group. No lack of respect toward any students is intended.

The typical *compliant student* is notably teacher dependent, conventional, and highly task oriented. Unlike other types, these students are comfortable with being dependent and are content simply to learn what the instructor wants them to know. Compliants speak in class most often to agree with the instructor or ask for clarification. They rarely pose problems or question the teacher's control. They are in class simply to understand the material. They often prefer lecture to discussion classes. Because they always do what is asked, compliant students usually do moderately well on exams, but they are unlikely to show much independence or creativity. As might be expected, the percentage of compliants (10 percent in Mann's sample) is greater among freshmen and steadily decreases with age. The most important characteristic of these students is that they are content to support the status quo and never question authority.

College teachers can help compliant students become more independent by initially accepting their dependency. Once the students come to believe that the instructor accepts them, the instructor can ask them to show more independence. For example, the teacher might write on an exam or paper, "You showed mastery of the material presented in class and assigned readings. Good work! I think you are now ready to add some of your own conclusions and critical evaluations to what you are learning so well. Include one or two of your own views next time in addition to presenting what others have said. Keep up the good work." This strategy supports what is admirable and effective about the students' preferred style while encouraging them to grow toward independence and maturity.

Anxious-dependent students are very common (26 percent of the Mann sample) and can be spotted early by their excessive concern about grades. Like compliant types, anxious-dependents want to learn exactly what the teacher wants them to know — but these fear that they will miss something. They are likely to ask the teacher to repeat definitions so they can get them word for word. Compliant students generally trust teachers and assume that the grades they receive are justified. In contrast, anxious-dependent students distrust teachers and expect trick questions or unfair grading practices. Their combination of high ambition, anxiety, and suspiciousness suggests that they feel angry about having less power in the educational setting than they would like.

Anxious-dependent types frequently hold low opinions of their own work, an evaluation not entirely unfounded; their verbal SAT scores were the lowest of the eight types studied by Mann. It is perhaps this self-doubt that leads them to make a great show of their academic effort. These students commonly come to exams looking frazzled and stay until the last possible moment, rechecking their answers or adding "just one more sentence" here and there. Because of their excessive anxiety and relatively limited abilities, their work is frequently unimaginative, mediocre, or erratic. It may be packed full of memorized details and definitions but be lacking in conceptual complexity. However, having their work evaluated poorly merely confirms their pessimistic expectancy and reinforces this pattern of overly anxious and dependent behavior. It is easy to understand why such students prefer lectures to discussion.

It is hard for a teacher to avoid becoming frustrated, angry, and rejecting of anxious-dependent students. Still, when one of these students whines, "But how are we supposed to know which of these names is important?" the wise teacher counts to ten. Responding angrily with "Come now, you should be able to figure that out for yourself" increases the students' anxiety and solidifies their belief that the instructor really does make a clear distinction between "important" and "unimportant" names. A better response might be, "That's a good question. I guess some of the people mentioned in the book have had more impact on the field than others and are more important, but I hope everyone appreciates that they are all notable authors (scientists, artists, philosophers, or whatever). I would rather that you decide how they are similar and different and what impact they have had on each other than try to guess how I might decide to rank-order them." The essential message in this lengthy comment is that there is no correct answer to the student's question but that the question is relevant. The comment does not reject the student for asking the question, but rather suggests a way to evaluate the persons being studied—and the comment is one useful for the entire class to hear.

Anxious-dependent students have a penchant for black and white distinctions, for simple right or wrong answers; a college teacher who expands their range of options aids their intellectual growth. Rejecting their questions or refusing to acknowledge their concerns simply raises their anxiety further and increases their need for specifics from the teacher. Suggesting a less dichotomous way of viewing the material, on the other hand, gives anxious-dependents reassurance while stimulating their intellectual development.

Discouraged workers, Mann's third category, make comments in class that communicate a depressed and fatalistic attitude toward themselves and their education. Like compliants and anxious-dependents, discouraged workers see themselves as having little control over their learning. Some may have worked so hard to earn high grades in the past that they no longer find learning pleasurable; they have burned out. Often they are older students coming back to school after a stint in the military or work force who find it hard to regain their youthful enthusiasm. Some have jobs or families and are more likely to be physically tired and preoccupied than the typical "college kid." Any of these circumstances can dampen curiosity and lead to joyless learning. Though classes appear to offer little pleasure to this small group of students (4 percent in Mann's sample), they can be made into active participants by an inspiring teacher.

Recognizing that certain students are chronically discouraged or resigned calls for a special effort to pick up their spirits. Written compliments on their best work (admittedly a difficult task if they have done poorly) are good, but face-to-face conversations are even better. The instructor should look for some excuse to engage them in small talk before class or ask them to stop by for a conference during office hours. Openly acknowledging that he or she has noticed their low morale and wants to understand them better may be the best help a college teacher can give discouraged workers.

Independent students take what instructors have to offer and pursue their own goals in equal measure. They are comfortable, (perhaps even detached or aloof) in doing what is asked of them, usually prefer seminar to lecture classes, and do not balk when asked to formulate their own thinking about a topic. The majority of independent students are high participators, make friends with instructors easily, and identify with them to some extent, much as many graduate students relate to their professors. They are ideal, mature students, the ones a teacher can count on to discuss and to perform at a consistently high level. In Mann's population, 12 percent of the students were in the independent group and, not surprisingly, they were more frequently juniors or seniors. Independent students rarely present problems for teachers, but, if the quality of instruction is poor, they are most likely to be selected as spokesmen for the group's grievances.

Independent students do not require much special attention other than the just desserts of their achievements. The instructor should acknowledge their independence and encourage them to use it to go beyond what might be expected of others. The key to dealing with such students is deciding whether they are exhibiting genuine independence or rebellion. The best test is their past performance on structured tasks.

Heroes resemble independents in their identification with the teacher and their preference for independent or creative work. They lack the detachment of the independents, however, and seem anxious to make the teacher notice immediately what great students and interesting people they are. Most critically, heroes routinely fail to deliver on their initial promise. They are the erratic, optimistic underachievers who initially excite an instructor with their intensity and grand plans for independent projects, only to disappoint later with poor execution. Heroes would very much like to be the independent, creative students they see themselves as being, but some underlying hostility toward authority figures or inability to maintain their commitment to a goal prevents them from playing this role to the end. Ten percent of Mann's students fit this classification, and almost every class has one or two.

Heroes make certain that the teacher notices them very early. They frequently stop by after the first class to let the instructor know how interested they are in the subject and how much firsthand knowledge of it they already have from previous reading or work experience. Their initial comments in class may impress the instructor and raise hopes that he or she has run across an unusually outstanding student. Heroes love discussion; they can be annoyingly argumentative, never admitting that they have lost a debate. Reflection on their comments, however, usually reveals that they have not done the assigned reading and are simply showing off previous knowledge or posing tangential questions that occur to them in class. Inexperienced instructors may be quite surprised at these students' poor performance on initial exams or papers. Heroes typically miss class more often than others once the novelty of the semester has worn off or they have begun to do poorly.

These examples suffice to make the point: Heroes promise much but usually deliver little. This is particularly sad because they are usually quite capable students with very high expectations for themselves. Their failure to live up to their potential often results from a fear that they might not be able to live up to their heroic ideal even if they try their best. Because they typically make friends with the instructor right off, they can be enticed to perform more consistently by skillful handling. Still, they are unlikely to work up to their intellectual potential until their impulsive temperament is stabilized by increased maturity. Though most heroes have poor academic records in spite of their high SATs, so-called late bloomers in this group sometimes settle down during their junior and senior years and receive better grades. Heroes occasionally drop out of school to work for a year or two and return as more mature and better students with high graduate or professional aspirations. Heroes typically have high, even grandiose expectations for themselves, and many are capable of outstanding careers if they lower their expectations slightly and resolve their ambivalence about authority and achievement.

Giving heroes the independence they claim to desire almost never improves their performance; it reinforces the special attitude they hold about themselves without making them responsible for living up to it. It is better to encourage heroes to channel their energies into meeting the more structured requirements of the course first. For example, instead of letting them select a term paper topic more ambitious than that assigned to the whole class, the wise teacher will suggest that they use their special skills or insights to produce a tightly reasoned, well written, polished paper on the common topic. Such a suggestion reinforces the high opinion these students have of themselves but says that they will not be free from the limits imposed on others.

Heroes are more likely to produce good work if given such special handling. To be successful in motivating heroes, a college teacher must maintain a good relationship with them over the term. Heroes are very prone to withdraw their initial investment in the course and put their energies elsewhere. If heroes believe that an instructor expects great things of them, they are more likely to live up to their own billing—but only if the instructor keeps close tabs on them and applies persistent, soft control.

A *sniper* is a hero who is hostile toward college teachers, unlikely to approach them, and filled with cynicism. Like heroes, snipers (9 percent in Mann's group) have very high expectations and positive images of themselves, but they have little hope that the world will recognize their worth or give them a fair chance to demonstrate it. Their hostility seems untempered by positive feelings. They are habitual rebels who sit as far from the instructor as possible and often comment with cutting remarks. Some also show their rebellion by wearing unusual or provocative clothing to class. Because they apparently feel guilty or fearful about their hostility, they retreat quickly when questioned about their sallies. Unlike heroes, who never seem to tire of debating, snipers strike their colors after the first salvo is fired.

As with anxious-dependents, the instructor's first task in forming positive relationships with snipers is to control anger toward them. Their hostile comments often should simply be ignored. Ignoring snipers does not break through their hostility to form a relationship likely to lead to work or change on their part, however. A more fruitful, but more difficult, approach is to respond enthusiastically to the snipers' comments, emphasizing what is positive and ignoring what is hostile. For example, suppose a sniper criticizes a nineteenth-century political leader for having racist, sexist, or elitist attitudes. The instructor might say in response: "That's an interesting point, and it raises an important dilemma for the historian: How can we look at distant events through the eyes of the people of that era, rather than coloring them with contemporary values? We will discuss historical methods again in a few weeks. For now, let me say that I very much sympathize with your concerns and I suggest that all of us try to imagine why this leader did what he did given the way that he and many others of his time viewed the world." This response relates the student's hostile comment to a critical issue in the field without rejecting the student. By expressing sympathy with the student's concern and suggesting that the whole class try to learn from it, the instructor also recognizes the student as a valuable class member. Admittedly, it is hard to respond at length to frequent sniper interruptions without showing irritation. Responding to some sniper comments and ignoring or laughing off others can reduce these students' hostility and make it easier for them to put forth their best efforts.

A smiling offensive — eagerly seeking them out — does not generally work well with snipers, especially early in the term. Approaching snipers makes them more uncomfortable, so they become more hostile in order to distance themselves from the instructor. A better strategy is to praise their class comments as much as possible, make lengthy and careful notes on their exams or papers, and wait vigilantly for chances to start personal conversations with them later in the course. By that time they can sometimes tolerate short conversations of a personal nature, but even then they will seek out the instructor only rarely. As the Mann study showed, snipers do respect authority, and they will become even more hostile toward a college teacher they see as weak. The snipers' hostility stems from discomfort with authority figures and protects them from close contact with them, but such students may actually desire closeness and welcome someone who makes contact without scaring them away.

Attention-seeking students (11 percent in Mann's group) enjoy coming to class mostly to socialize with other students or the professor. Like heroes, they are fond of discussion; they love to talk. For them, social needs predominate over intellectual ones. They are pleasant to have in class, and many will form close personal relationships with an instructor. Attention-seeking students are capable of good work if it is made clear that they must work well in order to be well thought of by the instructor or other students. These students like to organize group review sessions or class parties. Thus, they fill a useful role in class as what is known in group dynamics literature as "social-emotional leaders." Attention-seekers are no less intelligent than other students, just less intellectual. However, like discouraged workers, they are easily influenced by others, and a skillful instructor can interest them in intellectual as well as social discourse.

Because instructor attention is so reinforcing to attention-seekers, they are relatively easy to motivate. An instructor should give them ample attention with no strings attached at first to assure them that he or she thinks well of them. Then the teacher should reduce the level of attention and show it mainly for their academic work, especially good work. This strategy effectively motivates most socially oriented students to take intellectual content more seriously while maintaining their interpersonal engagement.

In the classes studied by Mann, *silent students* (20 percent) made so few comments that they could not be classified into one of the other seven mathematical clusters. Mann observed classes with heavy discussion formats, in which not speaking was a more revealing characteristic than it might have been in larger classes. Given this context, it is not surprising that Mann's silent students proved to be similar to each other in other ways as well. For example, their personal questionnaires and teacher evaluations revealed that they were acutely aware of the way the instructor behaved toward them. Of all the types, these students most wanted a close relationship and were most afraid that the instructor did not think highly of them and their academic work. Silent students respond to this fear with silence rather than hostility. Unlike snipers, silent students are usually aware of their desire for a personal relationship with the instructor. This makes them easier to reach.

The easiest mistake a college teacher can make with silent students is to ignore them, for they will not attract attention or pose problems. To guard against this, a good teacher goes through the class roster every few weeks, noting how each student has been behaving in recent meetings. Any students who have not made comments or approached the teacher individually by the end of the first third of the semester should be earmarked for special attention. Smiling warmly at them, walking to their part of the room before class, and making eye contact with them during lectures and discussions can help to bring them out. Silent students are often receptive to the direct suggestion that they come by during office hours to get acquainted. It is preferable to let them approach first, but if they have not done so well into the term, it is appropriate for the instructor to take the initiative. The instructor should guard against overdoing efforts to form personal relationships with silent students, however, because some may tend to become overinvolved with especially receptive teachers.

Students Under Special Stress. Some students enter classrooms under considerably more pressure than others. Though few college teachers advocate assigning less work to such students or grading their work differently, these students do require special understanding if they are to perform maximally. Regardless of the source of extra stress the students are experiencing, the instructor's strategy should be the same: Recognize the added stress they are under and communicate empathy with it. The teacher should not reduce requirements for these students because they are likely to be insulted by such an action. Forming a good relationship with them, being a willing listener without dwelling on their specific condition or asking less of them, is normally all the teacher needs to do.

Which students are under unusual stress? In the following I have expanded on a list proposed by Barnes-McConnell (1978). Students with chronic physical handicaps or diseases are obviously overcoming a greater number of obstacles to attend college. At some point early in the semester the instructor may ask if these students will need special consideration in connection with examinations, laboratory work, or field trips. Students under treatment for emotional problems also may need an especially understanding relationship, though it is important not to reinforce their symptoms by offering to exempt them from requirements.

Other high-stress groups to consider are identifiable minorities in class or on campus. Students of minority sexes, races, or religions greatly appreciate an instructor who acknowledges them as individuals. They are *not* likely to enjoy being called upon in class to speak "for" their group. Even students who choose to emphasize their minority identity by class comments also wish to be seen as capable of contributing ideas about other issues. Most minority students want simply to be treated like other students.[1]

Freshmen are under unusual stress, too. They are especially likely to feel uncertain at first and to need extra structure and reassurance from college teachers. At the other end of the age dimension, older students—many with family and work responsibilities— are also typically under added stress. They greatly appreciate the instructor's recognition that by their greater maturity and experi-

---

[1]These suggestions were adapted from those made in discussions held by the Black-White dialogue group at the University of North Carolina at Chapel Hill in 1981–1982.

ence they can make a valuable contribution to the class. Other groups to keep in mind are upwardly mobile students who are the first in their families to attend college, students on athletic teams (which require extensive time commitments and occasional missed classes), and students supporting themselves financially.

Students with Unusual Academic Abilities. It is especially important for college teachers to form personal relationships with students at the extremes of academic ability. Identifying such students is rarely easy, but the level of complexity and abstract thinking displayed in class comments and on exams provides useful clues. Especially bright students — the truly gifted, not merely the high-achieving "grinds" — are vulnerable to boredom and apt to slack off if they fail to find a class intellectually challenging. Besides offering stimulating lectures, instructors should actively cultivate personal relationships with these students and encourage them to think independently or creatively about the subject. They will resent extra make-work assignments, but they may welcome recognition of their talent and encouragement to read advanced works on their own. Some instructors invite very bright students to come by regularly to discuss their independent reading or ideas on the common work. Grades should not be given for such work; the teacher should let the students' satisfaction of their own curiosity and the pleasure of discussion suffice as reinforcement.

It is equally important to pay special attention to the student who finds college work extremely challenging or even overwhelming. Such students almost always work hard at their studies, and they are not likely to be helped by admonitions to work harder. Specific guidance on ways to study and organize material is more likely to support their struggle. The instructor should recognize their difficulty and empathize with their fear of flunking out of school but reassure them that doing well in college is not the only important thing in the world. He or she should teach these students as much as they can learn and support their efforts to survive this demanding enterprise. For some students, eventual failure may provide the needed understanding that higher education, or at least some aspects of it, is not for them.

In sum, college teachers should treat different kinds of students differently in terms of the interpersonal strategies used to form personal relationships with them, even though all students are assigned the same work and graded using identical criteria. To motivate each student fully we must necessarily modify the approach we use.

Miscellaneous Interpersonal Topics

Three additional topics, loosely related to each other and all within the interpersonal realm, are presented in this section: relating to students during office hours, especially those students asking (implicitly or explicitly) for extended counseling; the ethics of teaching, including the question of love and sex between teacher and student; and the importance of teacher tolerance of adolescent behavior. Some of the suggestions given here are adapted from W. J. McKeachie's *Teaching Tips* (1978).

Individual Meetings with Students. Even in small classes, most students will not drop by during office hours or call on the telephone. When one does, the way the instructor reacts will determine whether the student finds the venture satisfying or feels frustrated, even punished, for risking a one-to-one encounter (Eble, 1976). To begin with, an instructor should *always* be present during his or her posted office hours. Dropping by a professor's office is rarely a casual action for a student. To prepare oneself to appear "between 1:30 and 2:30 on Wednesdays or Fridays" and find the door locked or standing open with no sign of the instructor or explanatory note is disappointing, if not anger-provoking.

Nonverbal communications to students in the office are even more important than those in class. Offices are seen by students as very much "teacher territory," and entering them often stimulates authority conflicts. Consequently, it is imperative at least to *seem* eager to see a student, even if one is preoccupied with a research project or must leave for a committee meeting in fifteen minutes. Some instructors act impatient or irritated by a visiting student's interruption. One such person I observed was fully aware of this behavior and remarked that he used it "to make the students more independent and keep them from bothering me too much." Instructors may fear that students will take inappropriate advantage of their time, but if they wish to maintain high inter-personal rapport with students, college teachers must be skillful in the ways they limit accessibility to themselves.

How can an instructor seem eager to see a student who drops by right at the end of, or even outside of, office hours? The teacher might say something like, "Hi, Josh, I'm glad you stopped by. I'm sorry I only have a couple of minutes right now. Which would you rather do, talk briefly now or longer in a couple of days?" If given such a choice, the student is much more likely to feel that the instructor is in fact interested in talking with him than he would be if the instructor simply said that office hours were over or that he or she did not like to see students outside posted hours. A pleasant message is at least as likely to control a student effectively as a curt one. Similar considerations apply to telephone calls received at inconvenient times. Obviously no one can be available any time a student wishes, and limits must be imposed. But there is wide latitude in ways to set appropriate limits tact-fully, without rejecting students for wanting to see their instructor and taking the (for them) big step of stopping by.

What are some things to consider when meeting with a student when ample time *is* available? Two aspects of the instruc-tor's behavior are especially important: whether the instructor relates to the student as superior to subordinate or as adult to adult, and whether the instructor assumes that the student's chief purpose in coming is revealed in the first topics he or she brings up.

College teachers may unknowingly emphasize their power over students during office meetings. A common way of doing this is by appearing unconcerned when students drop by to see them. Some teachers avoid eye contact as a student stands at the door or enters. Some provide a place for students to sit that is distant from them or across a large and imposing desk. Answering phone calls or responding to colleagues in the hall as if the student were not there also tells a student that he or she is not considered important.

To deemphasize status differences, some instructors stand when students enter their offices, show them to a seat, offer to take their coats, or practice other common courtesies of our culture. Others find such actions too formal and prefer to behave more casually. Any courteous style that is personally comfortable for the instructor is likely to be effective. A conference in the atmosphere created by such behavior facilitates the development of a person-to-person relationship by downplaying the hierarchical relationship between student and teacher.

Reasons that prompt students to visit a teacher vary immensely. Many students are concerned about their performance on exams or papers. Occasionally students drop by in anticipation of doing poorly, but more usually they come after graded work has been returned. Anxious-dependents are especially likely to come by to express concern about grades, almost regardless of what marks they received.

Other students may visit for a variety of reasons. For example, compliant students may come by to have the teacher check a term paper outline, independents or heroes may come to share some insight they have had about the subject or a proposed project, and attention-seekers may want to chat or reveal personal things about themselves. By their choice of ostensible reason for coming, by the confidence or anxiety they show, and by the dependence or independence they assume, students will reveal what they expect from the instructor in a given meeting. They may also attempt to maneuver the teacher into treating them as they expect.

How can a teacher best handle these hidden agendas in student conferences? It is best to be accepting and egalitarian and also not to assume that a student's first statement about why he or she has come is a sufficient reason for the call. If the teacher waits patiently and lets a student talk or ask questions freely, he or she may be able to guess the student's underlying concern or interpersonal strategy. Then the teacher can respond in a way that both affirms the legitimacy of the student's desire and gently pressures him or her toward a more independent and assured attitude.

A teacher should not let an emotional response to a student's remarks dictate his or her behavior. The instructor who becomes angry or defensive about grading practices when a student questions a grade does not foster a relationship that is conducive to good work nor aid the student's subsequent study. Those who calmly listen to the student's complaint, indicate that they can see why the student might feel that way, and then reread the answers or paper in question communicate to the student that his or her concerns are taken seriously—even if the grade is allowed to stand as originally given. It is important that a teacher not feel guilty about a student's failure or identify to excess with a hard-working student's desire for an "A." As has been stressed throughout this chapter, an instructor's ability to be aware of and control his or her personal feelings is the first ingredient in fostering interpersonal rapport with students.

The emphasis throughout this book is on warm interpersonal relationships with students, but instructors still should set limits on recurring personal conferences. Students may on occasion raise topics of immense personal concern with their college teachers. For example, they may express the fear they are going crazy or will kill themselves, or they may describe troubling conflicts with roommates, friends, or family members. Troublesome eating or sexual behavior also are commonly revealed. Students talk about their troubles only to instructors they like and trust, so a teacher should be complimented if a student brings a personal concern to him or her. A college teacher needs no special training or professional skills to listen to what are usually transiently troubling problems (Strupp, 1980). The teacher should encourage students to talk about what is bothering them, but only on one or, at the most, two occasions.

An instructor should encourage students to speak with a professional counselor if their problems are interfering seriously with their academic functioning, if they want to change their behavior or improve a conflicted relationship, or if their health or lives are in danger from suicidal impulses, drug or alcohol difficulties, or physical abuse by another. In order to deal with such problems a student needs to form a specific counseling relationship. Even instructors who are trained as therapists or counselors should avoid becoming involved in recurring counseling sessions with their own students. If counseling sessions are to be helpful, the counseling relationship must be clearly defined by both participants as existing *only* for that purpose, and the evaluative role of a college teacher rules out completely the possibility of formal counseling.

Teaching Ethics. College teachers are responsible for controlling the considerable power they have over students and ensuring that it is used only to achieve educational objectives. Not surprisingly, written ethical codes for college teachers do exist. For example, the American Psychological Association (APA) has proposed ethical guidelines for its members.[2] Most APA guidelines are designed to protect students from various forms of abuse or exploitation. For example, instructors are admonished not to require students to reveal personal information that might be used selfishly by the instructors as research data (although having students collect or generate data in order to teach research methods or content is appropriate). The deciding question should be, "Does the activity (laboratory or library research, field observations) fulfill *educational objectives* for the students?" This group advocates giving disquieting information to students in order to stimulate them to think about both sides of complex issues, but it urges college teachers to respect students as persons and avoid being excessively shocking or provocative. Finally, the APA requires college teachers, as gatekeepers to careers in psychology, to advise students as accurately as possible on their probability of successfully entering that vocation. This precept applies to other disciplines as well.

Most college teachers could add to this list of ethical considerations, and I will propose two additions. The first is that teachers should ensure that evaluation and grading be as fair and objective as possible. The second is that it is *under no circumstances* appropriate for a teacher to become romantically or sexually involved with a student, even if the relationship is initiated by the student. Here are my reasons for taking this position.

All students are prone, and some students especially so, to react to college teachers — even youthful graduate instructors — as symbols of important persons in their lives, notably their parents. Though no teacher-student relationship is likely to have the intensity of a psychotherapeutic transference relationship, romance between instructor and student is no more likely to be mutual or rationally chosen than it is between therapist and patient. The difference in power is simply too great for a truly mutual relationship to develop. The student is responding to the instructor more as a powerful symbol than as an individual, and the instructor is likely to be using the less powerful student to meet a variety of

---

[2]A copy of this code may be obtained from the American Psychological Association, 1200 17th Street N.W., Washington, D.C. 20026.

selfish needs such as distraction, denial of aging, or affirmation of attractiveness.

An instructor implicitly or explicitly requesting sex for a grade would be rightly damned in anyone's ethical code, but as Eble (1976) notes, this is much less common than romantic involvement between generally willing, but discrepantly powerful, participants. The most common type of attachment is the one-sided one in which a student develops a crush on a professor or has frequent sexual fantasies about him or her. If an instructor suspects that a student has such romantic feelings, he or she should try to limit individual contacts with that student and discourage a more involved relationship. However, the teacher should not respond by giving the student *less* attention in class than is given to others. College teachers may also have romantic or sexual fantasies about students on occasion, but private fantasies need not lead to overt behavior.

Certainly, lasting and satisfying relationships have been formed between individuals who originally met as student and teacher. However, even if an instructor believes that he or she has found in a student a potential life partner, the worst possible time to begin the relationship is when the student is enrolled in that teacher's class. Both should wait until the end of the professional teacher-student relationship before exploring the personal relationship further. Each person will then be in a position to respond freely as an adult. Some colleges have explicit rules against faculty members dating undergraduate students under any circumstances, but administrators and colleagues generally would judge a relationship begun after a class is over less harshly than they would judge one begun during class.

Teacher Tolerance of Youthful Behavior. Between the ages of eighteen and twenty-one, most men and women complete the process of separation from their families that was begun in their early teens. The open struggles with parents during early adolescence result in increased physical freedom, but it is the private skirmishes of late adolescence that free individuals from the emotional vulnerability of childhood. Relationships with other adults during this period (teachers, military officers, supervisors) provide a useful setting in which to learn how to relate to important others as an adult.

Outstanding teachers have often expressed the sentiment that to be a great classroom instructor one must genuinely like college-age students and identify with their interests, both serious and foolish (Highet, 1950). Appreciating the emotional tasks facing college students puts their sometimes inappropriate, immature, or even self-destructive behavior into a perspective that makes it more tolerable. Remembering personal excesses when one was a similar age can curb tendencies to judge students too quickly. An instructor who likes college students and accepts their interests will find enjoyable the time he or she is required to spend with them and value even more the greater time needed to have a significant impact on their lives.

The suggestions presented in this chapter are based on the position that common emotional reactions will appear in college classrooms regardless of what the instructor does. Instructors familiar with these phenomena, aware of their own expectancies and contributions to them, and skilled at communicating will be able to individualize their approach to students so as to avoid stimulating negative emotions and to promote warm and work-conducive relationships with all. Knowing what emotional phenomena are likely to occur in the classroom over a term also prevents dissatisfaction resulting from incorrectly labeling transient behavior as permanent. Because most college teachers enjoy classes more when they have personal relationships with students, interpersonally skillful teaching improves the quality of instruction that students receive because a satisfied instructor is more motivated to do his or her best.

The preceding two chapters have dealt exclusively with maintenance or emotional concerns in classroom groups. The next two chapters deal with task concerns — with the techniques of speaking before groups that teachers need to learn in order to utilize the classroom as a dramatic arena, and with ways of organizing lecture content for maximum impact and learning.

CHAPTER 4

❧❦❧❦❧❦❧❦❧❦❧❦❧❦❧❦❧❦❧❦❧❦❧❦❧

Analyzing and Improving Classroom Performance

> Drama critic John Lahr (1973) argues that drama encompasses more than plays on the conventional stage; in his view, drama also includes the highly engaging and emotionally stimulating performances witnessed by thousands in the form of sports spectacles, rock concerts, or symbolic political gestures such as draft card burnings and self-immolations.

This chapter is based on the premise that college classrooms are dramatic arenas first and intellectual arenas second. Its objectives are to sensitize the reader to the critical importance of speaking skills to college teaching, to describe those skills fully, and to help an instructor evaluate and improve his or her performance in this area. Mastering traditional stage skills is in no way sufficient to attain excellence in teaching, but it is impossible to attain such excellence without considerable practice and comfort with these skills. The chapter that follows (Chapter Five) deals with the specifics of choosing and organizing lecture content and should be considered in tandem with this chapter.

College Classrooms as Dramatic Arenas

The fundamental setting of drama—a speaker or speakers before an audience, captivating their attention and stimulating their emotions — has long been a universal part of human experience. People today seek out a wide range of theatrical experiences and spectacles, both formal and informal, just as people always have. Whether observing a tribal storyteller, a narrator of an epic poem, a Greek comedy, an Elizabethan tragedy, a nineteenth-century opera, or a twentieth-century existential play, people have enjoyed being caught up in the spell of drama.

Even when the purpose of a gathering is not explicitly dramatic, speakers require the skills of the stage in order to be successful. Religious, military, and political leaders must be able to attract and hold an audience's attention if the message they convey is to have its desired impact (Stevens, 1966). If the speaker's skill is great, his or her presentation will create the involvement and feeling of suspense associated with theater. College teachers, too, need dramatic skills to ensure that students become fully engaged in class presentations and find them enjoyable.

In what ways do classrooms resemble theatrical settings? Many classrooms have stages or raised platforms in the front of the hall, and classrooms are frequently equipped with some kind of overhead stage lighting. Furthermore, the overwhelming proportion of college teaching follows a lecture format in which the instructor stands before an audience of up to several hundred students. Although teachers of large classes are relatively more dependent on speaking skills than are leaders of seminars, all college teaching is fundamentally public speaking.

College teaching is different from religious, military, or political leadership, but it is leadership nonetheless; and though it is far more than dramatic entertainment, it should resemble drama in being engaging and pleasurable. College teachers develop more involved relationships with their audiences than is possible from single appearances on the theater or lecture circuit, and instructors play themselves rather than having assigned parts as actors do. Still, teachers share with other speakers a fundamental reliance on an ability to engage an audience and to stimulate emotions.

Effective speaking in no way ensures that a college professor will promote wisdom or provide students with permanent intellectual growth. Professors — and the public at large — rightly have long distrusted speakers who appeal to the emotions for the purpose of closing rather than opening avenues of inquiry. But such need not be the purpose of an accomplished speaker. Distrust of demagoguery does not require that the college teacher avoid developing the skill of speaking powerfully and persuasively to students. Sound arguments are the prime ingredient of a fine lecture, but the skill with which they are delivered should be equal to the skill with which they were prepared if they are to have maximum impact on students.

Using Emotion in Lecturing

Capturing an audience's attention is the first thing required of any performer, college teachers included. Almost all students will pay attention to an instructor for a few minutes, but most students will not continue to listen actively to a mediocre lecturer, any more than they would be responsive to a mediocre theatrical performance beyond the opening scenes. But eliciting and maintaining attention is only a first step.

College teachers need to stimulate emotion, but their purpose in doing so differs from entertainers. The entertainer's goal is to stimulate emotion for its own sake, while the classroom instructor uses emotion to engage students' attention fully in the content selected for presentation and to transfer to them his or her own passionate interest in the subject.

Like most of us, college students remember images longer than they remember words, and instructors can aid their recall by pairing abstract content with emotionally tinged associations and vivid images whenever possible. Expressive speech, including changes in the loudness of the voice, also helps to punctuate a presentation and emphasize the organization of the lecturer's ideas.

In addition to using positive emotions, skilled instructors avoid stimulating negative emotions such as anger, anxiety, or — perhaps especially — boredom. The best way to keep students from being bored by a subject is to show them that *you* are not bored by it. Some professors can make anything interesting, primarily by conveying their own excitement about the topic. At the other extreme, some instructors show so little emotion when discussing their subject that their students may wonder why the professors bothered to learn it themselves. College students, like most other reasonable adults, are generally able to spot the shallow or fraudulent instructor who relies on emotional appeals to gloss over a superficial understanding of content or to present material in a slipshod manner. They will, however, respect and respond to a teacher's genuine enthusiasm.

Improving Classroom Speaking Skills

College professors can be effective classroom teachers in spite of physical handicaps. Most could continue to teach from a wheelchair or even after losing sight or hearing. However, unless a teacher had students who could understand signing, it would be almost impossible to continue teaching after losing his or her voice. Yet almost all instructors take their speech for granted. Unless they have a significant speech problem such as stuttering or speaking too softly to be heard, few college teachers evaluate the effectiveness of their speaking voices or actively work to improve them.

The purpose of this section is to present a framework within which an instructor can evaluate his or her speaking voice and to suggest exercises that may help in overcoming common speech weaknesses. The aim here is not to give professors the expressive range of Burton or Olivier by merely to describe what ordinary teachers can do to improve their speech in the classroom.

Increasing Sensitivity to Others' Speech. The first step in improving one's own speaking voice is to pay serious attention to the ways others use their voices in group settings (Machlin, 1966). Notice the variety of others' speech. Some people speak slowly and deliberately and others with speed and impetuosity; some speak softly, others with loud projection. Still others present great variety and change between these extremes. The tone of speech probably varies most, from deeply resonant to high or shrill. Tune, the musical quality resulting from patterns of rising and falling tones, also varies. You will find that voices and speech styles are almost as unique as appearances.

You are also likely to notice how certain speech habits distract you from the ideas being presented (Satterfield, 1978). Some

speakers habitually begin sentences with meaningless vocaliza-
tions such as "uh," "well," or "okay," as if their vocal cords could
not begin to vibrate without a warm-up. Speakers are often
unaware of how much their speech is interrupted by such unnecessary sounds. When observing one novice college teacher I was so
struck by her habit of beginning sentences with "okay" that I made
an informal count over the remainder of a fifty-minute class. In
discussing her lecture afterwards I commented on her use of "okay."
She agreed that she said it a lot, estimating that she had used the
word "about ten times" during her talk. The actual count was over
seventy-five!

Other speech qualities also distract listeners. For example,
some instructors speak in such low tones or with such poor articulation that listeners become fatigued from the effort needed to
understand what is being said. At the other extreme, rapid speech
or speech delivered in staccato bursts also can be tiring to the hearer,
especially if no breaks occur. Anything about vocal delivery that
takes the listener's attention away from the content of the speaker's
remarks will distract from the overall effectiveness of the communication.

Probably you have noticed that some speakers' voices are
easier and more enjoyable to listen to than others. From the first
few phrases, some voices capture the ear and produce a warm glow
of anticipated pleasure, while others create almost a dread of what
is to come (Machlin, 1966).

What voice qualities contribute to these markedly different
effects? Foremost among these is *pitch*. The degree to which the
voice varies in pitch is critical to engaging speaking. A voice rang-
ing melodically between high and low tones is much more likely to
keep listeners' attention than a monotonous voice that merely uses
one or two notes. The way a speaker uses *inflection*, giving more
emphasis to some words than to others, also contributes to audience interest. Speech with little or no emphasis is unlikely to
engage and maintain someone's attention.

Even something as subtle as the timing of a speaker's breathing can contribute to the overall quality of the speaking voice.
Silent or barely audible inhalations occurring at the ends of major
phrases are less likely to interrupt the flow of ideas than noisy inha-

lations stuck in the middle of important sentences. Ironically, some political speakers seem especially prone to break up their speeches with unnecessary pauses (Henry Kissinger is one example).

Though more difficult to pin down than other characteristics, the degree to which speech sounds relaxed or tense contributes significantly to its overall effect on listeners. When speakers have a relaxed or flowing style, when their speech seems to come easily, we say they are fluent. Hesitant or jerky speech causes the listener to share the speaker's tension, discomfort, or lack of confidence.

Noticing how differences in others' speech affect you is the first step in improving your own speaking voice. It does not matter how systematically you note speech qualities. Simply paying attention to them as you sit in meetings or lectures will increase your sensitivity as effectively as taking detailed notes on what you hear. Let your personal preference dictate your choice of method. There is, unfortunately, no choice about the next step to take in improving your speaking voice — you must listen to a tape recording of yourself talking.

Recording and Analyzing Your Speech. Speech teachers agree that a detailed analysis of a tape recording is an essential step in deciding how one's voice can be improved. Audio-only taping is preferable, because videotaping introduces visual distractions. The following method is adapted from those advocated by speech authorities (Machlin, 1966) and refined based on my experience with graduate student instructors. I recommend that you make *two* tape recordings of your voice, in the following way.

Ask a friend to help you in making the first tape. Set up your tape recorder in a small or moderate-size room. Facing your friend, begin a conversation by stating your name, your age, and where you were born. Then pick some topic that interests you — a recent movie or book you liked or hated, for example — and for four or five minutes tell your friend how you feel about it. Instruct your companion beforehand to ask short questions or respond briefly to what you say if he or she wishes, especially if you stop talking. The objective of this exercise is to record yourself talking in a natural, conversational style for a few minutes.

Within a few days (or immediately afterward, if you wish), move your recording equipment to a classroom seating between twenty and fifty students. Place this recording on the same tape immediately following the informal conversation so that both will be together when you analyze them. Bring a friend along as an audience and have him or her sit in the middle of the front row with instructions to remain quiet during this recording. Select a topic from your subject area and give a short lecture of five to ten minutes' duration, standing up.

Do not listen to either of your recordings right away. A few days after the second recording has been completed, set aside an hour for your analysis. The following steps may be useful in structuring your assessment of the recordings.

1. Listen to each recording without stopping to take notes.
2. Afterward, note your initial reactions to hearing yourself speak. What are your feelings (puzzled, ashamed, pessimistic, defensive, critical)? Try not to let your initial reactions, whatever they may be, discourage you.
3. Listen to the first recording a second time, jotting on a piece of paper the words that seem to best describe your voice. Try to think of it as a voice you have never heard before. *Stop at the end of the conversational recording.*
4. Rewind the tape and listen to the conversation segment for a third time. Using the Speech Assessment Rating Form (Exhibit 1 at the end of this chapter), rate your speech along each of the eight dimensions. Do not be too concerned about selecting a particular number on the scale, but note where in general you believe your voice fell on each dimension.
5. Within twenty-four hours, rate the lecture segment using the same procedure.
6. Consider differences between your speech in the two situations. Was it more relaxed and natural when in the informal setting? Did your speech become tighter and more highly pitched when you were lecturing? Was it louder and more precisely articulated when you lectured? In which setting were you more fluent, more enthusiastic? Any differences you note will help you decide how to improve.

The next step is to determine how your speech could be improved. There are several ways to do this. The best method is to take the tapes and rating forms to a speech coach or experienced speaker for review and critique. You might also work with another instructor who is interested in improving his or her speech and take turns speaking and listening. Each person can rate the other's voice as well as his or her own, and the two of you can compare notes.

Regardless of what other people listen to your recordings, *you* must make the final decision about what, if anything, in your speech needs improvement. It is important to note that no single voice quality (other than distracting speech habits, perhaps) will determine listeners' interest when you speak. Rather, the overall variety and expressiveness of your voice is the critical thing. A speaker whose voice is sometimes loud, sometimes soft, sometimes fast, sometimes slow, sometimes sharp and crisp, and sometimes mellow and melodic is more likely to keep an audience's attention than one whose voice has any one quality for too long.

In addition, remember that the impact of your speech on your audience may have as much to do with what you are feeling when you speak as with the technical qualities of your voice. If you are enthusiastic and eager to tell your audience what you know, they are more likely to be enthusiastic about hearing it. If you are fascinated about the topic at hand, they are likely to have their curiosity aroused, too. In addition to selecting specific speech characteristics to change, it is wise to attempt to experience what you wish your students to feel and trust your speech to model it for them.

The following section discusses a number of common speech weaknesses that can be improved. For best results with serious problems such as stuttering or extreme stage fright, you should consider consultation with a speech therapist. However, the self-improvement techniques that follow are helpful remedies for the most common minor weaknesses observed in the speech of college teachers.

Voice Improvement Exercises. Though you may not be fully aware of how often you use unessential words or phrases, it is relatively easy to increase awareness of their use and to eliminate them from your formal speech. Ask someone in the audience, such as a friendly and trusted student, to count your uses of certain words for a few days and report at the end of each class. The resulting information can help you gain control over this distracting habit.

Most college teachers speak too quietly. Developing a speaking voice that is strong and energetic enough to be easily heard and understood by students in the back rows is essential. Speaking loudly enough is especially important at the beginning of a class when the students have not yet settled down and become caught up in your ideas.

Projection refers to the combination of volume and energy that makes the voice carry well to the back of a room or auditorium. As any singer or actor knows, speaking with projection is more than simply speaking loudly. The following exercise can both illustrate voice projection and, when repeated on several occasions in increasingly large rooms, provide a technique for increasing it.

Position yourself and a companion in the middle of a room about the same size as the ones in which you typically teach. Standing only a few feet from one another, take turns reading several lines from a book. Speak your lines expressively, opening your mouth wide and saying them with vigor and conviction. Notice the sound of your own voice as it reverberates around the room and compare it mentally with that of your partner as he or she speaks to you. Each of you should then take two or three steps backwards and repeat the procedure. Even though you are now farther away, continue to speak directly to your friend as if it were critically important the he or she hear and understand what you are saying. Repeat this process until the two of you are standing against opposite walls.

During this exercise you probably noticed the need to take much bigger breaths when you spoke as you moved farther away from your partner. You may have also noticed that you needed to open your mouth considerably wider to project your voice over a greater distance. You may have become aware of a tightening in your throat as you were required to speak over a larger distance. If this was the case, your voice quality and comfort probably decreased as well.

A well-projected voice requires a sufficient volume of air to generate the vocalization and still have a reserve to support the sound. You must fill your lungs with more air than you need because lungs are much less efficient balloons when they are only partly inflated. To fill your lungs fully, inhale from your abdomen rather than your chest. Your "stomach," not your chest, should rise when you take a deep breath. (This is far easier to do if your posture is good—spine straight, shoulders back.) Singers and wind players learn "belly breathing" early in their careers.

Voice projection is aided by opening the mouth wide enough to allow the sound to escape easily. Singers know well the importance of opening their mouths to deliver a relaxed-sounding voice with high volume. The key to opening the mouth wide while keeping the throat (and therefore the sound) relaxed is to lower the jaw as far as possible rather than stretching the cheeks sideways. Making a wide, exaggerated smile ruins voice quality by creating tension in the mouth and throat. To illustrate how far your jaw will hinge downward comfortably, yawn several times. That is the type of mouth opening to use when you are trying to fill up a room with the sound of your voice. Except when speaking in very large halls, it will not be necessary to project to your maximum potential, but developing such power makes it unlikely that your voice will ever be underpowered in less demanding classroom settings.

No matter how well you project your voice, there are situations in which other factors will work against your being heard. Power to project your voice is especially important in poorly designed classrooms with poor acoustics. Because bodies and clothing absorb sound and thus reduce distorting reverberation, a room full of people will have better acoustics than an empty one. Avoid classrooms with especially poor acoustics if possible, and schedule your classes in rooms only as large as the number of students enrolled; decline the option of a larger but half-filled room.

It is almost impossible to be heard in some teaching situations. For example, on one of those first few lovely days of spring, students may persuade you to let the class meet outside. With no walls or ceilings to reflect your voice, it will be practically impossible for students spread out on the grass to hear you—even assuming that they are looking in your direction and not watching the passing campus scene. Giving in to earnest requests to hold class outside is a poor idea for a number of reasons, but the near impossibility of being heard is foremost among them.

To increase your voice projection, there is no substitute for practicing in actual classrooms. Begin in small rooms and gradually work your way up to the largest ones at your school. Bring along a friend or two to sit in the back row if possible; they can tell you how well your voice is carrying to where they are sitting. Whether you are alone or accompanied, the key to projection is speaking directly to a real or imagined person sitting in the back row. Some college teachers have learned to do this in actual classes by picking one or two students in the rear and pretending that they are speaking only to them.

Learning to speak with sufficient projection is relatively easy if practiced with commitment, but a few college instructors who had used these exercises still had difficulty in making themselves heard. Discussions revealed that the source of their difficulty was an underlying inhibition about speaking loudly. When they first tried the exercises, they were quite uncomfortable about speaking with such vigor and volume. The origin of this anxiety about hearing themselves speak with volume may have been excessive demands from parents and elementary school teachers that they speak softly. Do not be concerned if your voice sounds different or displeasing to you as you begin to project more. Such a reaction may simply reflect long-standing conditioning to speak softly, even in front of groups. Luckily, such (for a college teacher) maladaptive conditioning can be modified with practice.

Next to speaking too softly, poor articulation is the most common speech problem observed in college teachers. Speaking crisply and clearly takes considerably more effort than speaking conversationally. Speaking before others, especially as the size of the group and the necessary projection increases, requires proportionately more distinct and energetic articulation.

Well-articulated speech results primarily from the way the speaker sounds consonants, especially those that begin and end words. Such sounds result from lip movements to some degree, but primarily they result from the way the tongue touches the roof of the mouth and the back of the teeth. You can demonstrate for yourself how much activity occurs in your mouth when words are well articulated. Read any short passage out loud, slowly and with deliberate pronunciation of every syllable. Notice how much your lips and tongue must move to make all the consonant sounds.

The consonants that precede and follow open-mouth vowel sounds make possible the large number of sounds human beings can make.

Increased attention to forming consonants and to speaking more deliberately in front of groups is probably all you will need to overcome poor articulation habits. However, some instructors have also found it useful to practice saying tongue twisters that focus on different consonant sounds such as "p," "t," "s," "ch," and "ing." More than anything, a college teacher must make the conscious decision to speak as distinctly as possible.

Anyone can learn to speak with sufficient projection and articulation, but tonal quality is more difficult to improve. Voice quality is largely the result of the physical properties of the throat, mouth, sinus cavities, facial bone structure, and chest, none of which can be changed easily. There are, however, certain unpleasant and distracting voice qualities that college teachers can and should reduce or eliminate.

The first of these is *stridency*, speaking with a hard, metallic (usually loud and shrill) tone. This voice quality typically results from trying to speak loudly without breathing deeply. The attempt to gain volume in this way constricts the throat and produces the strident sound. Breathing deeply to achieve projection will usually help to produce a more relaxed, less strident tone. An additional voice exercise to reduce stridency is to yawn a few times and then make an "ah" sound for ten seconds or so, letting your voice gradually fall in pitch to produce a long, sliding sound. Stridency comes from tension in the vocal apparatus, and this tension will disappear when you learn how to produce volume while maintaining relaxation.

Excessive *nasality* or twangy quality results from directing too much sound through the nose. It is normal to send sound in this direction when we make "mmm" or "nnn" sounds, but doing so with other sounds, especially open vowel sounds, produces a result that is unpleasant to hear. Practice making long vowel sounds through the mouth rather than the nose to eliminate this problem.

Winter colds or excessive strain can give the voice a hoarse, breathy sound. College teachers should know a few stage tricks for speaking well in spite of a cold. Singers and actors learn to spot the beginnings of a sore throat and to avoid speaking or singing any more than they must at such times. It is also common practice for them to gargle with a mild soda and salt solution or to suck a lemon just before performing. This can reduce unpleasant voice tone and provide relief for an hour or so.

Though a masterful lecturer results from far more than an engaging speaking voice, the skill with which a college teacher uses this oral bridge to his or her students will strongly influence the effectiveness of the presentation. The visual dimension of a presentation, though of less importance than the spoken dimension, is another essential element in mastery of the classroom as a dramatic arena.

Gesture and Movement: The Visual Dimension

The gestures a college teacher uses do not communicate content to students directly, but they can greatly increase attention and emphasize relationships within the content. Most students will be as affected by what they see as by what they hear. What they see can distract from, enhance, or complement oral messages.

What might we see when listening to an outstanding college teacher? We are not likely to see a stiff, wooden figure solidly planted at a single spot on the floor. We are more likely to see a figure whose posture — shoulders back, head erect — conveys confidence in what he or she has to say. We are likely to see the speaker's arms and hands move in varied gestures, such as a single finger pointing upward for emphasis or palms extended toward the class just before a new idea is presented. At times subtle, at times sweeping, the speaker's movement is always coordinated with his or her speech to enhance the message.

Individuals prefer different movement styles, just as they use different speech styles. Many styles can be effective. Some speakers remain relatively stationary (standing behind a lectern and only occasionally moving to the side) and still visually captivate an audience through subtle movements of the head, upper body, and fingers. Other speakers prefer a more active style to convey their intense emotional state. They may pace across the front of the classroom and dart down the middle or side aisles on occasion. The movements of excellent speakers are intimately connected to what they are saying: The curved hand and arm gesture coming at the end of a major point accompanied by a drop in inflection and a slowing of speech communicates as eloquently, with as much ease and expressiveness, as their words.

Other than recommending good posture and teaching standing up (it is much more difficult to capture students' attention sitting), there are few formulas to offer for developing effective movement before a group. Try to increase your overall energy level and relax whatever inhibitions you may have about throwing yourself into a classroom presentation. If instructors are highly excited about the business of communicating to students, their bodies will automatically become involved in the process.

Noticing how your body takes part in your overall behavior is a useful place to begin. Making a videotape recording of yourself giving a lecture and watching it with the sound turned off is a good method of assessing what kinds of movement you use and their effects on observers. You can also note how you feel after teaching. If you feel relaxed, it is unlikely that your body was actively involved in the goings-on. Total involvement in a performance of any kind burns energy and creates temporary fatigue, but it has the benefit of producing gestures and movement from within, visual stimulation that appears genuine and unstaged.

This does not mean that every movement you make before a classroom must be totally fresh and original. When you find a movement that is effective, by all means make a note of it and hold it in reserve for another appropriate time. Accomplished actors have a variety of expressions and gestures that they use to communicate emotions, and the best players have the largest repertoires to draw upon. Actors typically experience the emotion first and let the movement follow naturally. The prevailing school of theater in America (and to an increasing degree in Britain) is one emphasizing the actor's experience of emotion as opposed to skill at mimicking it (Linklater, 1976). (Much modern stage training resembles experiential encounter groups more than speech classes.) Similarly, the accomplished teacher may have a large repertoire of gestures and movements, but the pantomime is more likely to enhance the point being made if it occurs spontaneously.

There are some exceptions to the general rule that gestures are more effective if they are natural rather than planned. Many excellent instructors step to one side of the lectern or table when expressing one side of an argument and to the other side when presenting the opposing view (Harris, 1977). Because presenting contrasting views is so common in teaching, this staging can be used by instructors of most subjects. Such side-stepping not only catches the students' eyes but also emphasizes an important logical relationship in the material and probably aids recall as well. College teachers who use this device are frequently unaware of it, but most do so deliberately. A similar tactic is to advance close to the front row when discussing administrative details, making anecdotal illustrations, or leading discussion, and retreat nearer the board when presenting new content. One professor I observed sometimes sat on a tall stool placed within a yellow square when he wished to speak as an individual rather than as a scientist.

In summary, learning to move well in the classroom results from involving the whole body in teaching in a relaxed but energetic manner that is consistent with one's personal style of communication. Natural and appropriate movements and gestures support the oral presentation.

Many static characteristics of classrooms have significant power over students' visual attention, and college teachers can increase the overall quality of their performance by being sensitive to these characteristics. The next section deals with some of these factors.

Sensitivity to the Classroom as a Stage

A number of physical features of classrooms enhance or detract from an educational performance. Taking stock of the physical classroom and making whatever adjustments are possible cannot offset unclear content or poor delivery, but it can make a significant if admittedly small contribution to your teaching performance.

Assess whatever classroom you use with a special visit to examine its theatrical characteristics. This is especially important when considering a new course, because you may wish to modify your initial plans after you have seen the room in which you will teach. Evaluating the hall increases the precision with which class presentations can be accurately planned.

Size is surely the first attribute to consider in evaluating a room. Compare the actual number of seats with the expected enrollment to determine room density. If you have many more seats than students, the acoustics will be poorer and your presentations will have less sense of intensity and intimacy. When faced with such a situation, consider using strands of crepe paper to close off the rear rows to encourage students to sit nearer the front.

Some beginning teachers are initially distraught to find seats bolted to the floor in their assigned classrooms, believing that they must be able to move chairs into small groups for discussion to occur. Movable chairs are not really a prerequisite for effective student interaction. Still, if you think your teaching plans require movable seats, a visit to the classroom will reveal whether you have them.

A room's acoustics are important, and it is a good idea to practice a bit of lecturing during your visit, even though you cannot make a final evaluation of the room's acoustics until it is filled with students. Also note other physical characteristics (room shape, distance between speaker and students, ceiling height, lighting) that will influence the ease with which you will be able to communicate with your audience. Most classrooms are adequate, but a scouting trip can help to anticipate possible problems while there is still time to complain and have them corrected.

When entering a classroom to teach, note the presence of anything that may distract the students' attention. Are the chairs in a state of disarray? Are there pizza boxes or coffee cups scattered across the floor? It is also a good idea to make sure that all the lights are on and that the area in front of the blackboard across which you will be moving is free of anything that might get in your way (chairs, electrical cords, trash cans). As a matter of routine, erase the board completely before beginning to teach to ensure that students are not distracted by the remains of someone else's outline and that you do not have to take time while in the middle of a lecture to clear a space to write.

Any good actress or actor knows the importance of entrances and exits to capturing the audience's attention. College teachers should also note the way they enter a classroom. (Exits are unimportant because professors in American colleges rarely leave before their students.) Noting by which doors you can enter the classroom and deciding on the mood (optimism, intensity, seriousness) with which you wish to begin will help you create an air of expectant excitement among your students from the very beginning. Though there are interpersonal advantages to arriving early for class, I have observed excellent teachers who habitually arrive a few minutes late: With a flourish, they begin to lecture as they dash down the aisle or in from stage left. Think about the way you begin a class to see if it is consistent with the effect you wish to have on your students.

Like actors on a stage, college teachers can effectively use various props on which to focus students' attention. Books are the most commonly used. Students are more likely to remember a book's title if the book is held up and passed around. Reading quotations directly from books also has a greater authenticity than reading the same quotations from lecture notes.

Books are not the only props that can be used effectively. Especially in science and art courses, numerous objects can be brought in to illustrate topics and break up the routine of lecturing, note-taking, and discussing. Props do not have to communicate anything directly; it is not even critical that students see them closely. Their primary value is a dramatic one: They add visual variety and refresh student attention. Slides, films, and other electronic props are a common means of increasing visual attention and emphasizing organization (see Chapter Five).

Even though college teachers cannot easily leave the classroom with flair, they can end their classes decisively. Stopping on time and with a strongly inflected concluding comment is far superior to yelling out a few additional points or suggestions about an assignment as the students file out. Conditioning students to expect a class to be ended as emphatically as it began will keep them from becoming restless when their watches (or stomachs!) tell them the end is near.

Actively Engaging Students

Speaking clearly with variety and projection helps to engage an audience; so does movement. An additional quality easily as important as these is *eye contact*. Except for stage asides, actors are taught to speak their lines as if the audience is not present. College teachers, by contrast, have a powerful additional resource in the opportunity to look directly into the eyes of their listeners.

Our faces reveal more about what we are thinking than any other part of our bodies. Though our eyes may not be literal windows into our souls, they do mark the spot of closest outside contact with our consciousness and emotions. Some instructors avoid looking at their students' eyes, habitually gazing to one side or the ceiling after a quick unfocused glimpse at the class. Even if they gaze out at the students, they rarely focus on single faces and allow that little spark of human contact to pass between them. Many students are equally uncomfortable with direct eye contact and will avert their eyes if the instructor looks directly at them. Over time, however, students can learn to be more comfortable with instructors who look them directly in the eyes. Making frequent and direct eye contact with individual students is as important as anything else discussed thus far to engaging their minds. Eye contact is also invaluable because routinely scanning students' faces is the best way to assess the impact of what you are saying or doing so that you can make small adjustments in your presentation.

An outstanding literature professor said that what contributed most to her teaching effectiveness was "where the students are sitting. I can capture the full attention of anyone who is seated in the first ten rows, but I will hook only some of the students seated farther back." Her rationale was that it is difficult to catch an individual student's eye beyond the distance usually covered by ten rows. So certain was she of this physical limit that she taught classes in rooms larger than this with great reluctance.

Even though actors cannot focus on individual sets of eyes, they are acutely aware of the necessity of maintaining that fragile connection between themselves and the audience. By "losing the house," stage directors and actors mean breaking or weakening that gossamer but all-important audience-performer bond. Actors are taught the importance of keeping their faces directed toward the audience as much as possible. Directors block actors' movements on stage so that they almost always face the audience (or are sideways to it) whenever they are speaking or are the center of action. The ancient admonition to "never turn your back to the audience" is no longer observed rigidly in contemporary theater, where thrust or round stages are common, but it is still followed when possible.

In college classrooms the traditional rule still holds. Every time instructors turn their backs to the class they risk "losing the house"; if they stay turned for more than five seconds, they will find most of their students looking elsewhere or thinking about something else. The theatrical tradition suggests that college teachers should maintain face-to-face contact with their students *at all times*. You can do this by turning sideways when writing on the board, regularly looking toward the class, and glancing around the classroom when a student is making a long discussion comment. When reading quotations, you can also read a phrase to yourself quickly and then deliver it with expression while look- ing directly at your audience, rather than keeping your eyes fixed on the page. This ability to read with what is called a leading eye can be developed by anyone with practice and was taught routinely to schoolchildren in nineteenth-century America (Machlin, 1966). The delicate visual bond so critical to facilitating understanding between instructors and students requires constant cultivation and protection.

College teachers must give exciting and moving perfor- mances day after day (though at least, unlike actors, they are not required to give the *same* lecture every day — with two presenta- tions on Wednesdays and Saturdays). Like other performers, col- lege teachers will find it difficult at times to "get up" for teaching. Being excited and fully motivated to teach is much easier at the beginning of a term than after the novelty has worn off and other demands on one's time increase. Luckily, college teachers can benefit from some of the techniques that professional actors use to give their best performances time and again.

The single most useful technique is to recognize that you must prepare yourself emotionally as well as intellectually before your "performance." No instructor is likely to go into a class without some idea or specific plan of what he or she wants to do and the necessary materials (books, props, maps, slides) to carry it out. Many college teachers, though, walk directly from parking lot or committee meeting into a classroom with only a short pause to collect their thoughts. The outstanding professors I interviewed typically set aside from five to thirty minutes beforehand to think about the class they are going to teach. Some close their office doors and hold telephone calls; others walk a longer route to their classroom building than necessary. However you can manage to find a few minutes of solitude before class (in the lavatory, if necessary!), recognizing the importance of emotional preparation, especially if you are tired or depressed, is essential to ensure a high-quality performance.

If you are emotionally prepared, you will have the energy to model the intellectual attitude you want your students to have. If you want them to be excited about the ideas you are presenting, you should be excited by those ideas as well—no small task when presenting fundamental concepts you first learned years ago and may have taught numerous times. If you wish your students to think, to push aside their emotional reactions and prior views to consider a problem objectively and rationally, you must wrestle through your own reactions again as well. If you wish your students to respond with emotional sensitivity to art, then you must be able to portray this response for them. Students will learn more about the emotional attitude they should (or could) have about a content area from what their instructor models than from anything else.

Several years ago I inadvertently learned the importance of preparation time when growing enrollments in psychology courses forced one of my classes, which met at a popular hour, to be moved to a building some ten minutes' walk across campus. As the semester progressed, I noticed that I was able to *begin* teaching this class with the energy and concentration I had come to expect only five to ten minutes after a class period had started. In effect, I had been warming up at the students' expense in the past. When I mentioned this to one of my students, a drama major, she said that no actor or musical performer would ever fail to prepare emotionally before going on stage, and she wondered where I had gotten the idea that college teachers were exempt from this rule!

Creating Dramatic Suspense

How can college teachers infuse their presentations with suspense, with a sense of dramatic tension and the excitement that comes from expecting something important or unusual? Instructors can create this sense of anticipation in their students by giving presentations as if they are telling a story, ordering and presenting their topics in ways that stimulate in their listeners a sense of unfolding and discovery.

To tell any story well, the narrator must become almost as caught up in the plot as the listeners. Even if they have told a story countless times, masters of the ancient storyteller's art grow excited at hearing the tale once again. They save the big surprises until the end, laying the groundwork early by posing questions from the opening moments and dropping clues along the way. The storyteller must approach the well-known plot as if telling it for the first time so that listeners will experience it afresh, even when they too have heard it before.

Superb lecturers share many qualities with storytellers. They, too, save the conclusions or most crucial points until the end, having teased the students along the way with key questions and preliminary findings or interpretations. Such instructors seem genuinely moved by the story they are presenting, the excitement of scientific discovery or historical events or the pathos and beauty of literature or art. These teachers have a well-developed empathic sense, the ability to imagine accurately the thoughts and experiences students are having as they listen to the story.

Some college teachers are natural storytellers who add a sense of drama to anything they talk about. But almost *any* instructor can learn to be a good storyteller if he or she relaxes inhibitions and reacts to the suspense inherent in most content. Practice in telling traditional tales to children can help college teachers add a sense of immediacy, spontaneity, and dramatic suspense to their teaching. Teachers who have tried this have reported good results. As noted psychology teacher James McConnell quotes an influential professor as saying, "If you want to capture the imaginations of young people, you have to tell them stories!" (1978, p. 4). Lecturing to college students is certainly a more intellectually demanding and complex business than telling stories around a campfire, but accomplished teachers are frequently skilled storytellers.

Exhibit 1
Speech Assessment Rating Form.

Speaker's Name _____

Date _____ Size of Room _____

  Instructions: Listen to the taped segment first to hear the content and gain a general impression of the voice. Then read the rating form completely. Keep the dimensions in mind as you listen a second time to the tape. Read the descriptions at the extreme ends of each of the speech dimensions and then mark a point on the line (with an X or ✔) to represent the part of the dimension that best describes the speech over the entire segment. You may have to listen to the segment a third time to be able to rate it on all eight dimensions.

  HINT: Try to ignore the content and to pay attention only to the speaker's voice.

1. *How frequently does the speaker begin or break sentences with unnecessary words or sounds* (such as "uh," "okay," or "well")?

1	2	3	4	5	6	7

Such words or
sounds are used
very frequently

Few, if any,
unnecessary words
or sounds
are uttered

2. *How relaxed is the speaker's voice?*

1	2	3	4	5	6	7

Voice sounds
very tense
and tight

Voice sounds
very relaxed
and free
from tension

3. *How rhythmic and fluent is the speech?*

1	2	3	4	5	6	7

Speech is very
halting, jerky,
and broken by
unnecessary pauses

Speech flows
in a naturally
rhythmic manner

4. *How noticeable or distracting is the speaker's breathing?*

1	2	3	4	5	6	7

Inhalations
are noisy and
occur at distracting
times (in the
middle of phrases)

Inhalations
are barely audible
and are well timed
(between sentences
or phrases)

Exhibit 1
Speech Assessment Rating Form, Cont'd.

5. *How varied is the pitch of the speaker's voice?*

1	2	3	4	5	6	7

Voice is monotonous, too consistently the same pitch

Voice uses a wide range of pitches, from high to low

6. *How appropriate and varied is the rate of speaking?*

1	2	3	4	5	6	7

Speech is either too slow, too fast, or too unvarying

Appropriate rate — speech is of varied speed and is easy to follow

7. *How meaningful is the stress put on different words?*

1	2	3	4	5	6	7

Stress is distracting — too light, too heavy, or inconsistent with meaning

Stress enhances rather than distracts from meaning

8. *Are the words clearly articulated?*

1	2	3	4	5	6	7

Words are frequently slurred or sloppily pronounced

Words are sharply and clearly articulated

CHAPTER 5

ᙓᙅᙓᙅᙓᙅᙓᙅᙓᙅᙓᙅᙓᙅᙓᙅᙓᙅᙓᙅᙓᙅᙓᙅᙓᙅᙓ

Selecting and Organizing Material for Class Presentations

> Scholarship must be accurate, whether it is interesting or not. But teaching must be interesting, even if it is not 100 percent accurate. *Highet (1950, p. 219)*

To many people the college lecture is a dinosaur, a holdover from a pretechnological age when books were scarce or nonexistent and the lecture was the primary way students could gain information. For some it represents some of the worst moments in their college educations, evoking images of fighting to stay awake while a distant professor droned on and on, his head buried deep in his yellowed lecture notes.

There is surely some merit in these points. The lecture is no longer needed for the purposes for which it was first created, and it can be an unsurpassed soporific for students when it is poor. Still, unlike the dinosaur, the lecture thrives as the dominant form of college instruction today. Why has the lecture survived?

Lecturing occurs whenever a teacher is talking and students are listening. It flourishes in an age of cheap paperback books and affordable videotape technology (Howe, 1980). Its survival is not solely due to the old-fashioned preferences of conservative college faculties. Many students, especially those who seek information and high marks, prefer lectures as well. Innovative course formats eventually fade from listings of departmental offerings when students are given a choice between them and traditionally taught courses. The lecture also survives because at its best it can be *magnificent.* Enough instructors at almost every school are accomplished lecturers for the form to remain the norm in spite of poor examples. The economic advantages of teaching classes by means of the lecture, especially those offering very large sections, are numerous, though they are insufficient to account for the lecture's popularity.

The model of teaching effectiveness upon which this book is based suggests that lectures survive because, like bullfights and "Masterpiece Theater," they satisfy the need for dramatic spectacle and offer an interpersonal arena in which important psychological needs are met. These assumptions suggest that the best way to improve college instruction, even in these technologically rich times, is for professors to master the enduring and traditional skills—art form, if you will—of lecturing.

The Many Forms of the Lecture

A graduate instructor I once supervised eschewed lecturing in favor of discussion. He said he didn't believe in lecturing. Asked to describe the lecturing he did not believe in, he realized that lecturing symbolized for him a rejecting, dominating attitude toward students, not a variety of teacher presentation.

What are the major types of lecture? At one end of a continuum is the *formal oral essay,* the tightly constructed, highly polished kind of lecture that presents information primarily to support a summative point or conclusion (Kyle, 1972). In this kind of lecture the professor has reviewed and selected from a large body of knowledge the theories, research studies, and arguments that support his or her conclusion. The most formal of such lectures are written out and read to the students.

At their best, oral essays are by no means boring. Listening to one can be an emotionally and intellectually significant experience. However, lectures such as these rarely occur in college classes for a very practical reason. A formal lecture for a fifty-minute class needs to be about 7,500 words long (Satterfield, 1978). At three classes per week for a fifteen-week semester, a teacher giving only oral essays would have to compose 337,500 tightly constructed words, producing over 1,000 pages of typed manuscript — a feat well beyond the powers of most faculty members.

There are other problems with this kind of lecture as well. Formal essays can achieve the highest level of Dimension I teaching, but a course consisting solely of them fails to meet educational objectives that require dialogue with students. Because formal lectures ignore the interpersonal dimension, they are not likely to fully motivate or satisfy most students. A long series of such lectures would wear out students' ability to concentrate on them as well as the teacher's ability to construct them. However, there are times in any course when formal lectures are needed. Tight, integrative presentations are especially useful near the end of a course when the fundamental content has been mastered and the desired interpersonal climate of the class has long since been established.

The most common kind of college lectures are called *expository lectures* because they primarily define and set forth information. Most students think of this sort of lecture when they hear that a professor "lectures a lot." In these lectures the instructor does most of the talking, with only occasional questions from the bolder students. Such lectures are less elaborately planned than oral essays, but nothing prevents them from being outstanding and satisfying to students if they are skillfully prepared and delivered.

A related form is the *provocative lecture*. As in formal and expository lectures, the instructor does most of the talking, but here there is more intention of provoking thought. In these lectures the teacher challenges students' existing knowledge and values and helps them to form a more complex and integrated perspective. Provocative lectures are better suited to the humanities than to the sciences, but lectures that challenge and question student assumptions are appropriate in any discipline, especially near the end of a term when a common set of knowledge has been shared. Instructors rely more on discussion than on lectures to help students question their personal values and attitudes, but a first-quality provocative lecture can achieve the same objective. If the class is large, a lecture is in fact more likely to be effective than discussion.

Most college classes are variations on the lecture theme in which the teacher does more than talk. A common variant is the *lecture-demonstration* class, in which an instructor uses props to illustrate the subject at hand. Such classes are essential in most music, art, and science courses.

In another common lecture variant, the teacher spends most of a class period lecturing in response to questions posed by students. The teacher answers each question with a short, straightforward lecture that relates the inquiry to other course content or shows how it illustrates a fundamental issue in the field. This *question-lecture* is a variant of the lecture rather than of the discussion format because during it the instructor does not interact a great deal with students; he or she simply uses student questions to determine which lecture points to explain further. Students' involvement is still fostered, however, because their questions are being answered.

In a *lecture-discussion* the college teacher encourages students to comment or express concern rather than simply raise questions. The typical lecture-discussion class begins with the instructor speaking for five to fifteen minutes and then stimulating a few minutes of discussion around a key point in his or her remarks. During such discussion the instructor offers brief clarification or integration between student comments, but students do most of the talking. Lecture-discussions vary in the amount of time spent in lecture and in discussion, but most instructors using this format pause for discussion at least twice in a period. Discussion skillfully interspersed with lecture need not interrupt the flow of the lecture organization, and it encourages students to think about the content being presented as well as heightening their involvement in the lecture part of the proceedings.

Another common variation of the formal lecture is *lecture-recitation*, in which the teacher stops to ask specific questions or request students to read prepared material aloud. Lecture-recitations are the reverse of question-lecture classes because in this case the teacher provides the questions and the students share what they know or have prepared. Class time in American colleges was once spent almost exclusively on recitation (Kyle, 1972), and some teachers and subjects (especially languages) still use it heavily.

A final variation is the *lecture-laboratory*, in which students follow short lectures by making their own observations, experiments, or other independent work. Science courses most often use this method, but studio art and writing classes can be lecture-laboratories as well.

What the Lecture Can and Cannot Do Well

A common criticism of lectures is that if a speaker does not write out a lecture beforehand, what is said is likely to be inferior to something already written in a book; and if a lecture is already written, why bother to read the words aloud rather than simply assigning students to read the text?

This is indeed a conundrum if one accepts the premise that the sole purpose of a lecture is to present information. Available research consistently concludes that lectures are one of the *least* effective methods of conveying information (Bowman, 1979; Thompson, 1974). Though lectures sometimes produce better immediate recall than reading, tests of recall several hours or days later indicate that a single lecture does not produce more learning of information than a single reading of the same material. Since most students can read faster than a lecturer can talk, it is easily argued that lectures are an inefficient use of students' and teachers' time. Individualized teaching methods were developed in part because of this evidence of the lecture's relative ineffectiveness at transmitting information.

Fortunately, this narrow view of the objectives of the lecture is neither universal nor necessary. Lectures do much more than readings. Research suggests that a first-rate lecture is better than written material at emphasizing conceptual organization, clarifying ticklish issues, reiterating critical points, and inspiring students to appreciate the importance of key information. The high clarity of an excellent lecture aids understanding, as do the emotionally tinged associations created when students learn in a state of intellectual excitement.

The lecture is probably most effective at motivating students to learn more about a topic. Good lectures are very difficult to ignore. They are, above all else, *engaging*. Any student's mind wanders more often while reading assigned chapters or articles than when listening to an instructor who makes his or her knowledge about a subject seem exciting and important. The intellectual excitement resulting from good lectures can make students more likely to read assignments attentively. Thus, lectures can be very effective at creating an emotional set that aids students' learning indirectly by motivating them to apply their energies fully.

Lectures, then, are not superfluous. When formal essays, expository lectures, or provocative lectures are combined with any of the modes requiring student participation, such as discussion or laboratory, a number of educational goals can be accomplished. Students can question their values and attitudes and increase their problem-solving and thinking skills. A professor can model the kind of thinking he or she wishes students to emulate and then give them an opportunity to try it themselves.

To organize lectures well, teachers must consider how students learn. The next section contains a brief summary of what psychological research has demonstrated about learning. These general principles apply to all human learning, but they are especially relevant to the way content should be selected and organized for presentation in a college lecture.

Summary of Relevant Learning Theory

While many theorists stress the importance of events outside individuals for learning, the position taken here is that human learning is heavily mediated by internal events — thoughts or cognitions. The following principles of human cognitive learning are sufficiently well established to be used by a college teacher desiring to organize and present lectures in ways most likely to produce learning (Bugelski, 1964; Eble, 1976).

1. It is better for college students to be active seekers than passive recipients of learning.
2. For students to be fully engaged in learning, their attention must be focused on the material.

3. Differences in intellectual ability among college students will influence their speed of learning; these differences will be more noticeable when the information to be learned is abstract and complex than when it is simple and concrete.

4. Students increase their effort if rewarded rather than punished; however, students differ in the teacher behaviors that they find rewarding.

5. Students will learn and remember information better if they have many cognitive associations to it; learning of isolated information is more difficult and less permanent than learning of information that is connected to a network of other material.

6. It is difficult to learn ideas that are very similar unless the differences between them are emphasized. Conversely, it is easier to learn disparate ideas if their similarities are emphasized.

7. Students learn images as well as words, and images are more easily remembered, especially if the images are vivid and emotionally tinged.

8. Students enter every class with positive and negative emotional attitudes that can interfere with learning or can increase motivation and provide an associational network for new learning.

9. A moderate amount of anxiety or challenge activates most students and increases learning; however, excessive anxiety interferes with learning.

Choosing What to Present in a Lecture

This section deals with ways of organizing outstanding lectures. The preparation is the same whether the instructor only lectures or combines lecturing with other activities. My recommendations in the remainder of this chapter concern both *what* a college teacher chooses to present in a lecture and *how* he or she presents it.

Deciding How Much to Present. As instructors quickly learn, only a small number of major points can be presented effectively in a single class meeting. Research on what can be remembered following classes indicates that most college students can absorb only three to four points in a fifty-minute period and four to five in a seventy-five-minute class, regardless of the subject being taught (Eble, 1976; McKeachie, 1978). Students can remember details about each point, but the number of general ideas that can be absorbed is limited. Attempting to cover too much causes the coverage of each point to be superficial and the pace to be rushed for the instructor and frantic for the students. Time to answer questions or to pause for individual ideas to sink in will be eliminated. Most critically, squeezing too much into one presentation will reduce the amount of learning because people store information much less efficiently when their minds are temporarily overloaded.

Selecting Points for Presentation. Since relatively few major points can be presented in each lecture (and in a semester), choosing what to present becomes critical. A first choice is whether to survey course content comprehensively or select only key or critical topics for presentation. Though most teachers in theory endorse concentrating on points of fundamental importance, in practice they seem to believe that if they do not cover everything, their teaching is somehow suspect, shoddy, or superficial. Introductory or survey courses particularly evoke this feeling. When, as is common, beginning college teachers fall hopelessly behind schedule near the end of the term, they wrestle in obvious discomfort over which important topics to omit. Without guidelines on ways to select material, the easiest course for an instructor to take is to attempt to present it all, however sketchily. Neither college teachers nor students, however, are likely to be satisfied with this solution to the problem.

Experienced instructors know that lectures cannot carry the major responsibility for conveying information. Readings should do that. Points for lectures should be chosen using the following criteria:

1. *Central points or general themes* that tie together as many other topics as possible should be presented (Highet, 1950). Details will be associated to central points more easily. The lecturing practice of placing topics in brief historical perspective is common because of this advantage of organizing points.
2. Points should also be selected for their *high interest* to students.

If the most provocative topic in the assigned reading for a given class is ignored in favor of more theoretically critical topics, students are likely to be disappointed. Satisfying students' initial curiosity about certain topics is a good way to lead them to appreciate the importance, beauty, or relevance of other ideas that seem less appealing at first and to motivate them to read assigned materials outside of class.

3. A teacher should occasionally choose a topic because it is *especially difficult* for students. Though class time would be drudgery if it were spent only on difficult or abstract points, selecting commonly misunderstood topics is frequently appropriate.

4. Of most importance in choosing what to present is the *depth and complexity* of a given topic. A lecture should not be so simplistic or obvious that students are unlikely to learn anything new from it (especially if they have done the assigned reading); neither should it be so sophisticated and terse that many will be overwhelmed with the intricacy of the remarks. Finding the appropriate depth of presentation for a group whose members differ significantly in ability is one of the greatest challenges in giving fine lectures. Experience can help a teacher calibrate his or her presentation, but careful observation of student reactions is the most effective way to fine-tune the level of complexity on the spot. The clearest exposition should seem eminently sensible to most listeners and should involve some new thinking or reorganization of what they already know.

Organizing the Lecture. A lecture should begin by stimulating students' curiosity. Any playwright, screenwriter, or novelist knows the importance of starting with a "grabber," a tension-producing statement or juxtaposition that attracts the audience and holds their involvement as the plot and characters are developed further. The opening of a lecture should also create in students an expectation that something important will follow.

Many lecturers begin with a key question or paradox that the day's lecture will attempt to answer or explain ("What can we learn about changes in British images of the heroic through comparison of nineteenth- and twentieth-century novels?"). Another option is to call attention to an intriguing example of or exception to a general phenomenon ("What does the treatment of immigrants at Ellis Island immediately before World War I suggest about class and race attitudes and political power in early twentieth-century America?"). Sometimes lecturers approach a familiar concept from a fresh direction ("Today we will examine evidence supporting the idea that our culture's emphasis on romantic love is a major cause of divorce"). Lectures aimed at students who have had considerable prior coursework in a subject are especially appropriate for beginnings that reexamine familiar ideas.

After the attention-getter is chosen, there are several options for organizing the remaining points in a lecture. A common method is to proceed in a linear and logical fashion, gradually building to a final concluding point. Some lecturers, however, prefer non-linear organization, in which students may not understand at the beginning where the lecturer is heading. Jacob Bronowski, in his television series "The Ascent of Man" (1974), typified nonlinear organization. Another common tack is to present two separate topics in some detail and conclude by contrasting and comparing them. Proceeding chronologically is frequently appropriate in history courses, but in other subjects this approach can bore students unless the chronology is important in its own right.

Whatever the organization of a given lecture (and one should vary the approach from one class meeting to another), it is advisable to approach the structure of the formal lecture as much as possible. Ploughing through loosely related topics without emphasizing the relationships among them promotes neither understanding nor satisfaction. When organizing a lecture, the instructor should remember that it is a dramatic presentation needing boundaries: an engaging beginning and a concluding ending. The best lectures can be completed in a single class, but if a lecture must be continued, the speaker should bring the first installment to an end decisively.

Lecturing to Promote Independent Thinking

The professor who wants students to think and reach conclusions on their own must first model such thinking for them (Harrison, 1969; Satterfield, 1978). Explicitly pointing out the thought processes involved helps to ensure that all students will notice what the instructor is attempting to demonstrate. Students should be told *how* conclusions were reached or theories constructed rather than being given only the finished products. Students can also be encouraged to think by asking them how they would interpret given data and by putting conflicting ideas before them for debate or consideration whenever possible.

Students will think more critically about a subject if an instructor exhibits a healthy skepticism at times about the field's assumptions and methods. One outstanding instructor told me, "I always begin the semester with optimism and enthusiasm about the material and usually have the students well enough informed by about two-thirds of the way through that I can be more skeptical and show them the limits of our methods, can bring them down to earth a bit. It's hard for some of them to take — a few become disillusioned — but it's the best way I know to teach them to think critically on their own."

Finally, college teachers can encourage independent thinking in students by addressing value issues directly rather than shying away when they appear. An instructor who openly admits that his or her conclusions are at times influenced by personal values is more likely to teach students to examine value influences on their own conclusions than is one who perpetuates the myth that knowledge can be value-free.

What an instructor chooses to present in a lecture and the way the material is organized will affect students' understanding of what they read and their eventual sophistication in a subject area. The *way* the teacher gives the lecture will affect the students' motivation to pay attention in class and to complete assigned work.

Presenting Content Effectively

This section focuses on general lecture style and the use of audiovisual technology to enhance interest and organization. Carefully selected and organized points constitute a lecture of only moderate quality unless they are delivered well. Increasing the interest value of a lecture is the best way to prevent students from dozing off in class or staying away altogether.

Lecturing with Immediacy and Spontaneity. Classical Greek orators spent an incredibly large amount of time preparing their speeches for contests (Highet, 1950). Every word, every gesture, and every inflection was planned and practiced beforehand so it would have the desired effect on the audience. Yet the effect the orators sought was the appearance of speaking extemporaneously to express genuine emotions. In effect, Greek orators worked exceedingly hard to appear not to have prepared at all! Contemporary college teachers can learn a useful lesson from them.

Regardless of how carefully a teacher has prepared a lecture, the actual delivery should have a sense of immediacy, as if the speaker is having for the first time many of the thoughts he or she is sharing with the students. This quality of conversational intimacy involves the students more readily in the flow of ideas than does a didactic style. The instructor should avoid at all costs the stern, moralizing tone commonly associated with a lecture from a disapproving superior. Instead of speaking *at* or even *to* students, the teacher should strive to speak *for* them (Satterfield, 1978). This approach is more likely to sweep them along fully in the interesting story that the instructor has to tell.

Beginning college instructors sometimes indicate that they plan to prepare for their courses by writing out all their lectures beforehand. Such energy would be highly misplaced. The elegance of written lectures is admirable, but such lectures take too much time to prepare and cannot seem spontaneous when delivered. Rather, teachers should think first about the major points they wish to present. If they want to plan specific classes ahead of time, they should write brief outlines for *at most the first three class meetings*.

Until an instructor has actually used notes, he or she will not know how much detail is needed or how much material can be covered in a given class. Because most beginners fear they will not be sufficiently prepared and will run out of content before the class hour is up, they almost always prepare too much and write notes in too much detail. After a few months' experience, they gradually shorten their lecture notes and come to realize that their initial fantasy about writing out all lectures ahead of time was quite impractical.

Lecture notes should contain in outline the major topics selected for presentation and the key points under each (Highet, 1950; McKeachie, 1978). Experienced instructors know that complete sentences in notes are both unnecessary and difficult to read quickly. Words or brief phrases suffice. Any formulas or definitions to be read to the class may be written out, though quoting from memory or reading them from a book is often more impressive to students. The purpose of lecture notes is to remind the instructor of what he or she thought about while preparing the class, not to provide something to read. There are no definitive criteria for the length of lecture notes for a single class, but less than one page is probably too short and more than three is surely too long. To achieve a sense of immediacy and spontaneity, a college teacher must *create* a lecture to some extent while presenting it, and writing notes out in too much detail risks sapping creativity and making the speaker too dependent on them. Many outstanding teachers report that they commonly have new ideas or insights into their material while actually giving a lecture. They also rarely consult their notes during their better lectures. The notes are there if needed, but the presentation comes from the teacher, not the notes.

Introducing Variety. An instructor must not only capture but also hold students' attention throughout each class meeting. "Never do any single thing for very long" is a good rule for keeping attention. Students will tire of anything, even humor or anecdotes, if it is done for too long without a change of pace. A lecturer should plan for some change in format every ten minutes or so. The organization of content need not be broken, only the manner in which ideas are presented.

An instructor might vary a presentation by giving a specific example of the topic under consideration, asking a series of rhetorical questions, or saying something humorous. Humor is an especially good way to introduce variety and let everyone (the instructor included) relax a bit. A teacher should note, however, that the best humor in college classes is not canned jokes; satirical or witty comments about the subject, individuals studied, or oneself are more appreciated. (Humorous comments about students are not advised because students may well take them as hostile unless they are delivered sparingly and with just the right touch.)

Seeking Feedback During Class. Fortunately, college teachers need not worry about sensing when they should shift gears to maintain the class's interest — the students will tell them. All that instructors need do is note the messages that students send their way. Students' faces give the best indication of the way a presentation is being received (Highet, 1950). Students signal when they are no longer caught up in a lecture and are having to work to pay attention.

Yawns, chair shuffling, sighs, or whispered asides to fellow students clearly tell an instructor that it is time to do something different. More subtle cues give the same message. There is a certain glassed-over quality in students' eyes that shows they are no longer fully engaged. The wise instructor looks for it constantly to fine-tune the pacing of a lecture and to indicate when it is time to ask a question, give an example, or in some other way break stride for a short while.

Another technique to solicit feedback from students is to ask questions such as "Am I going too fast?" or "Should I slow down a bit to let all this sink in?" Highet (1950) suggests keeping a running joke with the students in the back row of a large room: Every week or so the teacher can break up slow spots in a lecture by suddenly asking, "Can you people in the back row still hear me okay?" Occasionally asking students for such feedback keeps them alert and lets them know the instructor is concerned.

Emphasizing Organization. A good lecturer tells the class what he is going to tell them, tells them what he wants to tell them, and then tells them what he has just told them. Though boring if done to excess, previews and recapitulations are particularly useful ways to emphasize organization and key points. Students have thought about many other things since the last class meeting and can benefit from brief statements connecting the day's topic to what went on before. Mentioning the objectives for the day's lesson provides a context within which students can organize what they hear, especially if a major shift in the course has occurred.

A college teacher can also emphasize organization in a lecture by reviewing at the end of major sections and at the end of each class. A few sentences of recapitulation can help students notice that a transition is occurring and a somewhat different point is now going to be addressed. At the end of class, the teacher should take five minutes to tie things together and anticipate what will happen next time (Eble, 1976). The best lectures are well enough paced and include few enough points to allow an instructor three to five minutes at the end to put what has been said into perspective rather than desperately trying to cram in a few more details while the students are disengaging mentally, if not filing out the door.

Excellent students can take useful notes from the lectures of almost any professor, but the best lecturers are those from whom it is easy for every student to take well-organized notes. Though research indicates that taking notes is not really related to the amount students learn (Howe, 1980), factors such as intelligence and motivation probably mask the role of note-taking skill *per se* in the studies thus far reported. Despite the lack of empirical evidence, many instructors believe that taking notes does aid learning by helping students organize what they see and hear in lectures. If notes simply detailed what went on in class, a teacher might hand out photocopied lecture outlines or encourage students to subscribe to a note-taking service. Many students concur with this view, believing that the only purpose of coming to class is to leave with a set of notes or that borrowing another's notes is a suitable substitute for attending a lecture themselves. However, completed notes are not the only goal of note-taking.

It is the *process* of taking notes that is most important, though the notes do have some value as later reminders of what went on. Just as a teacher's notes are no substitute for all that should go on in an instructor's head during a top-notch lecture, so no student's notes can completely capture what went on in his or her mind. A completed set of notes is no substitute for having been in class to make them.

Using Visual Aids

Handouts. Many college teachers distribute handouts — such as lecture outlines, listings of definitions or formulas, or diagrams. Because the teacher prepares them, they are more accurate than what some students would record in their notes. Little time is required to produce handouts, so they are cost effective.

Some ways of using handouts are better than others. If given a detailed lecture outline at the beginning of class, many students simply examine the handout, develop a false sense of security, and pay little attention to the lecture, knowing they can refer to the outline if they miss something. Handouts, like student lecture notes, should provide organization and a reminder of what the students heard in the lecture. Thus, the teacher should distribute handouts when presenting the material they deal with. They are no substitute for a clear and engaging lecture from which a student actively creates a personal set of notes, but they do constitute useful souvenirs of the experience.

Blackboards and Flip-Charts. Whether green, beige, or white, blackboards are a universal feature of classrooms that are easily taken for granted. Because using them can soil hands and clothing, many teachers disparage and sometimes avoid them, but their educational value is substantial even in our electronic era. Nineteenth-century educators appreciated the blackboard's value. In 1841, Josiah Bumstead wrote, "The inventor or introducer of the blackboard deserves to be ranked among the best contributors to learning and science, if not among the best benefactors of mankind." Boards are still one of the most effective visual aids available.

The act of writing on the blackboard focuses student attention on the lecture. Research indicates that most college students will copy into their notes virtually everything the teacher writes on the board (Howe, 1980). Unfortunately, students sometimes omit key words when they take notes, totally missing the meaning of a lecture point. Thus, the blackboard is an excellent place to write key words or names used in a lecture — if for no other reason than to make it more likely that students will learn to spell them correctly.

Writing a definition on the board draws students' attention to it and is most appropriate if the teacher wishes to comment on various words and components of the definition in some detail. If the instructor's sole purpose is to be sure that students write the definition correctly, class time can be better spent dictating the exact wording. Writing on the board takes time (especially if material is written clearly enough to be read easily by students in the back rows), and it is possible to use the technique to excess. Basic rules are to write nothing unimportant on the board, nothing that one does not refer to in some detail, and nothing overly lengthy.

Many excellent teachers routinely write an outline of the day's lecture in one corner of the blackboard before class begins. This provides a useful preview of what is to come. A teacher should not write a great deal on the board before class, however. Students will simply copy it all down at the beginning of class, sit back, and relax. It is the process of writing on the board *during* a lecture that keeps students' attention and prompts them to organize content.

Flip-charts of newsprint are another popular method of accomplishing the same ends. They allow different colored marking pens to be used (colored chalk is difficult to read), and the notes need not be erased during or after class.

Electronic Aids. Electronic audiovisual aids in college classrooms can greatly enrich a lecture, but they are neither necessary nor sufficient for lecturing virtuosity. Electronic devices are essentially previously prepared blackboards with a greater range of sensory stimuli and power to attract students' attention. Their additional power results from the auditory, colorful, or moving graphic illustrations that can be used. Such enrichment is especially needed in very large classes (over 120), where the impersonality of the situation makes students less involved. The decision of most importance concerning any audiovisual aid is whether its advantages outweigh its cost and justify using it instead of handouts and blackboards.

Overhead transparencies are the most commonly used electronic aids because they are so easy to prepare. Many teachers routinely employ them in place of the blackboard, using photocopy machines to transfer material to transparencies before class or writing directly on the transparencies with specially designed pens.

Slides are much more difficult for most teachers because support personnel must photograph materials and develop film, but their visual quality is superior to that of transparencies. When the course content requires photographs of important objects or scenes (paintings, buildings, villages, geological features), 35mm slides are indispensable. Like transparencies, however, they are all too often used to present electronically what could have been written on the board.

Motion pictures illustrate content vividly, and the best contemporary educational films are conceptually complex and of high interest to students. Showing a long film takes up scarce class time, however. Given the relatively limited educational benefits of films, many teachers choose to show them at night or have film clips produced by media centers showing just the part needed to illustrate a lecture point.

Videotape cassettes have many of the advantages of motion pictures, although TV screen sizes severely limit the number of students to whom they can be shown effectively. Modern video projectors are a decided improvement over standard monitors. Cassettes have the advantage of allowing the instructor to show desired segments easily.

An ideal method of showing films or videotapes, available at many schools, is to have them housed at the library (typically in the reserve or nonprint section) where staff can show them to students individually or in small groups during regular library operating hours. Some library media centers will tape selected lectures for students as well.

Electronic methods of focusing student attention, presenting content, and facilitating student organization can enrich the lectures of an already-proficient instructor. However, they have disadvantages (including, but not limited to, cost) that must be weighed against what they offer over simpler methods.

Advantages and Disadvantages of Visual Aids. An instructor must consider a number of things when deciding which visual aids to employ and how frequently to use them. *Availability* is a primary concern. Blackboards are almost always present, and flip-charts are inexpensive and easy to carry. However, unless a classroom is permanently equipped with a transparency, slide, or movie projector or a videotape player, using these electronic aids requires prior scheduling, transportation, and setup in the classroom. Audiovisual machinery is not difficult to learn how to operate, and every college teacher should devote the minimal effort required to learn how to present each kind of visual aid. But something *will* go wrong on occasion — someone else will have taken the overhead projector without checking the reservation list, the bulb will blow out on the slide or movie projector, or the videotape cassette will jam. Purchasing one's own equipment to escape the hassle of ensuring its availability is expensive, but instructors who have come to depend on these devices sometimes take that step. Having electronic aids available when one needs them does require planning and introduces the risk that they may on occasion not be there. (The availability of chalk in classrooms cannot be assured either, but it is easy to carry chalk to class routinely.)

Another consideration is the amount of *advance preparation* required. All visual aids require some advance planning; even diagrams drawn on the board must be planned beforehand. Films, film clips, and 35mm slides require more lead time — frequently weeks, sometimes months — because of the assistance from others that is required.

A final consideration is the degree of *disruption* in lecture delivery resulting from the use of audiovisual aids. Turning to write on the board disrupts the proceedings little if the teacher does not lose eye contact with the class, but writing out a lengthy chart is guaranteed to lose students' attention. Turning on a videotape player already wound to the desired segment also introduces little disruption. The major disruptions caused by electronic aids are the noise they make and the necessity to dim classroom lighting. Both make it more difficult for a teacher to keep students' attention.

Some teachers must lecture almost exclusively with the lights off while students look at slides. One teacher of introductory art history I interviewed believed that his success resulted in part from his ability to maintain involvement by conveying emotion in his voice and skillfully coordinating the flow of slides and lecture. He did express regret at feeling more distant from such in-the-dark classes and not getting to know as many students personally. Though it is possible to teach effectively in the dark with the noise of electronic aids in the background, a heavy use of such aids makes facilitating interpersonal rapport more difficult because little eye contact between students and teacher is possible.

General Principles of Using Visual Aids. The first principle is to use visual aids frequently enough to keep student interest high but not so often that students become distracted or have no time to think about what is being said. One outstanding college

instructor I observed has perfected a lecture style that uses a daz-
zling array of electronic methods, primarily alternating between
35mm slides and film clips. His presentations sometimes average
one slide or short film clip for every 90 seconds of class time.
Though his classes are highly engaging, students in them may not
have sufficient time to think about the implications of what they
have observed. Many may simply sit back and wait for the next
display. This particular style is most effective with extremely
large classes (over 300) and cannot be duplicated without considerable technical expertise or support personnel. In deciding on the
appropriate amount of visual stimulation, an instructor should
remember that the thoughts that go through students' minds are of
more importance than the artful displays passing before their eyes.

A second general principle is to reveal visual material gradually, as it is referred to, rather than displaying it all at once. This
keeps students' attention focused on one major point at a time.
The teacher should write concepts on the blackboard one at a time
to stimulate student thought and memory rather than putting
them up all at once and then commenting about each individually.
With overhead transparencies the instructor can use a blank sheet
of paper to cover the parts not yet discussed. The same kind of
thing can be done by preparing a series of 35mm slides, each identical to the one shown before except for the addition of one new
topic at the bottom. However, using slides in this way requires
considerable advance planning and cannot be modified easily
during a presentation.

This section has touched only briefly on the possible ways
that diagrams or outlines can be presented by using visual aids.
The educational applications of electronic technology are expanding rapidly and will undoubtedly become even more sophisticated
in the future. Even today there is nothing except expense to prevent a college teacher from programming a small computer to display on a projection video screen lecture outlines or diagrams that
change as the lecture progresses. Such materials could be stored
on easily carried floppy disks, presented to the class as the instructor wishes, and modified on the spot if desired.

Regardless of the specific methods used to present material
visually, the psychological and educational purposes of the lecture

remain the same: to ensure that students concentrate fully on the presentation and that they understand and organize it maximally. It is important for a college instructor not to let "gee whiz" technology obscure these fundamental and traditional purposes, objectives that can also be accomplished by a masterful teacher equipped with a single piece of chalk, a board, and a reasonably quiet place in which to teach.

Intellectually Exciting Lectures: A Recapitulation

An outstanding lecture is many things. Primarily it is content that has been carefully selected and organized to capture the essence of a topic, complement what is presented in readings, and motivate students to learn the rest. The best planned content, however, will have little impact on students if it is not delivered well. To achieve all the potential of a lecture, the instructor must use variety and tension in his or her voice, movements, and visual enrichment to keep the audience captivated and stimulated and to aid their memory of what went on.

Two short lists loosely adapted from Kenneth Eble's *The Craft of Teaching* (1976) conclude this chapter. The first is a set of guidelines on how to be a particularly bad lecturer, and the second, an especially good one. These summarize by negative example and by explicit suggestion many of the fundamental points of this chapter.

Suggestions for Bad Lecturing.

1. Begin a course with no introduction to the subject or to your own bias. Simply start with the first topic you wish to present.
2. Make no references to the broader context related to the specific topic being considered.
3. Do not acknowledge the students' interests or previous knowledge and experience.
4. Become preoccupied with the historical context of a topic, neglecting the central subject of the course.
5. Give excessive attention to the trivial details of the subject or to those parts that most interest you; omit topics of more central importance or interest.

6.   Dwell extensively on your private scholarly quarrels with other authorities over esoteric points without showing how your concerns relate to the larger subject.

7.   Qualify terms so excessively that students will not be able to explain them to a friend immediately after class. Be so specific and sophisticated in the definitions you present that students will have to memorize what you say word for word and will be unable to define terms meaningfully in their own language.

8.   Present learned quotations without connecting them to the content.

9.   Justify conclusions on the basis of tradition or authority without explaining why the authorities believe as they do.

10. Use arcane terms and make no attempt to define them; do not acknowledge that students may not know what you mean.

11. Rarely look at your audience. With a fixed posture, keep your eyes on your notes, the floor, the ceiling, or the side walls.

12. Speak in a monotonous voice, showing little emphasis, force, or enthusiasm.

13. Hesitate frequently in the middle of sentences, but rarely pause at the end of major lecture sections.

14. Show little sense that time is passing and insist on presenting points in the orderly manner you have planned, even if individual classes end in midtopic or you fall far behind the course syllabus.

15. Indicate that you know the students are confused or impatient, but then do nothing differently.

Suggestions for Good Lecturing.

1.   Fit the material you present to the time you have available.

2.   Seek concise ways to present and illustrate content. Express concepts in the simplest terms possible and define technical terms when using them.

3.   Begin each course and class by pricking the students' interest, expressing positive expectations, and sharing the objectives you have for them.

4. Follow a prepared outline but include improvised material or illustrations. Appear spontaneous even when you are following the outline closely.

5. Break up the monotony of lectures by varying methods of presentation.

6. Use a wide range of voices, gestures, and physical movements, but be yourself: Develop a varied and interesting style consistent with your values and personality.

7. Give students regular places to catch their breath and ask questions. It is "better to talk too little and stop short than to go on for too long" (Eble, 1976, p. 53).

8. End each lecture with a conclusion that connects what has happened today with what will be covered during the next meeting.

9. Be guided by your students during your lectures. Continually observe their reactions, acknowledge them, and modify your approach when indicated.

10. Remember in your relationships with students that all of you are persons first, students and teacher second. Remember that you, as a teacher, "are both host and guest" (Eble, 1976, p. 53).

CHAPTER 6

Enhancing Learning
Through Classroom Discussion

> A useful classroom discussion, unlike a dormitory
> bull session, consists of student comments separated
> by frequent probes and clarifications by the teacher
> that facilitate involvement and development of
> thinking by the whole group. Dynamic lecturers
> captivate a class by the virtuosity of their individual
> performances. Master discussion leaders accomplish
> the same end by skillful guidance of the group's col-
> lective thinking processes.

College teachers who lead successful classroom discussion say
much more than "Any questions?" or "What do you think about
this?" In their hands, discussion (any verbal student response to
instructor questions or comments) is an active intellectual process
as emotionally involving as the most dynamic lectures.

Discussion requires interaction between student and teacher,
so its effectiveness depends heavily on the quality of student-
teacher relationships. Because discussion is much more unpredictable than lecturing, it requires considerable instructor spontaneity, creativity, and tolerance for the unknown. Whether it is held in
small seminars or in larger lecture-discussion classes, discussion
requires a teacher to have excellent communication and interpersonal skills. If done well, discussion can promote independent
thinking and motivation as well as enhance student involvement.

Like the lecture, discussion produces in many college teachers (and students) strong positive or negative attitudes that are based more on philosophical or political values than on experience. For many, discussion seems desirable because using it implies that students have important thoughts and experiences to contribute. An instructor who allows classroom discussions recognizes students as active participants in their own learning as well as passive recipients of the information and insights that the teacher has to share. Some people value discussion because the instructor seems more egalitarian or democratic during discussion exchanges than during lectures. A few go so far as to denounce other forms of instruction—especially the lecture—as insulting, even dictatoral. For many advocates, discussion embodies the humanistic educational philosophy (Brownfield, 1973). Yet all college teachers are not so enthusiastic.

Faculty members who view education as the acquisition of information or explicit training rather than the development of thinking skills or critical perspectives find discussion of little immediate value. These instructors believe that the positive motivational benefits of discussion are overrated and that it is more appropriate, given limited class time, to let the person speak who has the most to say: the instructor. Others see discussion as an abdication of teacher responsibility to share superior knowledge or as a shortsighted pandering to students' need to feel important and desire to hear themselves talk.

Though there are valid philosophical objections to classroom discussion, many college teachers have negative views of discussion simply because they have never observed good discussion or been able to use it effectively themselves. Like the lecture, discussion at its worst is painful and frustrating for all involved. Long silences, averted faces of students fearing they will be called upon or pressured to volunteer comments, or angry outbursts toward other students or the instructor so commonly characterize poor discussions that many college teachers abandon the technique after one or two unsuccessful attempts, rationalizing that their students "just aren't interested in discussing."

Discussions must be well planned in order to be effective, but their quality also depends greatly on how well the instructor performs. Leading an excellent discussion demands just as much

stage presence, leadership, and energy as presenting a lecture —
and considerably more interpersonal understanding and communication skill. Because of these additional requirements, some
educators believe that leading an outstanding discussion is more
difficult than giving a lecture of comparable quality (Eble, 1976).

In this chapter the many ways of using discussion in college
classes are considered, and instruction on developing discussion
skills is offered. Topics covered include educational objectives that
can be achieved by discussion, different kinds of classroom discussion, general characteristics of outstanding discussion, specific
instructor skills that facilitate dialogue, and ways to handle special
discussion problems.

Educational Objectives for Discussion

Course Content. As McKeachie notes, "Discussion is probably not effective for presenting new information which the student
is already motivated to learn" (1978, p. 35). Though not effective
for presenting content *per se*, discussion does aid its mastery by
encouraging students to actively process what they learn as they
sit in class. Asking a few students to think and speak out loud encourages all students to think more fully about content. Discussion helps students assimilate and integrate information they have
initially acquired from readings or lectures.

A skilled lecturer can walk the class through an application
of a general concept to a specific problem or example, but this can
also be done via group discussion. Though the students' solution
may not match the instructor's, it is more likely to be at a level of
understanding appropriate for the class as a whole. Lecturing to
students about a method of literary criticism, research design, or
computer programming is fine as far as it goes, but asking them to
apply in class what they have learned requires them to demonstrate understanding, not merely memorization. Applying general ideas also promotes independence and is good practice for the
time when students will be expected to work on their own. Class
discussion is a safe way for students to try their wings while the
instructor hovers close by.

Students can also be asked in discussion to compare and
contrast different concepts. Focusing on the similarities and differ-

ences that always exist between specific ideas helps to link the ideas in an associational network. Such networks are remembered far longer than isolated concepts. Discussion is useful for emphasizing the connections between new and old knowledge.

Though each of these content objectives can be achieved to a similar degree with a skillful lecture, discussion is desirable because of the other objectives that it can meet, some of which it meets more easily than does lecturing.

Thinking Skills. The objectives discussed thus far deal with knowledge as product — with *what* students learn (Axelrod, 1973). Discussion is most useful to teach the *process* of learning, that is, thinking. A rhetorical question in a lecture may stimulate students to think for a few seconds, but a provocative question that sparks a group discussion can stimulate thinking for several minutes. Discussion is especially stimulating for students who speak, but thinking is also stimulated in those who merely listen to their classmates and consider what they might have said themselves.

What can students learn about thinking during class discussion? They learn to approach a problem or topic rationally, monitor their own thinking processes, and question their implicit assumptions. As with learners exposed to the Socratic method, they may discover that they are not as open-minded or rational about some topics as they had thought. By modeling a desired way of thinking within the content area, a skilled discussion leader can gently guide and shape students' thinking. College teachers thus prompt students to think like literary critics, biologists, political scientists, or mathematicians. Practice in "as if" thinking can lead to better and better intellectual discourse.

Because discussion requires some students to demonstrate their understanding of concepts, it also tells an instructor how completely the information he or she presented was absorbed. Feedback from discussion is less systematic and representative than feedback from exams, but it is more immediate and enables the instructor to correct, expand, or reiterate important material on the spot. This is another, indirect way in which discussion aids student mastery of content.

Attitudes. Discussion is particularly good at revealing students' attitudes. The question presented by the instructor as a stimulus for discussion—the probe—frequently focuses on students' emotional predispositions or values. For example, a teacher might ask, "Are you or are you not in favor of capital punishment, and how did you arrive at your position?" or "Do you believe the ideals of socialism can be put into practice, given human selfishness?" Whether they participate in the discussion or not, students become more aware of their own attitudes and values by comparing them with the values and attitudes expressed by others. Exposure to different views can lead some students to question or even change their implicit assumptions.

Though especially useful in the humanities and social sciences, discussion is an ideal way to demonstrate to students of any discipline how knowledge may be evaluated. For example, students can be asked to assess the social benefits resulting from basic research and technological innovation, or how one theory or observation leads to fruitful subsequent inquiry. Because evaluation is personal, discussion is ideal for encouraging it.

When students have strong and differing opinions about course concepts, it is relatively easy for a college teacher to bring these out in discussion. Students are more likely to jump into discussion when a distant or historical topic is connected to a local or contemporary issue about which they disagree. Skilled discussion leaders heighten differences in any group and use them to teach valuable lessons about the role of affective judgments in intellectual endeavor.

Student Involvement. In addition to clarifying content, teaching rational thinking, and highlighting affective judgments, discussion is particularly effective at increasing student involvement in classes. Some instructors believe that only those few students who get a chance to speak become involved in discussion, while others are left out. If discussion consists only of isolated student and instructor dialogues, this point may be valid, but for the kind of group discussion featured in this chapter it is not.

When a college teacher initiates discussion with a provocative comment or question, every student must shift gears. Discussion breaks up the lecture routine, increasing involvement by its novelty alone. Students pay closer attention for a while, merely to see what the instructor is going to do or what others have to say.

They probably will think about what they *might* say if they were to enter the discussion, even if they do not actually speak out. Those who comment receive a lot of attention, and many of their classmates enjoy this vicariously. Discussion in itself increases involvement only briefly, however. A discussion leader who lets students talk on and on with little control or direction will soon lose the group's attention.

Interpersonal Objectives. Discussion can promote student rapport, independence, and motivation in ways unattainable by lectures alone. Motivation to learn is increased because students want to work for an instructor who values their ideas and encourages them to be independent. An instructor who by discussion asks for students' opinions communicates that he or she cares about their reactions to the course.

Discussion enhances rapport between student and teacher partly because it gives instructors so many chances to show acceptance of student ideas. When students offer comments or raise questions, they risk being judged critically by their professor and their classmates. Student comments are offered to the instructor in the hope of approval and verification of their academic competence. The quality of the instructor's response potently influences both the student offering the comment and those observing the interchange.

Over an academic term, interactions between college teachers and students during class discussion reflect the morale of the whole group. Early in the term, discussion gives students an opportunity to determine how much to fear their instructor. A few will bravely test the waters, offering questions or comments whether the professor invites them to or not. Most students will simply stand by and watch what happens to those who invite dialogue with the lecturer. During periods of lower morale, all students will be less willing to participate, and especially provocative questions will be needed to stimulate discussion. Because it is decidedly interpersonal, discussion becomes a focus of the class's shared emotional concerns about the instructor and each other and an arena in which the group's development is demonstrated.

Discussion is also important because it requires students to demonstrate independence. For the most part, students must come up with responses on their own during discussion. They may say how they feel about a topic or give specific arguments supporting or opposing those presented in readings or by the instructor.

Instructors who are skilled facilitators achieve both educational and interpersonal objectives with discussion. If they are perceptive of student communications and skilled in the specific techniques of leading discussions, they can balance a critical attitude toward students' contributions with acceptance of their individual worth. Instructors who reinforce student comments while correcting their errors educate as well as reassure and make the individual attention students receive during discussion something to be sought rather than avoided.

Types of Discussion

The ways college instructors use discussion vary in the amount of time students talk and the number of students involved. Some instructors allow only one or two students to respond to a question before changing the focus or resuming their lecture. Others give up to six or seven students a chance before moving on. All successful discussion leaders direct the group's thinking by following a series of student comments with brief remarks or additional questions that build on students' comments.

Though it is difficult to make generalizations about the optimal length of discussion, ten to fifteen minutes per class meeting suffices to achieve most of the benefits of class discussion. More than thirty minutes of discussion at one stretch can develop greater intellectual independence among the few speaking students, but extended discussion can also frustrate the majority, especially the more conventional and dependent students. The type of discussion and the attitude with which it is conducted are more important than the length of time spent on it.

Discussion also takes different qualitative forms. In one, an instructor listens to student complaints on administrative matters. Gripe sessions give the teacher important feedback and promote interpersonal rapport by letting students "blow off steam" and showing the teacher's interest in their problems (McKeachie,

1978). Because this kind of discussion deals exclusively with group maintenance concerns, however, frequent use of it can be counterproductive because it takes time away from the group's task.

Two types of teacher-student interchange are sometimes called discussion. In one, the instructor gives students an opportunity to clarify content or ask for opinions on related issues. In the other, the instructor asks questions requiring specific knowledge of course content, frequently from the readings. In isolation, neither question-and-answer form is really discussion because student remarks do not build upon one another. Isolated dialogues or recitation can, however, be used as a springboard for additional discussion or explanatory comment by the instructor; thus, questions and answers can be the start of involved and thought-provoking sessions. College teachers using this approach should remember that the questions they or the students ask are of much less importance as ends than as beginnings.

Because discussion is difficult in groups of over fifty, a common practice is to divide the class into "buzz groups" of five to ten students, each of which discusses questions or issues separately for several minutes before the class is reformed. This practice allows many more students to talk, but less group learning will occur, and the instructor cannot use individual comments to make points to the entire class. Buzz groups can be especially useful when an instructor wishes students to become acquainted or to consider personal values or attitudes. Students get into discussion more quickly if someone, whether appointed by the instructor or selected by the group, acts as a leader. Because this kind of discussion requires a minimum of twenty to thirty minutes to be effective — just moving chairs to form the groups takes several minutes — it should be avoided in smaller classes or if the same purpose can be accomplished with a less time-consuming technique.

If a substantial portion of a class session is to be devoted to a controversial issue, a short role-playing activity may be especially effective. The instructor describes a setting and gives volunteers characters to act out. One popular form of role playing is a "minidebate" between students: Those sitting in one half of the room argue for one position, and the rest assume the opposing view. If a show of hands indicates an equal split on an issue initially, one variation is have each side assemble and argue for the position they do *not* endorse, *against* their own beliefs. This is guaranteed to produce a lively exchange and a fresh consideration of the topic by all.

Though students enjoy occasional role playing immensely, getting them started requires instructor confidence as well as skill. The teacher should assume that many students are secretly eager to participate and will volunteer if he or she expects them to and waits them out. An instructor should avoid communicating doubt or uncertainty by making jokes about student eagerness, or lack of it ("Don't everyone rush to volunteer at once!"). Above all, the teacher must not give up. Students resent an instructor who gives up on getting volunteers and "drafts" students to participate. Students will volunteer more quickly if told at the start of class that role playing is going to occur ("Some of you will get to role-play an interesting situation later on today").

Some college teachers engage the class in a group problem-solving discussion that is designed to teach decision making. Regardless of the specific method of problem solving that is taught, this discussion format requires considerable time (part or all of several class meetings) in order to be effective. Most problem-solving methods are complex, with a number of separate steps, from "identify the problem" to "check the results" (for example, Wales and Stager, 1976). Less involved discussion can model and promote problem solving without occupying so much class time, but more structured methods should be considered if the primary objective of a class is to teach decision making.

The most common type of discussion is the kind in which instructors ask in the midst of lectures for student comments on specific issues. From thirty seconds to fifteen minutes may be spent in such discussion before the lecture is resumed. Simple discussion like this is common because it is so flexible and, depending on the specific questions asked, can meet all the objectives discussed in the preceding section. A teacher can decide on the spur of the moment to give a breather in a fast-paced lecture, to focus on a particular paradox in the content, or to increase students' involvement by asking them to guess what happened next. Discussion generally should be planned, but this type can be introduced spontaneously when it seems needed. Brief periods of discussion scattered throughout help to give a lecture variety. Instead of changing voice characteristics, bodily movement, or pacing, a lecturer can use student comments to enliven a presentation. Particularly effective college teachers commonly use this form of discussion.

Techniques for Leading Discussion

However a college teacher uses discussion, a common set of fundamental communication skills are required. Some of these are general principles that apply to most situations, while others are quite specific and have more limited value. In the following section general considerations are presented first, followed by specific techniques for starting, shaping and guiding, and ending discussion.

General Considerations. Discussion techniques should fit desired objectives; brief discussion suits limited objectives. For example, if an instructor sees the class's attention waning, he or she might say, "Can anyone guess what happened next?" or "What might be the next point in the argument?" Even if no one responds, encouraging students to anticipate in this way increases their involvement.

Sensing student discomfort or confusion, an instructor might remark in a slower, more reflective voice: "We've covered several important points today. What do you think of them thus far? Are you persuaded or troubled by this line of thinking?" Such questions let students relax and communicate the teacher's concern about their reactions to the content.

A similar tack is to make a transition to a new topic by saying, "Any questions about these ideas before we move on?" Raising your own hand slightly and slowly scanning the room for about five seconds lets students know that the teacher seriously wants to hear their questions before proceeding. Knowing this is their last chance, students with genuine questions will ask them; but even if no one responds, as often happens, the pause for questions punctuates organization, gives everyone a breather, and demonstrates instructor concern for students.

When classroom discussion occurs for more ambitious purposes than these, the specific technique used must still fit the desired objective. For example, a college professor wishing students to appreciate the thought processes of a famous person they have studied might ask them to imagine how that person might have felt or acted ("What might have been at the source of Freud's strong desire to become famous?" or "If you were Franklin D. Roosevelt recovering from polio, what sorts of things might you think about as you contemplate resuming a career in public life?"). This technique increases empathy and identification with the persons whose lives or ideas are being studied.

When using discussion to promote independent and critical thinking, an instructor should stimulate objective thinking rather than personal identification. He or she should ask questions such as "What are some problems with that line of reasoning?" or "If we assume that the author had these two purposes, how else might she have brought the plot to resolution?" Such discussion promotes general reasoning and can teach the type of scholarly arguments favored in a discipline.

Asking students to compare and contrast concepts, theories, and individuals orally in class helps to clarify the relationships within a content area. This discussion technique is highly favored because it encourages students to form associational networks, thereby increasing understanding and retention of details. For example, an instructor might ask, "How does the French Revolution illustrate the influence of both Enlightenment and Counter-Enlightenment ideas?" or "How were the themes of early twentieth-century American artists of the 'regional schools' similar and dissimilar to American composers of the same period?" Questions that students may not have considered before increase understanding of content as well as critical thinking.

College teachers who want to increase students' awareness of value controversies relevant to content should design discussion to reveal differences in student beliefs. Such discussion is most effective when students are already aware that they disagree about a topic, and a skillful discussion leader will phrase the question to maximize disagreement. The instructor both stimulates controversy ("Let's you and him fight!") and creates an atmosphere of acceptance that promotes tolerance ("Is it necessary that we all agree on this?").

To illustrate, suppose a sociologist wishes students to recognize that the benefits of affluence and middle class membership often come at the expense of underclass labor. South African apartheid is chosen as a notable contemporary example. If the instructor simply assigns readings and discusses apartheid, little disagreement is likely to ensue. Students might disagree on appropriate government action to combat apartheid, but no student is likely to favor such an obviously exploitative racial caste system. Even though the class might participate in a lively denouncement of apartheid, none would be sensitized to the universal importance of class and power or the role of these issues in their own lives.

A more effective approach would begin by asking why apartheid was bad, in effect generating a list of agreements rather than differences. Then the instructor could shift the focus from South Africa to the role of class privilege and exploitation in the students' own lives. He or she might ask, "How does each of us benefit directly from the cheap labor of exploited dark-skinned people?" Some students will think of the fruits and vegetables picked by migrant laborers; others may notice their fashionable running shoes, sewn by poorly paid Asian workers. The teacher should have a few examples in mind in case they are needed to get the students going, but students can usually think of their own instances quickly.

Students will try to relieve the class discomfort generated by a personally relevant discussion in a number of ways. Some will justify the class system in this country, using standard democratic society notions; others will argue against such points. Personalized discussion forces students to encounter the inconsistency between their social values (especially as applied to distant, largely symbolic examples) and their personal behaviors and interests. Students are not likely to change their values overnight because of such a discussion, but they will gain a fuller appreciation of the concepts under study and may become less smug about their moral superiority.

The first general principle of discussion, then, is to use it for an intended purpose, not simply because there is something inherently beneficial about hearing students' voices. A second principle is that the advantages of discussion must be weighed against what can be accomplished given a number of realistic constraints.

Discussion always represents a tradeoff of time and objectives; the instructor must decide if a particular objective is better met with discussion than with lecture, demonstration, or some other activity. Class size is one of several constraints that influence this decision: The number of possible objectives satisfied with discussion decreases as the number of students increases. In classes of less than twenty students, discussion can fulfill any purpose. Extended problem-solving sessions, class projects, or student presentations are easy in a small class. Discussion can also be used in larger classes to increase student involvement, emphasize times of transition, promote critical thinking, and increase value awareness.

Physical space can be an inhibiting factor. Discussion is easier when all students can see each other and the instructor. Many teachers arrange classes in circles or horseshoe formations to facilitate eye contact. Seat arrangement affects the quality of discussion less than does the instructor's skill in eliciting and guiding it. However, because extended group problem-solving or value-clarification sessions require that students make eye contact with each other easily, a course with such objectives should be taught in a classroom with conducive seating.

The largest constraint on the use of discussion is time. The most satisfying college classes are painfully fleeting for students and instructor alike: There are so many ideas to present and things to learn and so little time. College teachers must weigh judiciously the task against the maintenance objectives that can be met in a given period. Lecturing in every class might give students more short-term knowledge of principles and facts, but it would also dampen motivation and satisfaction over time. On the other hand, designing entire courses around group discussion might promote high emotional involvement and independent thinking, but more dependent students would find such classes frustrating, and the instructor could not be certain that essential content would be mastered.

Most outstanding college teachers resolve the time dilemma by mixing their objectives and methods in varied and interesting sequences. Their students learn facts and principles, improve critical thinking skills, and assess subjective judgments through both lecture and discussion. The specific combinations of these methods that an instructor uses result from what he or she senses the group needs at the moment, weighed against the amount of time that remains.

How can a college teacher create an atmosphere conducive to discussion? First, he or she should formulate questions that give students as much permission to be wrong as possible (McKeachie, 1978). Questions such as "How does the text define entropy?" or "What is the definition of existentialism?" leave little room for error. Even if a student is fairly sure of the correct answer, he or she may not feel certain enough to respond. Instead, the teacher should ask, "What about entropy stands out in your mind?" or "What does existentialism mean to you?" or "Are you an existentialist?" Including qualifying terms such as "what you know," "what stands out," or "mean to you" emphasizes that it is students' personal thoughts the teacher is interested in, not their ability to produce a "correct" answer. For every objective discussed in this chapter, it is more desirable for students to give their personal opinions or arguments than factual answers. Phrasing questions so that students have little to lose by speaking removes much of the anxiety that students have about responding to requests for discussion.

The way college teachers respond when students offer comments has an even more critical effect on students' anxiety. Every student should be reinforced or treated positively for making a comment in class—even if the comment seems dead wrong. The key to doing this is to select and emphasize the parts of what students said that were insightful or creative, so as to reinforce them for making the comment, while indicating that it was not quite what was expected. For example, a student might respond to the question, "How does the Fed regulate the money supply?" with "They print more money and burn less." The teacher might smile and say, "Yes, in a way that's the basic idea; they allow more money to be available by letting more out and calling in less. But they do it through their power to regulate loans to other banks, not through control of the United States Mint." When responding to students, an instructor should always reward them for trying ("Thanks for taking a stab at it") or highlight something positive about their contribution, even if he or she must reinterpret it a bit creatively to do so. The class has a common stake in knowing how much to fear the instructor, so all students will notice closely how each other's comments are treated. Because of this, the way an instructor handles a seemingly stupid comment is more critical to communicating an accepting attitude than the way he or she responds to an apparently brilliant comment.

Nonverbal messages also influence the way students feel after offering comments. Instructors need not scowl or throw up their hands to indicate displeasure. Merely looking away when the student is speaking or sighing slightly afterward gives the same message. An instructor should make eye contact when listening to student comments and display whatever nonverbal cues (smiling, nodding) he or she habitually uses when showing interest in what another is saying.

In addition to showing that students have little to fear and much to gain by participating in discussion, college teachers should show that they themselves are participating as well. Classroom discussion should be much more than recitation—students showing off what they know or that they have done the reading. Instructors can strengthen a spirit of mutual inquiry by deemphasizing as much as possible the hierarchical relationship between themselves and their students. Questions that indicate, or even hint, that the professor already has a good answer and that the students must guess what it is should be avoided. Instructors who respond with "No, that's not quite it" may inadvertently convey this attitude. In mutual, egalitarian discussion, the topics and issues seem important to all concerned (Barnes-McConnell, 1978), not just something the powerful teacher has put foward to test the students' mettle. A teacher might begin with something like "Let's see what we can discover about. . . ." or "What are we to make of this?" to emphasize that he or she, too, is participating in the process. Discussion of this sort can be exhilarating for college teachers and students alike.

It is important that students be conditioned to participate in discussion from the outset of a course. The instructor should indicate during the first class that a number of provocative issues will be coming up and that he or she is sure the students will have something to say. This works much better than simply announcing that he or she "wants to see a lot of discussion." If a teacher plans to use discussion during a term, he or she should devote part of the first two classes to discussion in order to condition students early to respond when asked. Because discussion promotes interpersonal rapport better than lecturing, using it early on also helps to put the class on a good footing.

The specific techniques presented in the following section are some of those used by especially skilled discussion leaders. But the general points just described are more important, and they should be kept in mind regardless of the specific techniques a college teacher uses.

Specific Techniques. College teachers commonly complain about the difficulty of beginning discussion. Not surprisingly, many instructors attempt discussion less and less often when they find they are unable to elicit it reliably. Actually, starting discussion is relatively easy if an instructor sets the stage in the general ways discussed in the preceding section and applies a few key techniques.

First, ask for discussion when the class is emotionally involved. Students are far more likely to want to respond to an instructor's probe if they are emotionally aroused (Barnes-McConnell, 1978). Stimulating students' emotions "primes the pump" and motivates them to vent some of their emotional energy. Giving the class a common emotional experience (via demonstration, case study, news clipping, provocative film, or intriguing reading assignment) is the most reliable way to ensure that they will be ready with something to say. Students' emotions can also be activated by reference to common experiences. For example, ask them to think for a minute about a relevant contemporary event or common personal experience. Alternatively, ask students to think about the way they *might* feel in certain circumstances. Whatever method is used to provoke emotions, remember that emotions are fleeting (discussion must follow immediately) and have little educational value in themselves. They aid learning by enhancing students' involvement in subsequent discussion and making what is said seem more salient.

Class discussion need not always be a major production. Once students have become accustomed to frequent discussion, an engaging lecture will suffice to create the necessary emotional involvement. The optimal level of emotional arousal depends on the reason why discussion is used. Brief discussion requires little emotion, but if you wish to spend a considerable portion of a class in discussion, the strong emotional involvement produced by a provocative stimulus may be required. A corollary is that students will want to discuss more following a particularly arousing experience than following a mild one. Thus, you should stimulate students to an appropriate level and allow enough time for the energy created to be expended.

The second skill essential to eliciting discussion is wording the query appropriately. Experienced instructors know to avoid questions that can be answered with short factual answers or simply "yes" or "no" responses and to keep their queries short and simple. There is an inverse relationship between the number of words in an instructor's probe and the length of subsequent student comments. If students must work to decipher your question, they are less likely to respond to it. Avoid especially the habit of asking a second (or third) question before students have responded to the first. Neither new questions offered in succession nor the original question reworded and prefaced by "in other words. . ." is likely to elicit productive discussion. Discussion questions should be easily understandable by students, put forth decisively, and followed by silence.

Even though an instructor follows these first two suggestions carefully, student discussion may not be assured. You must also learn to *wait* patiently for the first student response. Here class conditioning becomes especially important. If a class knows that the teacher will pause only three or four seconds before going on to something else — and many instructors stop no longer than that — students are likely to wait it out, knowing that the pressure to respond will soon be over. If a class sees from the instructor's worried or uninterested expression that little discussion is really expected, they are also unlikely to respond. If the instructor is openly angry at students for not discussing, responses are even less likely to occur. Several instructor behaviors, then, tell students *not* to respond to discussion. Fortunately, it is quite easy to replace these behaviors with more effective ones.

The following method of training a class to discuss following well-phrased questions has been successful for a large number of college teachers. Begin by stating your question in a relaxed and confident manner. When you finish, start counting silently to yourself: "one thousand and one, one thousand and two," and so on until you get to "ten." By then, approximately ten seconds will have elapsed. Ten seconds is *not* a long period of silence, though it will seem like an eternity unless you mark its passage. Scan the room slowly, remaining calm and relaxed, as you count. If students are in an aroused state, you will not have to wait long for the first response, but you can expect to get to ten several times during a term, especially during the first few classes when your control over the class is not yet well established.

If it seems that no response is going to come before you get to ten, begin moving slowly toward a table, chair, or wall. When you finish your count, remain calm and repeat the question in a shorter and slightly modified form — a "reprobe." If you wish, you may reduce even further the students' fear of giving a wrong answer ("Give any associations at all"). As you finish the reprobe, calmly, patiently, and slowly lean or prop yourself against whatever solid object you have maneuvered near and begin your silent count once again. You can be confident that your nonverbal message — "See how comfortable I've made myself; I can wait here all day!" — will prompt students to respond. Teachers using this two-probe technique almost always see student response before they pass "five" on their second count. Once the class has become conditioned to discuss when you ask for it, you will rarely need to use this maneuver again.

The first student comment is by far the most difficult to obtain; after the first student breaks the ice, others are usually eager to jump in. Once discussion is underway, a number of techniques are useful to keep it going and guide it gently. As has already been noted, using eye contact, smiles, and gestures to reinforce student speakers makes others more likely to offer comments. The following suggestions illustrate other ways to encourage student response.

After the first response, summarize the student's comment and say something mildly positive about it ("I hadn't thought of it in quite that way before"). If you are uncertain about the comment's meaning, add a questioning inflection to your voice or qualify your summary with something like, "If I understood you correctly, Janice, you are saying that. . . ." You might also ask the student to expand on the comment, but do so with utmost care so as not to make the student feel that he or she is being examined, especially if the student speaks in class rarely.

It is important to summarize students' remarks in order to be certain that everyone heard them clearly. One of the biggest drawbacks to discussion is the difficulty students often have in hearing each other's comments. The summary also encourages students to listen to each other's points before firing off rounds of their own. However, although summaries are necessary early in the term and at all times in larger classes where hearing is difficult, an instructor can easily turn off students' motivation to speak up if he or she talks for more than fifteen seconds between their comments. Thus, make your summaries very brief, and avoid launching into comments of your own unless you are ready to shift focus or bring discussion to a close.

Many college teachers habitually arouse their students with an engaging example and initiate discussion with a well-formulated question, only to frustrate them by delivering a spontaneous two- to three-minute minilecture after the first student comment. They do not realize that the reason they rarely get a second response is because the readiness to talk that they created in students was dissipated during their own lengthy response. Instructors should wait for at least two or three student comments before moving the discussion along with another query or shifting back to lecture. On the other hand, a class's enthusiasm for responding usually wanes after five or six comments, and the instructor must then exert leadership once again.

For discussion to progress smoothly toward thoughtful conclusions, the teacher must control the proceedings; sometimes overtly directing traffic, sometimes indirectly encouraging students to interact with one another by saying little. There are times when silence is the best instructor behavior. More than anything else, control during discussion should be indirect and lightly delivered.

The single most useful technique for controlling student discussion is the age-old practice of having students raise their hands to speak. This method lets you decide who will talk and makes it less likely that only the loudest and most assertive students will get the floor. In large classes, students will need to raise their hands throughout the semester because it is hard to maintain adequate control without this procedure, but hand-raising can be faded in smaller classes that have been conditioned to discuss in an orderly manner. Hand-raising also reminds students that the instructor is in charge and will decide who will talk and when.

A few principles are important to remember when calling on individual students. It enhances morale to use students' names when recognizing them. (It also provides good practice for remembering their names.) Morale is seriously harmed, however, by calling on students who have given no indication that they wish to speak. Unless you are giving a recitation class or a class in which students are supposed to learn to think on their feet (as in law school), calling on students takes away far more than it adds. Even if you force only the outgoing students to talk, others will become anxious about being called on. All students prefer to choose when they speak, and for students who are fearful about speaking out, worrying about being called upon can seriously impede motivation and learning. If a student is looking puzzled, you might observe, "Dina, you look perplexed," and ask if she has a question, but otherwise you should never call on individuals who have given no indication that they wish to speak.

Scan the classroom frequently to be sure you notice students who wish to speak. Many will raise their hands high, even wave them, but others, especially quieter students, raise their hands tentatively. A few raise only a single finger in front of their questioning faces. Unless you watch students closely, you are likely to miss subtle cues or hands in the rear of the room.

Get as many students as possible to participate in the discussion by recognizing students who talk infrequently before those who have little hesitancy about speaking out. In almost every class a few students can come to dominate discussion unless the instructor actively recruits other speakers. When asking a question, scan the entire room before calling on the first person whose hand went up. Delay recognizing a frequent contributor in the hope of a sign from a quieter student. When several students raise their hands at once, always pick the one who has spoken the least. However, also remember which students were not called on and go back to them when the first student is finished, even if they no longer have their hands up. Even students who like to talk respect an instructor who lets as many students participate as possible.

College teachers should control group discussion to make it as easy as possible for every student to participate. Once students are talking, instructors must use their control to shape and guide individual student comments toward common intellectual conclusions. Steering discussion is clearly the most difficult part of leading fruitful classroom discourse. How can it be done?

Instructors to a large extent must let the discussion develop in its own way (Eble, 1976). You can set the stage and focus attention on a provocative issue, but then you must wait for discussion to begin. Anxious for students to reach certain conclusions, wanting them to realize the logical problems of an argument, college teachers sometimes force the process, state their own position too quickly, and deny students the chance to come to independent conclusions. Thus, requisite skills for teachers in guiding discussion are patience and willingness to let students think on their own.

You must also listen carefully to what students say in order to comprehend what they really mean (Eble, 1976). Without listening closely it is difficult to remember and summarize student comments for the class. Give careful and complete attention to discussion, noting the essential point(s) in each comment and, from associated nonverbal messages, the way the student felt about the topic.

In guiding a discussion you should organize individual student comments into a mosaic of related ideas, into themes mean-

ingful to the group as a whole. Teachers commonly do this by jotting comments on the board as students offer them and indicating
later how the different ideas illustrate the overall dimensions of
the topic or varying theoretical approaches to it. Student comments that reveal underlying assumptions may be highlighted to
promote thinking.

The following example illustrates both methods. In a course
on social deviance, the instructor asks students at the first meeting
to suggest examples of behaviors they would call deviant and lists
them on the board. Within five minutes the board has ten to
fifteen examples. The instructor points out that several of the
examples given represent groups who violate social or moral
norms and asks if the board entries might be compressed into
general categories such as political extremists or religious eccen-
trics. After students have worked for a few minutes at combining
individual examples into categories, the instructor summarizes
the dimensions they have generated and points out that these
categories are similar to lists proposed by others. The students' list
may be similar to what the teacher would have presented, but the
students are certain to remember the groupings better than if they
had simply heard them in a lecture and copied them down.

To follow the example further, the instructor could then
ask *why* each category is considered deviant. As the students
struggle with this question, the instructor can help them discover
their underlying assumptions about deviance, sometimes asking
them to say more, sometimes exaggerating a point to emphasize
difficulties ("So you're saying that our society considers anyone
who doesn't believe in Christianity a deviant?"). Negative discussions in which assumptions are questioned require that instructors
become highly involved in the group's problem solving as gadflies
or devil's advocates, working to keeping the group moving.

Guiding discussion is much more difficult than eliciting it
and requires considerable interpersonal sensitivity, enthusiasm, and
intellectual sharpness. Students learn most from struggling with a
problem or issue, so you should not propose a solution or reveal your
own position too quickly even if directly asked. It is much more productive for a college teacher to shape the students' ideas and withhold
personal comments until the end, if not completely.

When discussing, most students address the instructor, but students occasionally refer to each other's comments or speak to one another directly. Student exchanges more often occur in small seminars and later in the term when students have become less dependent on the instructor and more invested in each other. Student debate is encouraged if instructors are silent after student comments to give other students a chance to respond. Using students' names when referring to their argument ("As Julie was saying") also promotes student-student interaction. The degree to which students talk to each other is mostly a function of class size and the amount of teacher talk during discussion. In extended discussions, experienced instructors know to encourage the group to develop as an independent unit by being less active from the start, letting students' discomfort with silence pressure them to relate to each other as well as to the instructor.

However discussion is guided, the class's emotional arousal and investment during discussion must be maintained. An instructor can use humor, spontaneity, or a sense of irony or tragedy at different times to keep the discourse lively (Barnes-McConnell, 1978). Instructors contribute to good discussion indirectly through subtle control and stimulation of students' thinking processes.

College teachers must also know when to end discussion or guide the discourse in another direction. The way an instructor ends discussion (to return to lecturing or to end class) affects the amount students learn from the exchange of ideas and the eagerness with which they will discuss next time. Instructors sometimes find it difficult to close discussion when students are highly involved, but the skills required to end discussion well are simple.

First, give students some warning that the discussion is about to end. Asking, "Are there any other comments before we tie these ideas together?" lets students with more to say and those who have not yet spoken know that they need to speak now or never. It also communicates that you plan to go on to another topic unless students have something else important to say. Students will close discussion more decisively and quickly if they are warned that the end is coming.

When you do shift the focus to another discussion point or

return to lecturing, begin talking with the forceful voice and strong bodily movements you normally use in lecturing to let students know that you have shifted gears and they should now only listen. This is an excellent time to summarize the major points of the preceding discussion. An instructor's final review of the discussion frequently appears in student notes and is remembered. All discussion, of whatever duration, should end with a summary.

Ending discussion well makes it easier to initiate discussion again. This is because instructor summaries show students that the teacher was listening carefully to what they had to say and also because a firm ending reminds students that the instructor is in charge. Ending discussion before students run out of steam also preserves their eagerness to discuss again; no one enjoys discussion that goes on for too long. Like the seasoned performer, the skilled discussion leader stops while the audience is still eager for more.

Special Discussion Problems. Other than the difficulty of initiating discussion, the most frequent problems associated with discussion occur when the class strays from the intended topic, students become so emotionally involved that they get angry with each other or the teacher, or some students dominate the proceedings while others withdraw. Though a college teacher may never encounter all of these problems, it helps to know how to deal with them should they occur.

Skilled discussion leaders select their comments and questions to have an intended effect on students and to lead them in a particular direction. But no one can always predict how students will respond. The excitement many instructors feel during discussions probably comes partly from this unpredictability. It should not be a surprise if a discussion veers off the intended course when the comments of individual students take a different direction than expected.

When you notice that the discussion is drifting, ask yourself whether the group is leaving important points dangling, perhaps avoiding coming to terms with a difficult issue, and whether the new direction appears to have potential. If the group has not sufficiently fleshed out some important point, you might refocus the discourse "Let's tie up the point about the economic causes of the revolution before moving into this interesting new hypothesis"). If the original topic is exhausted, offer a concluding comment to tie together what was said. Do not automatically assume that the new direction is of little value just because it was not planned. When deciding whether to follow the students' lead, ask yourself whether the direction suggested by their comments is as useful as what you planned to do next. Of course, sometimes the group must be reined in simply because insufficient time is available to go in the new direction.

A second special problem in discussion results from uncontrolled emotion. Some college teachers avoid discussion altogether because they fear angry outbursts from students. First-rate discussion *is* intense, though student anger is unlikely to become unbridled if you are alert for signs of excessive emotion in students' voices and faces. If such signs are noted, reassert control by shifting the focus or get students to achieve distance by asking, "Why do you think you feel so strongly about this topic?" Making the potential or actual outburst an object of study both controls emotions and leads students to understand the power of attitudes and values.

Classroom discussion allows students to display personality characteristics openly, and students at both extremes of talkativeness can present problems. Students who talk too much may dominate a discussion unless the instructor curbs their talking. Constant talkers typically want above all else to impress the teacher, and they never notice the way other students look away or whisper to each other when they begin a comment ("There he goes again!"). Whatever the quality of a verbose student's comments, the instructor must end his or her monopoly of the floor to preserve class morale and the overall quality of discussion. Other students expect the teacher to control such a classmate, but they will be disappointed (and frightened) if the instructor treats the student aversively.

How do you control an overly talkative student without bruising other students' sensibilities? First, avoid looking in the talkative student's direction when asking a question. Turn your back to the student slightly, scan others' faces, and wait for another student to respond. Do not go too far, however, and never recog-

nize or look at such a student. Call on the student quickly sometimes, but systematically ignore him or her at others. Let the
student know instantly whether you are going to call on him or
her this time around. This practice will bring the student's talking
under your control more quickly than trying to ignore him or her
altogether. Another technique is to slowly walk away from the
student when he or she is talking. Do not turn your back on the
student entirely, however. Look around the room at the whole
class as the student talks, occasionally making eye contact with
him or her as well. This reduces the one-to-one nature of the student's communication and makes it more of a comment to the
group, something more likely to involve others. (Incidentally,
slowly walking away from the speaker makes *all* students speak
more loudly when making class comments.) These two techniques
usually suffice to control a dominating student. Occasionally you
may need to talk with the student privately, however. If this is
necessary, compliment the student for his or her willingness to
share ideas before suggesting that others be given a chance to participate as well.

College teachers are less likely to notice the extremely
uninvolved or withdrawn student. Just because students are not
offering comments does not mean they are uninvolved. One of the
beauties of engaging discussion is that the observers can be as
involved and intellectually active as the participants. Some students do withdraw from discussion proceedings, however. To
recognize such students, scan the faces of the class regularly during discussion, noting how interested each person seems to be as
well as which individuals seem ready to make a contribution. Try
to make eye contact with any student who consistently seems preoccupied. Lecturing in that student's part of the room or speaking
to him or her casually before class may keep the student engaged.
Some students are so information oriented and grade conscious
that they find discussion an unpleasant waste of time. If more
than 10 percent of the class seems withdrawn at any time during
discussion, consider whether too much time has been spent in discussion or whether the topic is really important enough to justify
using class time in this way.

A Final Note

Classroom discussion can be a waste of time for everyone and as boring as the worst of lectures. When focused on appropriate course material and when done with a class that has been trained to participate, however, discussion can produce unmatched involvement and opportunities for students to practice critical, independent thinking. Discussion can be planned, though not with as much certainty as lectures or demonstrations. Discussion is the most interpersonal of all classroom teaching methods; thus, it is the first to reflect a rise or drop in class morale or teacher enthusiasm. Because discussion requires so much energy, creativity, and spontaneity, college teachers should work just as hard during discussion as they do during a lecture and not be surprised if they feel just as emotionally drained afterward. Though courses vary tremendously in the extent to which their objectives may be attained by using discussion, skilled instructors use it whenever it is indicated.

The next chapter describes how college teachers decide what to include in a course and how to present the chosen content. Guidelines for planning entire courses as well as individual class meetings are offered. As has been clear throughout this book, the best laid plans do not ensure high quality teaching, but planning does force the instructor to consider as many options as possible when deciding what to present in the limited class time available.

CHAPTER 7

೭೮೩೭೮೩೭೮೩೭೮೩೭೮೩೭೮೩೭೮೩೭೮೩೭೮೩೭೮೩೭೮೩೭೮೩

Planning Course Content to Maximize Interest

> Suppose you wanted to get to know a tract of
> country. The worst way to do it would be to jump
> into a car, drive straight from one end to the other,
> then turn your back on it and walk away. Yet that is
> what many teachers do with complex subjects, and
> that is why their pupils seem stupider than they
> really are.... How much better would they learn
> the country if, before setting out, they were briefed
> and given maps to study; if they were rested and
> reoriented once or twice during the trip; and if they
> were shown photographs of the best spots and taken
> once more over the map when they reached the end
> of their journey?
>
> *Highet (1950, pp. 79–80)*

Many college teachers are ambivalent about planning. Though
most would endorse in theory the value of educational planning,
few plan their courses creatively and independently, stepping outside the traditional curriculum to select the concepts they believe
to be most fundamental. Like compliant students who do only
what is asked of them, too many college teachers adopt a traditional outline or prescribed syllabus or follow the chapter headings
in a textbook without considering what students should actually

learn from their courses. Most excellent instructors, on the other hand, plan very seriously, fully aware that lecturing skills cannot offset superficial or poorly organized content.

This chapter deals with planning college courses in terms of both the whole course and individual class meetings. The suggestions offered here apply to any course; see Cahn's collection of essays (1978) for guidelines on teaching specific content areas.

Before planning is discussed, it should be emphasized again that although thoughtful selection of content and objectives contributes significantly to a course, still, as in warfare and athletics, the value of a battle or game plan depends most on how well it is executed and whether it is flexible when surprises occur. No matter how carefully thought out and detailed, course outlines and lesson plans do not captivate students; college teachers with well-honed classroom skills do that. Nonetheless, teachers who carefully consider what content should be presented and how it should be organized are more likely to give virtuoso performances than those who leave everything to improvisation.

Before launching into course design, think of the complexity of those for whom the course is being planned. Students in every course have different abilities, interests, and expectations. Many students are high achievers and wish to be challenged fully. Others merely hope to get by without doing poorly. Some students are greatly interested in the course's subject, while others, hopefully few, approach the content with dread. Yet all students must be offered the same class meetings, given the same assignments, and evaluated using identical criteria. How can you adjust for student differences when planning a course?

The initial topics chosen for lecture should attempt to engage *all* students, the least as well as the most motivated and interested. Once the course is underway, topics of less obvious interest can be introduced with a greater probability of acceptance. When previewing a course for students, you should describe a wide range of objectives to maximize the probability that every student will be seeing something of personal value in the course. From what kinds of objectives may you choose?

Determining Objectives

Different Levels of Objectives. Benjamin Bloom's taxonomy of educational objectives (1956) has been widely accepted by educators since the 1950s. Most teaching involves some combination of the six different categories or levels of objectives Bloom describes, though some involves only one or two levels. Introductory courses often involve only the first few levels; higher level courses, only the last few. As is clear from the following presentation of Bloom's taxonomy, the levels become increasingly complex and difficult to specify, attain, and evaluate as they rise from one to six.

Some college teachers are interested only in having students (1) *recall and recognize* information. Committing to memory facts, theories, and principles is the essence of level 1 in Bloom's system. Almost every instructor has some information for students to handle at this level. Most teachers also desire students to (2) *comprehend* what they have learned, to understand and be able to explain specific concepts in their own words and images rather than as memorized definitions of others. Neither recall nor comprehension is sufficient for those who expect students to be able to (3) *apply* what they have learned. For such instructors, a student's mastery of a topic is incomplete unless he or she can apply it correctly to examples. Still others want students to think about what they have learned in an active way: Students should be able both to (4) *analyze* the subject, to break it down into its constituent parts, and to (5) *synthesize* it into a unified whole once again. Finally, some college teachers are not content unless students (6) *evaluate* their knowledge critically. For such teachers, learning is incomplete unless students have come to grips with underlying value issues and are able to judge the importance of what they have come to know.

By way of illustration, a professor of abnormal psychology I observed desired to achieve objectives at all six of Bloom's levels. For a section on schizophrenia, he wanted students to be able to define in their own words a number of specific concepts and research findings relating to the theory that biological influences are at the root of this disorder. He also wanted them to be able to apply this hypothesis to other disorders and to use it to interpret the results of studies stressing family influences. It was his wish that students be able to critique various kinds of supporting research (neurotransmitter studies in animals, genetic studies in humans, clinical effects of drugs) and also be able to bring them together in an integrated argument showing how all could result from a common source. Finally, this instructor wanted students to form a personal opinion on the persuasiveness of the biological argument—especially in contrast to competing hypotheses stressing the effects of experience—and make some educated guesses about what future studies might demonstrate. Though this professor knew of Bloom's system only generally, the objectives he had for his students fit it nicely.

Though Bloom offers a range of potential objectives, they cannot be selected haphazardly. Success at the first levels is necessary for later levels to be achieved: Students must master basic concepts before they can begin to think about them critically. An instructor preparing a course must decide what mixture of objectives he or she will seek and in what order they are to be sought, and at what point in a term he or she should shift from presenting new concepts to comparing, contrasting, and evaluating old ones.

Specifying Objectives in Advance. Since Bloom proposed his taxonomy, professional educators have advocated that instructors specify their objectives for a particular course in advance (Barry, 1978). Advocates of this position have added two corollaries to Bloom's taxonomy. The first is that college teachers should be accountable—that they should commit themselves ahead of time to what they are going to accomplish. The second is that teaching should produce observable behavioral changes in students. Unfortunately, behavioral objectives are most easily written for the concrete, factual levels of Bloom's taxonomy. As one moves up the list, it becomes increasingly difficult to specify what students will be able to *do* differently.

A third corollary of the educational objectives movement is an emphasis on minimal standards of achievement for a class, that is, the objectives that should be met by all. This rule fails to recognize the sizable individual differences in talent and motivation present among college students. What were designed as minimal expectations for all can easily become maximal accomplishments for those students who could have gone far beyond what was expected of others.

Some educators advocate that instructors spend the first part of each course helping students formulate their own objectives for the course rather than dictating objectives to the class (Barry, 1978). Though students may initially like being involved in course planning, this approach does not capitalize on the instructor's greater expertise, and it wastes precious class time that might be better spent. Class consensus on a set of objectives is also very difficult to achieve. Most students actually prefer to have the instructor formulate objectives rather than going through the exercises of wording objectives and seeking consensus.

The best college teachers offer a wide range of challenges for students, spanning all levels of Bloom's system. They expect students to master facts, demonstrate that they can think about what they have learned in a personally meaningful and intellectually complex way, and apply their learning to the real world. Designing a course that has a wide range of goals ensures that students with different interests and abilities all will find something of interest and challenge. More importantly, a wide range of objectives will stretch students' intellects and pique their imaginations more than will stressing the acquiring of information alone. The following section offers specific suggestions on ways to plan a course with a range of objectives.

Designing a Course

Selecting Topics. The first step in planning a course is to make a large, tentative list of topics that might be included. From this comprehensive list eliminate the least desirable topics, using two criteria: how essential the topics are to the course as a whole and how interesting they might be to students. As less essential and less interesting topics are eliminated, a mixture of especially important or interesting topics will emerge. Another option is to select the most desirable topics first, rank-ordering each according to these same criteria. A final list can be constructed by alternately selecting topics high on each separate ranking, particularly those high on both lists. The final selection of topics depends

ultimately on your subjective judgment about what is most important in your field and what students' interest in various topics
might be.

Forming Topic Objectives. You must next consider what
you would like students to learn about each topic. Sometimes you
will simply want students to define a concept correctly; at other
times you will want students to apply an idea. In deciding how to
treat each topic, consider what you want students to know, be
able to do, or feel following the course. Thinking about objectives
is particularly useful in deciding what reading or written assignments to include. Formulating objectives is admittedly a difficult
process and, other than the advisability of putting them on paper
for inspection and revision, no rigid guidelines are proposed. This
stage of course design requires careful instructor judgment and
maximum creativity.

Adjusting Goals to Reality. You should remember that
stated course objectives are goals to be pursued, not sacred injunc-
tions. They must be fitted to realistic constraints.

Time is the major constraint on what can be accomplished
in a course. A sixteen-week semester allows only forty hours of
class time at most. The first and last classes deal largely with
administrative or group maintenance concerns, and one to two
additional classes will be taken up by exams, so a better estimate
of available class time is thirty-five hours.

As experienced college teachers know, the first step in
fitting their goals to the available time is to list all class meetings.
Fill in this schedule with tentative topics, including at either end
the predictable administrative concerns. It is advisable to schedule exams first and to leave open the class just before each exam to
allow for catching up or review. The number of available class
meetings rapidly shrinks. In fitting lecture topics into the available meetings, begin if possible with high interest topics and those
that must be mastered before others can be introduced. Particularly complex or difficult concepts may take several meetings; on
the other hand, several simple ideas may be combined in a single
session. Because the initial list of topics is almost sure to be larger
than what can be accommodated, you will have to eliminate
topics. Strive to arrive at a varied schedule, changing the format

every three or four classes and mixing lecture, case study, demonstration, or discussion to maintain high interest and prevent predictability.

When scheduling, remember that several classes are especially important. The first and last classes and the classes just before and after exams have a great impact on class morale. Attempt to make these classes especially interesting or provocative. The last two or three classes are highly suited to integration and evaluation of what has been covered in the whole course.

Other important constraints on planning are class size and the time students have to devote to the course. Objectives requiring extensive discussion are much more difficult to meet in large classes; large lecture classes require more dramatic methods of presentation. Planning for small seminars and for very large lecture classes is discussed in a later section of this chapter. You should also remember that students have other courses and demands; make your requirements reasonable in light of common practices at your school. Balancing intellectual objectives and the need for maintaining student interest is difficult, but seeing the difference that good planning can make in the quality of the course offered has convinced many college teachers that it is worth the effort.

Sharing Objectives with Students. Stating objectives openly is a good way to tell students specifically what is desired of them. They are much more likely to meet expectations if these are clearly stated well in advance of expected performance. During the first class meeting, present orally (and perhaps in writing as well) the objectives you have formulated for the course. Full details need not be presented, but a few minutes spent on objectives at the very beginning gives students an idea of where they are headed and why it is important to go there. Some instructors state objectives as questions that the students should be able to answer when the semester is over (James Maas, Psychology Colloquium, University of North Carolina at Chapel Hill, 1980). Going back to the objectives during the last class meeting reminds students what they should have gotten out of a course and makes a good basis for a final discussion.

Planning for Special Types of Classes

Very Large Classes. Few college teachers prefer large sections to smaller ones. But if practical considerations require that a large class be taught, an instructor can adapt effectively by recognizing how the objectives, methods of presentation, interpersonal atmosphere, and administrative problems of a large class differ from those of a small one. Instructors should bear in mind that large classes are offered only for convenience; they have no educational advantages over smaller ones. The relevant question is whether large classes are *less* effective than small ones. (To review the research on that question, the variable of "class size" must be quantified. I will define *very small* as classes with 15 or fewer students; *small*, classes with fewer than 35; *moderate*, fewer than 60; *large*, fewer than 120; and *very large*, over 120. Like all qualitative labels, these are approximate and are used for convenience.)

Student achievement and satisfaction have been compared in small and large classes. Research suggests that college teachers can achieve many educational objectives in large classes just as well as in smaller classes. Scores on final exams do not differ because of class size, for example (McKeachie, 1978). Large classes cannot, however, realize objectives best facilitated by discussion, such as retention, critical thinking, or attitude change.

Research on class size indicates that large classes are less effective than small ones for students who need interpersonal attention from teachers in order to do their best (McKeachie, 1978). Highly dependent, less academically able, and poorly motivated students do not do as well in large sections. Thus, large sections are not as effective as small ones for a significant percentage of students.

Though most students and instructors prefer smaller sections, skillful lecturers can offer exciting and meaningful educational experiences and can compensate for the liabilities associated with large class size. In planning for a large or very large section, wise instructors recognize that most objectives must be met using lecture and that the lectures must be more dynamic and engaging than they would have to be in small or moderate-sized classes.

Brief discussion can be used to answer questions, involve students momentarily, or break up a lecture (as with a rhetorical question); extended discussion is unlikely to be effective, however. Thus, the objectives for a large section should be primarily to present and evaluate information rather than to encourage students to evaluate their personal values or to think independently. Written assignments can be used to encourage thinking, and provocative lectures can be used to achieve limited affective goals.

Because large classes are less personal and intimate than small ones, teachers of large classes should offer as many opportunities for individual contact with students outside of class as possible. Some instructors invite small groups to observe their laboratory or field research ("Sign up on the sheet by the door if you would like to visit my laboratory on Wednesday afternoon" or "I have room in my car for four students to accompany me on a two-hour trip to collect botanical specimens this Thursday afternoon"). Others invite students to sign up for group conferences in which students can comment informally on the course.

Requiring students to take advantage of such opportunities for personal contact is not a good idea, however. Doing so increases their fears of both intimacy and autocratic teacher control and weakens rapport. It also takes away students' opportunity to make their own decision to seek closer contact with an authority figure. Furthermore, requiring student attendance necessitates monitoring to see which students appear and deciding how those who do not will be treated. None of these outcomes is desirable. It is better to offer attractive events that students, even those who are most afraid of teachers, will want to attend. All students appreciate having such opportunities available, and those who take advantage of them will feel more personally involved in the course.

It is also important to maximize opportunities for personal contacts with students during class. Instructors of large classes can come to class five to ten minutes early, stroll around the room, and chat informally with students. They can walk up and down the aisles frequently when lecturing to make eye contact with every student several times during each class. Occasional personal disclosures also add intimacy to large lecture classes. The techniques for maximizing rapport given in Chapter Three are especially needed with large classes. Just as lecturing to a large audience requires a more forceful and energetic delivery, fostering rapport with a big group requires more aggressive interpersonal strategies.

College teachers planning large sections should be aware that administrative nuisances increase with class size (McKeachie, 1978). Not only does it take longer to score the exams of a large class; it also takes considerably longer just to hand them out. If handouts are to be used, they may need to be placed in stacks near classroom entrances before class because of the time that would otherwise be required for distribution. Access to reserve readings may be difficult in large classes unless sufficient copies can be produced. Several problems associated with evaluation also become more troublesome in large classes. Students are more likely to cheat in a large class where they feel little personal involvement, and it is more difficult to prevent them from doing so. Teachers are also more likely to be annoyed by large numbers of phone calls on the night before an exam. All the irritations of teaching are magnified as the number of students increases, and greater instructor patience and tolerance is required in large classes.

A traditional method of easing the burden of large sections is to have one or more teaching assistants (TAs). The argument for this practice is that assistants can do much of the "grubby" work—especially grading—and free the professor to teach. TAs can help with the busywork, but they cannot promote interpersonal rapport as well as the instructor. They also require considerable supervisory time if their labors are to be satisfying to everyone concerned. Teachers who have TAs hold office hours for them fail to recognize that office hours exist for interpersonal reasons as much as academic ones and that students want a relationship with the professor—the group leader and symbolic parent figure— more than with an underling. If TAs assist *only* with technical matters (running audiovisual equipment, setting up demonstrations), they are unlikely to create problems. If TAs grade students' work, they must be integrated into the class from the beginning. Ideally, TAs should help to plan the course, attend all class meetings so they will know what was presented, and make occasional presentations of their own to establish relationships with the students. Leading small discussion groups is an ideal use of TAs and is a good training ground for their own teaching skills. Teaching assistants can boost the instructor's morale, but they can do only so much to offset the disadvantages associated with large sections.

Very Small Classes. Extremely small classes (fewer than fifteen students) will be more involved and emotional social settings than larger classes, regardless of what the instructor does. Psychological research has demonstrated reliably that group members become increasingly emotionally responsive to each other as the size of the group decreases (Cartwright and Zander, 1960). When class size drops below fifteen, interpersonal involvement among group members, including the leader, becomes noticeably more intense.

Close involvement is not always pleasant, however, as the conflicts that occur within families demonstrate convincingly. In extremely small classes the instructor's leadership role is of great importance. In small classes instructors' attitudes are more obvious and their methods of control more crucial to classroom atmosphere. How should college teachers adjust their presentations and treatment of students to the interpersonal intensity of small classes?

Getting to know students personally is even more important in small classes than in average or large ones. In a class of 100, being unknown is not as aversive as it is if there are few other students from whom to be distinguished. Even if an instructor does not ordinarily seek familiarity with students, he or she must at least learn students' names in a small class. Instructors must also adjust their goals and preferred methods of presentation for very small groups. The interpersonal closeness of small classes allows instructors to increase students' comfort with independent thinking and likelihood of attitude change, but it rules out a course geared to learning facts and theories from instructor lectures. When planning small courses, experienced teachers know that students in such courses expect less lecture and more discussion.

College teachers who ordinarily use discussion frequently will find the small class delightful, but they too should adjust the way they use discussion. Many students are comfortable being silent in a large class, but it is the unusual student who will sit through a very small class without speaking. Thus, leading discussions in small classes can take more time because more students expect to speak. In smaller classes students often speak without raising their hands and interrupt each other's comments — sometimes even the instructor's — so it is also more difficult to control the discussion and make it possible for quieter students to hold the floor. Leading successful discussions in smaller classes requires a sense of when to let the students go and when to exert control. In small classes it is still important for the teacher to set the stage for student comments at the beginning and bring things together at the end.

Small classes have many advantages. It is extremely easy to get to know students in such classes and to evaluate their work closely. It is also easier to stimulate discussion and to use it to promote independent thinking. Less factual, more complex objectives are easier to achieve in small classes. However, the greater personal contact in small classes can be uncomfortable at first for teachers (or students) who prefer or are accustomed to more distant relationships.

Greater flexibility is required in planning for very small and very large classes. A college teacher who tried to use discussion exclusively in a class of over 100 would be just as unresponsive to the setting as a teacher who lectured for an entire semester to a group of 10.

Some courses require special planning because of their atypical format. Such courses include individual instruction resembling the traditional tutorial and innovative courses based on contemporary technology.

Tutorials. Individual or small-group tutorials are the backbone of graduate education, and every college teacher is likely to encounter an individual teaching situation at some time. A student may ask an instructor to direct honors research, independent study, or a program of guided reading. An instructor may even be asked to offer a formal tutorial involving regular group meetings of three or four students who submit weekly essays in the British style. Teaching students individually requires skills different from those needed for traditional group classes.

Individual courses are commonly given for purposes not easily achieved in typical group formats, especially to help students expand library or laboratory research skills. They usually have the goal of encouraging students to think, to create and express their ideas independently. Students should be aware of the purpose of the course and in agreement with it when signing on.

Because students are expected to act differently in tutorials, they should be told how tutorials differ from ordinary classes. They should be warned that they must work more independently and learn to use the instructor as consultant rather than as supervisor. They should also be prepared for the critical nature of tutorials and reassured that comments about their ideas or work should not be taken too personally. Few undergraduates have learned to value negative criticism as an aid to future improvement, and they can benefit from discussion of critical methods. Sharing one's own difficulty with criticism helps students develop a mature learning attitude.

When more than one student will be participating in a tutorial, the teacher should instruct them in how to *give* criticism. Most students will copy the teacher's style of offering criticism, but explicit instruction in how to criticize constructively can eliminate beginner's mistakes and get the tutorial group off to a good start.

Teachers direct the proceedings less in tutorials and give students more time to talk. As with regular class discussion, though, a college teacher must structure the dialogue if a tutorial is to be instructive. Regular meetings are one important way to structure independent student work. Even the best-intentioned students will have trouble if they are instructed to appear "whenever they have work to present or questions to pose." A tutorial instructor should schedule weekly meetings and have the student(s) attend even if they have nothing new to report or present. If no one has anything to present at a scheduled meeting, general discussion of research methods or theoretical issues can be profitable. Because college teachers rarely receive teaching credit for individual courses, they may not treat them as seriously as regular courses and may tend to avoid formal structure. A successful tutorial, however, should meet as regularly as other courses.

Instructors can further structure students' independent work by focusing on the subject and avoiding a drift into casual or social topics. The intimacy of tutorials makes the student-teacher relationship personal, which is generally advantageous. However, this personal quality increases the temptation to engage in conversation that can take the tutorial off track if allowed to occupy too much meeting time. The instructor must monitor the amount of time spent on personal concerns and refocus the discussion when indicated. ("It sounds like you had a particularly interesting trip to New York City, Kathy. What did you learn at the libraries there that you want to focus on today?")

Some tutorials follow the traditional British format, which routinely begins with a student reading his or her essay and the don interrupting at will to make points or ask questions. Individual or group music lessons (especially master classes) also follow this traditional pattern of student performance and instructor critique. Even in such structured cases, the tutor must keep the group on track and resist temptations to avoid serious artistic, intellectual, or scientific inquiry by lapsing into social or irrelevant discourse.

The major responsibility of a tutor is to set limits within which students can exercise independence and responsibility. Experienced college teachers know it is tempting to be overly controlling. It requires tremendous patience to watch students struggle with a problem or learn a skill one has long since mastered without doing it for them, rescuing them too quickly from their intellectual quandary. Most good teachers are compulsive sharers, and a tutorial requires them to hold back for as long as possible before revealing their own ideas. For students to learn independence, the instructor must facilitate their thinking and problem solving by giving them ample opportunity to find solutions on their own. To many, nurturing intellectual growth makes the tutorial more satisfying than lecturing; but tutoring is frustrating to others because it requires unusual teacher restraint.

More than anything else, tutorials require that college teachers be sensitive to the *process* of their interactions with students. A successful tutor constantly monitors what is happening interpersonally—whether the students are being independent or asking the instructor to do too much for them, whether they need direction or freedom, whether they take criticism well or become defensive. Sometimes an instructor must keep a student motivated by commenting on his or her behavior ("I get the impression, Mark, that you are finding it hard to do what we agreed you would do at the start of term"). Most of all, tutors must remain flexible and modify their approach when indicated. Whether they are formal tutorials, writing workshops, reading courses, or independent research, individual courses require the most interpersonal sensitivity and skill of all teaching settings.

When planning a tutorial, the most important consideration is the objectives. Teachers should be sure that they and the students are clear and in agreement on the purpose of the class. Beyond the motivation and abilities of the individual student(s), the success of a tutorial depends most on the teacher's ability to structure an effective consultative relationship.

PSI and Computer-Assisted Classes. To many, the most popular and promising teaching innovations of recent years are individualized teaching methods that capitalize on current technology. PSI, or Personalized System of Instruction (Keller, 1968), is based on behavioral learning principles and requires students to master each unit of content on their own or with the assistance of an undergraduate proctor before proceeding at their own pace to others. A number of college courses are taught each year using PSI methods, and for four years (1976–1980) *The Journal of Personalized Instruction* was published by the Department of Psychology of Georgetown University to disseminate research articles devoted to this approach. Though research on PSI affirms its effectiveness as a means of conveying information (Kulik, Kulik, and Cohen, 1979), it has not revolutionized higher education as its proponents had originally hoped (Fred Keller, Psychology Colloquium, University of North Carolina at Chapel Hill, 1980). Some research suggests that the PSI format is best used in conjunction with lecture-discussion methods to help students measure how well they are mastering content (Williamson, Sewell, and McCoy, 1976). A great deal of what is known about PSI is assembled in a single volume (Sherman, Ruskin, and Semb, 1983).

One of the many ways computers have been used in higher education has been as electronic tutors to present information and correct the mistakes of students seated at terminals. In its earliest and most primitive forms, computer-assisted instruction offered little more than a means of using a $1,000,000 computer instead of a $15 textbook to present material to students. Interactive programs available today, however, teach students to think as well as to know. Predictably, the use of computers in education has drawn serious attention, most of it friendly and optimistic but some of it concerned (Oettinger, 1969; Rockart and Morton, 1975). As the number of microprocessors in schools, businesses, and homes continues to mushroom, the educational applications of computer technology in colleges are sure to outstrip what is known today.

These promising technologies are too complex and quickly changing to be presented in detail here. Though future research will establish its limits, a good guess is that technology-based individual teaching is best used in tandem with more traditional lecture-discussion formats. Computers and behavioral approaches may be the best means of ensuring that students master basic facts, freeing class time for instructors to pursue high-level objectives.

Considerable planning is required if these individual approaches are to be effective, and the instructor should remember that they in no way negate the importance of human interaction between student and teacher. Students still need living teachers to inspire, to motivate, and to reassure them. As O. P. Kolstoe notes, "To learn, students must react to the presentation, whether that is a person, place, or thing. The successful teacher is apt to be the one who honestly faces the fact that communication is a very personal thing between each instructor and each student. . . . Universal (alternatives to this) simply are myths pursued by naive teachers and technology hucksters" (1975, p. 72).

Planning for Individual Class Meetings

Though a college teacher will have noted objectives for each class meeting when planning a course, these will be too general to use for specific presentations. College courses are too unpredictable to be planned completely, even by experienced instructors, and they would be lifeless affairs if they were so thoroughly planned. To be fresh and involved and closely connected with the previous topic, each class meeting should be organized only a few days to a week beforehand. What should be considered when planning for a specific class?

Selecting specific objectives from available options is the first task. An instructor might want students to know a topic in a number of different ways—to develop historical perspective, to remember and understand difficult details presented in readings, or to see the applicability of a concept to their experiences with contemporary events and issues. A teacher might wish to present a relevant theory or piece of literature or to show how others have tested or criticized the topic. Because the possibilities are almost endless, instructors should carefully select both what is most important and what is most needed dramatically and interpersonally on a given day.

In planning single classes, review the topics just presented and those scheduled immediately afterward. A useful technique to select the focus for a given class is to imagine what you want students to tell their friends about the topic over lunch or after class. Thinking about topics from the students' perspective can give you clues as to what you want most to accomplish with a given topic. This in turn can help you decide how to present the topic.

You should first list three or four major points you wish to make in a class meeting (McKeachie, 1978). You must then decide how to make the points. Here creativity, a sense of drama, and sensitivity to student interests come into play. If lecture is to be used, remember the guidelines about variety and timing when deciding how to present each point and where in the presentation it should appear. If discussion is appropriate, note potential queries and where in the presentation they can be raised. Demonstrations or slides must, of course, be prepared well in advance. When constructing a presentational outline for a given class meeting, think of the meeting as an artistic event needing an overall theme, an engaging beginning, and a buildup to a decisive ending.

Modifying Plans

This chapter began with the premise that planning is valuable because it helps college teachers anticipate classroom events. But how rigidly should course plans be followed? The answer depends on a number of things.

It depends on the college teacher's experience. Not surprisingly, experienced instructors are better able to plan accurately, but even the experienced may find their plans for a new course disappointing in application. Anyone teaching a course for the first time should view his or her plans with considerable skepticism and be willing to drop or add topics if too much or too little was planned for the time available. An instructor may also need to adjust the relative amounts of time spent on discussion or lecture. The first set of exams can indicate whether too little or too much was asked of the students.

If an instructor has successfully taught a course at a given school before and finds it difficult to stick to the planned schedule, he or she should look for reasons for the difficulty. Occasionally instructors may notice themselves being unnecessarily wordy or tangential when lecturing or too willing to let a class wander from the point or discuss too long. This may be because the teacher is preoccupied with personal concerns, physically tired, or simply bored by teaching on that day. Whatever the cause, teachers who have difficulty sticking to their class plans should examine their own attitudes and increase their motivation to teach well, rather than assuming that the plans need changing.

If a college teacher senses on a given day that what was planned is not going well, he or she should definitely consider doing something different. The methods of presentation are more likely to need change than the planned topics. Perhaps the class has not gone well because of an unanticipated drop in class morale or a consuming campus issue that has affected the students. Whether the malaise rests with the students or with the instructor, increasing discussion, presenting humorous anecdotes, or energetic lecturing may turn things around. A rule of thumb is to be wary of changing course outlines unless you are new to a course, but be quick to modify your behavior in a given class when things do not go as expected.

One exception to this position about changing plans deals with requirements and evaluation. Students will become upset if requirements (exams, significant readings, or papers) are added after the semester is well under way. All major work expected of students should be announced on the first day of class. College teachers should also avoid decreasing assigned work unless it is apparent that a serious error of planning has occurred. The teacher should not ask students if they would like requirements changed. Asking indicates that the instructor is not confident and raises the possibility that other requirements are negotiable. An unconfident instructor raises students' anxiety about class leadership and reduces their motivation to complete assignments. If an instructor decides to combine two short papers into one long paper, he or she might ask students to vote their preferences and then announce the final decision later. The work expected of students in a college course is a solemn social contract, and modifying it significantly risks reducing student satisfaction and motivation to assume work responsibilities.

Plans, then, generally should be carried out once a course is underway. They represent (or should represent) the results of careful thinking about the topics of the course, the objectives to be pursued, and the methods to be used. But planning involves more than classroom presentations. Student course requirements and the means of evaluation must be planned as well. This chapter has dealt with planning generally. Chapter Eight focuses on course requirements, including assignments that students are asked to do outside of class, and Chapter Nine details methods of evaluation and ways to use them to increase motivation.

CHAPTER 8

❧❦❧❦❧❦❧❦❧❦❧❦❧❦❧❦❧❦❧❦❧❦❧❦❧❦❧❦❧❦

Integrating Learning
In and Out of the Classroom

> Attending class is akin to regular religious obser-
> vance: The ritual or sermon is less important for
> what it teaches directly than for its motivational
> impact on what believers do between services.

Coming to class is essential to mastering the content of a college
course, yet most learning actually occurs outside the classroom
(Eble, 1976). Recall and recognition of specific information most
often result from solitary reading and concentrated study. Independent thinking about course content is also fostered by written
assignments that students complete on their own. For some subjects, firsthand observation of the phenomena, research methods,
or artistic performances under study provides an essential
framework in which to organize learned facts. Most courses can
benefit from occasional field trips or observations that students
make on their own. Do not let this book's emphasis on college
teaching as artistic performance in an interpersonal arena obscure
the fact that the abilities to read and write critically have long
been the fundamental skills of an educated person, and these are
developed largely through individual efforts outside the
classroom.

Students do learn some content details during class, but

such learning is superficial and temporary if their only exposure to information is lecture. To get the most out of class presentations and to master the content most easily, students should read something about the topic both before and after class. Even if assignments are read after the lecture or when an exam draws near, reading gives students a second exposure to the ideas presented in class. Having written materials available is essential for learning of depth and permanence.

If so much learning occurs outside class, why do we hold classes at all? Coming to class introduces students to a mature lecturer's perspective and models the thinking skills they need in order to evaluate what they read. Skilled instructors can demonstrate ways to pose a literary or intellectual argument or design a scientific study and to view the results from the distance of time and competing explanations. Nothing aids students' understanding and evaluation of what they read so much as a professor who reveals the way he or she thinks about a content area. Whether lectures or discussions are used to increase students' intellectual appreciation of a topic, the end result makes coming to class a valuable aid to what students learn on their own.

Still, most of the benefits students gain from attending class are motivational. College classes at their best have an aura of magic — they are exciting and pleasurable experiences that engage students' attention and stimulate their imaginations richly. Such classes create a positive emotional response to the subject that makes it much more likely that students will eagerly perform what is asked of them outside of class. If nothing else, coming to class regularly reminds students they *are* taking a course and have duties to perform, assignments to complete.

Because coming to class is never sufficient, however, college teachers should give careful attention to what they ask students to do on their own. This is the subject of this chapter. Three kinds of outside activities instructors commonly require of students — reading, writing, and observing — are discussed in the material that follows, and specific suggestions are offered on ways to integrate these activities with classroom lectures and discussions to produce superior learning and motivation.

Reading Assignments

Like the topics chosen for a course, readings should be selected both for their importance and for their interest. Considerable deliberation is required to assemble reading assignments that meet these dual criteria. Readings should be clearly written and at an appropriate conceptual level for the students being taught.

One initial decision is whether to use prepared textbooks or a collection of individual readings chosen by the instructor. Most reading for college courses is done in prepared texts. Yet some instructors are reluctant to use textbooks, believing that they will appear shallow or unintellectual unless they assign original sources or put together their own set of readings. Contemporary photocopy technology has made it easier than ever for teachers to design their own texts, though tightened copyright guidelines have restricted this option. The choice of a prepared text or original sources should be determined by one's objectives more than anything else.

In lower or introductory level courses a college teacher must ensure that students master a body of information. The reading skills of freshmen, especially, are usually not sufficiently developed for them to work independently for most of the semester. For these courses a single comprehensive text is probably best (Eble, 1976).

If an instructor wants students to increase thinking skills and gain mature opinions, he or she should have them read original materials. The abilities to weigh evidence and to contrast various points of view are most easily taught by having students read isolated materials and discuss them in class or in writing (Eble, 1976). For this reason, original materials rather than textbooks are usually used in advanced courses or small seminars.

Many courses fall in between the introductory and advanced levels. Fortunately, factual and evaluative objectives are not mutually exclusive. Both goals can be pursued if the characteristics of the students and the nature of the content are taken into account. For many courses the best choice is a single text to present the meat of the content, supplemented by readings to give students a taste of the original sources, to enhance their interest, and to serve as the basis for critical thinking. Having thought out course objectives makes choosing readings a much more rational process.

Which readings should students own individually and which should they share? Reserve readings save students money, but waiting for available copies at the library costs them valuable time. Sharing readings also decreases the probability that students will read and study them sufficiently. Many students dislike going to the library and devote little time to reserve reading. Experienced instructors usually ask students to purchase major works (texts, literature), but they place on reserve short supplemental papers (critical essays, research reports, newspaper or magazine articles).

Other considerations are important in deciding which readings students should buy. For example, cost is always of concern to students. A teacher should always find out what various books cost and choose the cheaper work of comparable quality. A hardcover book should rarely be assigned if a paperback version is available. If an instructor believes a book should become part of students' permanent libraries, he or she should order both covers so students can choose. Having a personal copy of a book increases the probability that a student will reread and underline it, so most teachers encourage purchases. However, if the book chosen is much more expensive than other texts, many students will not buy their own copies.

Size is another consideration. Heavy, large texts are unwieldy to use and difficult to carry around. Some publishers have experimented with smaller texts, so a variety of sizes may be available. Readings of an appropriate level of difficulty should be chosen. Many teachers compare sections on the same topic from different texts to select the best text for their course and students. Finally, books and other readings should be attractive and engaging to undergraduate readers. Texts vary greatly in terms of layout, photographs, and graphics, and these features should be evaluated as much as the quality of information and writing style.

Readings should be integrated with class activities. A teacher should tell students why particular texts and reserve readings were chosen and what he or she expects the students to do with them. Students are more likely to read assignments day by day (rather than just before exams) if the readings are pegged to particular lectures. A written outline handed out on the first day that pairs class meetings with specific reading assignments will help students pace their reading. As much as possible, instructors should avoid skipping around in texts (McKeachie, 1978), because some students will inevitably read straight through and thus cover the wrong chapters for class or exams. In addition, the organizational transition provided by the text author will be lost (or confusing) if many sections are read out of order.

Students are more likely to read assignments on schedule and to relate readings to class content if instructors show that readings are important by mentioning them frequently. The content in the book need not be repeated, merely alluded to. For example, a teacher might say, "Your text gives a number of explanations for the decline of the Ottoman Empire, but let's consider only the two most compelling." For those who have read the assignment, such statements connect the readings with the lecture; for those who have not, it begins an organization of what they will learn later from their books.

This example raises the question of how much of the readings a college teacher should cover in class. Repeating textbook material in class will bore students who have done the reading and kill for everyone the incentive to read before class. An instructor should use lecture, Fritz Machlup (1979) suggests, to elucidate what the text leaves obscure and to elaborate what the text leaves incomplete. No text is likely to present every topic to a teacher's satisfaction, and the classroom is a good place to correct a book's weaknesses. Class lectures can be devoted to interpretations different from those of the textbook writer. Lecture is better than discussion for comparing interpretations because students often are not prepared and feel called on the carpet during discussion; at least, students should be warned if such comparative discussions are going to occur. An instructor should select topics from the readings about which he or she has special expertise or which can be related to current events or key issues in the field. In general, the teacher should use class time to tie together topics in readings with each other and with the students' experiences, rather than attempting to present them in detail.

Students' motivation to read assignments can be increased in a number of ways. As many as 20 percent to 40 percent of the class will not have done the reading before class, but a teacher should not acknowledge this openly. Sarcastic remarks about student failings ("I'm sure everyone has done the reading, as usual") make students feel guilty and suggest that the instructor does not expect them to prepare for class. Instead, the teacher should state a positive expectation and try to pique students' curiosity. ("I'm sure many of you will find Chapter Seven of particular interest" or "The article we will discuss in the next class is one of my favorites, and I'll be interested to find out what you think of it"). Interesting and enjoyable class lectures and discussions closely connected to assigned readings will motivate students to read the chosen assignments with enthusiasm and concentration.

Written Assignments

Term papers are common in college courses, but many students — and instructors — do not enjoy them. Independent thinking and clear writing are very difficult for many students, so they avoid subjects or courses that require substantial written work. Even students who write successfully may be reminded of past difficulties with choosing a focused topic, finding materials in the library, or simply getting themselves to begin writing. Written assignments put stress on all students because they involve independent thinking, self-revelation on paper, and, inevitably, evaluation.

Many college teachers also are ambivalent about written work. Some avoid assigning papers at all; most dread grading them. For some, disappointment over the worst papers more than offsets the pleasure of reading the best ones. Late or sloppy papers are nuisances, and possibly plagiarized papers can kill enthusiasm for ever assigning certain topics again.

In spite of these drawbacks, written assignments are unmatched for getting students to think independently and critically (Eble, 1976). Students will improve their writing only by continuing to write long after freshman composition courses are over. Fortunately, it is possible to overcome many of the negative aspects of written assignments. First, a word is needed about the objectives papers can meet.

Objectives for Written Assignments. One objective for written work is to help students hone their writing skills. Writing is an essential skill of educated persons, and its development is the responsibility of all college faculty.

Many faculty members also want students to read more than textbooks. Requiring students to select additional readings from a list or from their own search and to summarize or critically review the material is a useful way to meet this goal. The content of the writing is less important than the independent reading preceding it.

A similar technique involves asking students to keep a journal of their experiences in class, while reading, or while observing a subject on their own. Critical autobiographical notations are particularly useful when teachers ask students for their personal reactions or attitudes (Hettich, 1976). For example, students in a criticism course may be asked to evaluate their reactions to plays or films seen on their own rather than to simply list those reactions. Again, what students write is less important than the fact that the journal motivates observation and evaluation of their own experience.

Teachers commonly assign written papers to teach students to use the library. Written assignments may require students to search card catalogues and research indexes, locate books and scholarly articles, and scan various works for passages relevant to their topic. The quality of the students' conclusions may be less important to the instructor than the intimate familiarity with library resources gained in the process.

Some instructors ask students to apply course concepts to specific problems or issues through written assignments. For example, students may be given literature to read and evaluate using the methods demonstrated in the course. In the sciences, students may be asked to solve specific theoretical or applied problems. For any subject, students may be asked to contrast and compare different research methods or theories and draw independent conclusions. Bloom's objectives of analysis and synthesis are both met by these "thought papers." In such application assignments, the complexity, sophistication, or creativity of students' thinking is of most concern.

In some papers college teachers require critical evaluation, not just analysis. They give students a research study, a philosophical or historical treatise, or an artistic work and ask the students to evaluate it. In completing such an assignment, students consult and consider other perspectives but ultimately must form their own opinions regarding the topic. Philosophy is particularly suited to evaluative assignments.

As instructors' objectives for students' written work become more abstract and complex, grading criteria and procedures change. Logs or journals are most appropriately graded pass-fail: students either did what was asked or not. Though an instructor may be tempted to grade research papers on their length and on the amount of library research a student appears to have done, it is better to assign grades on the quality of the student's organization and integration of ideas. Grades on thought papers are typically based on the quality of original thinking—a very difficult determination. Evaluative papers are even harder to grade, and it is critical that a teacher evaluate students' thinking processes rather than the degree to which they share the instructor's opinions.

College teachers may assign written work for many reasons. In assigning a paper, the first step is to state one's objectives for doing so. Many students do not recognize that there is more than one type of written assignment, so it is wise for the teacher to spell out what type of writing he or she has in mind. Clear objectives and instructions help students understand an assignment and complete it properly.

Using Written Assignments. College teachers traditionally make very broad, even deliberately vague, paper assignments. The most common assignment is simply, "Write a paper on some topic relevant to the course." Even if an instructor clarifies the request by saying something like "Write a term paper on cultural relativism," students still have considerable freedom to choose theorists and compare them in any manner. Skilled students may be able to handle such loose assignments and produce first-rate pieces of research, thinking, and writing, but most undergraduates will write papers that better meet a teacher's objectives if the teacher avoids vague and general topics and guides their work (McKeachie, 1978).

How much guidance is sufficient? A paper assignment can easily be made so specific that little creativity or independent thinking is required. For example, if an anthropology instructor asks students to write about four ways in which the ideas of Ruth Benedict and Margaret Mead on cultural relativity are similar and dissimilar, students need only list what is asked. Such assignments create less anxiety in students initially, but eventually they seem like drudgery or busywork because they do not allow for creativity or independent thinking. Teachers should find a middle ground between overly broad topics and mere exercises in word choice and grammatical form.

Paper topics should also fit course objectives and treatment. If students are asked to integrate lectures with readings and apply that knowledge to specific examples, the papers will be relatively unique to the particular course. Such written assignments promote independent thinking and are also exceedingly difficult to buy or plagiarize.

A college teacher must decide how many written assignments should be made, how long the papers should be, and when they should be due. For most courses, educational objectives can be met by a single written assignment during the term. This is the traditional academic practice because it fits most courses well. However, term papers inevitably create anxiety in many students and administrative hassles for instructors concerning timely delivery and grading. Some instructors therefore assign two short papers in an attempt to soften the negative impact of one long paper and to keep students from putting off writing until the end of the term and staking their grade on a single piece of work. Two papers usually multiply rather than reduce the problems, however. Students feel anxious twice, and instructors must hear double excuses about tardy turn-ins. A written assignment is a major emotional event in the life of a class regardless of paper length. Teachers should remember this when considering more than one assignment and avoid assuming that the interpersonal costs of written assignments can be reduced by spreading them out over shorter tasks.

To be sure, sometimes multiple papers are appropriate. When a course emphasizes independent student thinking, papers are the most appropriate method of evaluation, and students are typically asked to submit two or three during a term. Papers are commonly used as the major method of evaluation in small advanced seminars and many graduate courses. But in most undergraduate courses content mastery is a major goal, and examinations best measure that. Many professors do not assign papers at all in such courses, and those who do most commonly assign a single one.

Some students invariably ask, "How long should papers be?" In theory, length depends on the instructor's objectives for the paper; in practice, length is more often a function of individual students' writing styles and what they are accustomed to do for other faculty. Most term papers are between ten and fifteen double-spaced typed pages, though there is considerable variation in every class. This norm probably occurs because it is difficult to say anything meaningful in less than five pages, and twenty pages suffice for most topics that undergraduates choose. A good way to respond to the student who asks about length is to say, "Length depends on how concisely you write and how ambitious your topic is. I would prefer that you express yourself concisely — say what you have to say — rather than attempting to fill up a certain number of pages. I do not count pages, and I hope you will not focus on length either." Many instructors suggest a range of lengths, however. (As a way of deemphasizing length, Eble (1976) advocates telling students not to turn in handwritten papers that end at the bottom of a page!) Students will learn to be more independent if a teacher emphasizes that *they* are the most important judge of what is enough.

Collecting Written Assignments. One of the more irritating administrative nuisances college teachers encounter is getting students to turn papers in on time. Whatever a teacher announces about due dates rarely brings all the work in on time. Some college teachers take a casual attitude about due dates, suggesting that students "turn the papers in sometime before the end of the course" and responding to student queries about dates with, "whenever you've finished." Such instructors can expect papers to dribble in throughout final examinations and for a number of students to request extensions or incompletes. Because writing papers requires so much student initiative and discipline, a college teacher actually helps students by giving them a due date.

In contrast, some teachers adopt a police mentality and set elaborate punitive policies for late papers ("I will subtract one half of a letter grade for every day your paper is late after 5 P.M. on the due date"). This approach does bring in most papers on time but at a considerable cost in student morale. Even with hard policies, some students will fail to turn papers in on time or will request exemptions ("I have a note from the infirmary" or "My typist got the flu!"). An occasional student may casually turn in a good paper several days late and force a teacher to enforce his or her overly harsh rules and assign a low grade to an otherwise very acceptable paper. In addition to damaging interpersonal rapport, "tough-guy" policies do not encourage students to work more independently. Rules of any kind tend to be seen, especially by the young, as limits to be tested or circumvented. The more elaborate an instructor's policies about late papers, the more some students will attempt to get around them.

How can a college teacher provide structure that helps students complete written work on time without denying them independence or stimulating rebelliousness? First of all, a teacher should give a definite due date for papers. A date about two weeks before the last class allows ample time to grade and return papers before the term ends. Secondly, the instructor should remind students during the semester when they should be "thinking about," "researching," "beginning," or "polishing" their papers. Thirdly, the teacher should *not* announce penalties for late papers, but simply say, "I would like the papers by the date listed on the syllabus so that I'll have plenty of time to read them carefully and return them by the end of the course." Typically, a few weeks before the due date, some student will ask what will happen if a paper is late or if he or she can have a typing extension. The teacher should try to look more surprised than angry and respond with something like, "Gee, I don't know. Papers usually come in when I ask for them. As I said, I want them by that date at the latest so I can give them the attention they deserve. I simply can't do that if very many are late." This response emphasizes that the date selected is reasonable and consistent with students' wishes to have their papers read carefully and returned promptly. Treating deadlines this way deemphasizes the authority issue between instructor and student, making the due date a matter of personal convenience rather than control.

Most students will respond well to a deadline presented in this way. But some students, especially the immature or anxious-dependent, find such vague consequences uncomfortable and may try to pin the instructor down or receive personal assurance that they will not be harmed if their papers are late. They should be calmly and firmly told that the teacher will be pleased to read their papers whenever they are ready but cannot declare them on time if they are late. If such students still seem concerned, tell them that you will *attempt* to grade late papers the same as those coming in on time. To facilitate their personal growth, an instructor should put gentle pressure on dependent or anxious students to take responsibility for turning in their papers on time or facing the mild consequences — the teacher's inconvenience or displeasure. More mature, less conflicted students will appreciate a teacher who confirms their independence; only rarely will a student attempt to play games with deadlines presented in this way.

A variation on this method is for the teacher to announce that he or she wants all the papers by a particular day but would like as many of them as early as possible. Students can be told to turn in papers any time during the two weeks preceding the final date. Though some students will chuckle at the notion of anyone turning in papers early, a few will do so with this mild encouragement. Returning these papers as quickly as possible in clear view of the whole class effectively motivates other students to turn theirs in a day or two early as well. Seeing one's classmates turning in papers is a powerful motivator to students who habitually do things late. These techniques of getting papers in on time are based on the assumption that students are more likely to cooperate with and appreciate subtle methods of teacher control than more autocratic and less respectful ones.

Evaluating Written Assignments. Though the virtues of written assignments are many, their substantial liability is difficulty in fair grading. Even when students write on similar topics, the accuracy, complexity, and originality of their ideas vary tremendously. Their writing skill varies even more. There are no agreed-upon formulas or guidelines for assigning specific letter or number grades to term papers. Paper evaluation inevitably reflects the college teacher's professional judgment and subjective opinion. However, instructors can ensure that other factors such as halo bias (assuming a student's paper will be excellent because previous work has been good) or fatigue do not enter into the grading process. They can also make their evaluation instructive to students.

Written work can be graded more fairly and objectively if the teacher does not know which student's paper is under scrutiny. Though blind grading is easy — one can have students use school identification numbers in lieu of names — some instructors believe that such precautions are unnecessary and are confident that they can separate the paper from the student. In fact, a large body of research has demonstrated that many factors affect teacher judgment of papers, and in some instances the effects can be considerable (Cronbach, 1970). For example, instructors tend to grade the paper of an attractive or personable student higher than one belonging to an unattractive or disagreeable student. Grading has also been shown to be influenced by the quality of a student's other work during the course: It is harder to believe that a poor paper came from an "A" than from a "D" student. Though in practice such biasing effects are usually slight, blind grading eliminates them entirely. It may be difficult to forget a previous discussion of a paper's topic with its author, but without a name one cannot be absolutely certain who wrote the paper.

Another reason for grading student work blind is interpersonal. Students tend to equate evaluations of their work with evaluations of themselves, as indications of the degree to which the instructor likes or respects them. More experienced and mature students can separate teacher evaluations of product from those of producer, but all students may occasionally take criticism personally. Using ID numbers instead of names assures students that it will be the paper, not the student, that receives the grade.

Grading papers fairly and objectively is easier than grading them reliably. Experienced teachers know that reading, thinking about, and evaluating a ten to fifteen page paper will take between fifteen and forty-five minues of concentrated effort. Every instructor becomes fatigued by several papers in a row and is more likely to grade them with different criteria once concentration has lapsed. Most professors have had the experience at least once during nonstop paper grading of realizing they have been staring at a single page for five minutes without the slightest idea of what they have read!

To ensure that every paper receives the same attention, an instructor should grade papers in small batches spread out over several days. Some instructors do as few as two in one sitting, and few look at more than five without taking a break. Ideally, one should grade each paper twice and compare grades, but because it takes so much time to grade a set of papers once, few are likely to attempt this regularly. Except for periodic reliability checks, grading time can be better spent in giving detailed feedback than in increasing reliability.

Once an instructor has read several papers of varying quality, the dimension along which papers vary becomes clear. It is wise to begin by reading through four or five papers quickly without assigning grades to get an idea of this baseline. Some instructors make this dimension concrete by putting graded papers in piles of similar quality and then going back through each stack before assigning final grades, particularly pluses and minuses. They may write down the characteristics of each group of papers in order to apply the criteria consistently across grading sessions and to explain them to students afterwards.

Comments on papers can tell students a great deal about the subject and about ways to write effectively. Letter grades are mainly for teacher convenience and are of limited use to students in themselves. Students are understandably disappointed when a paper is returned with only a letter grade on the title page. They expect at least an explanation of the grade they received. Noting the criteria used in assigning grades can serve this purpose. Instructor comments on returned papers should be carefully phrased to show students how to improve on future written work and to avoid discouraging them. Seasoned instructors know that students are more likely to use whatever negative criticism or suggestions a teacher has to offer if they are also complimented for what they did well. If an instructor has the time to make comments within the body of the paper too, so much the better. Some instructors find that doing so helps them maintain their concentration as they read; occasional comments at least show students that their papers were actually read to the end. Most students spend many hours preparing written assignments, and college teachers should recognize this by taking a few extra minutes to give them detailed feedback on their work.

For college teachers who are serious about helping students to improve their writing skills, giving feedback is not enough — they encourage students to *rewrite* papers. Such teachers tell students that they can resubmit their papers for another grading, using the teacher's detailed feedback to improve them, and offer to count the higher grade if the grade is changed by rewriting. If the whole class is offered this option, students do not consider it unfair. The teacher should have students interested in this option turn their papers in early and note on them that they intend to rewrite. (One is likely to have more suggestions for the student who intends to rewrite.) College teachers offering this option report that 10 percent to 40 percent of their students elect it. Ideally one should require rewriting of all students, but competing objectives usually prevent this much emphasis being given to even such a worthy goal. Encouraging students to volunteer to improve their writing is a reasonable alternative.

Even if effective written expression is not emphasized, every college teacher must decide on the extent to which writing skill will affect his or her evaluation of papers. Depending on the subject, an instructor may consider it appropriate (English classes) or unfair (science courses) to penalize students for mediocre writing. Whatever decision is made about this, it should be communicated as clearly as possible to students beforehand.

Every college teacher will occasionally encounter a student whose writing is unacceptably poor. Some encounter poor writing frequently. How can a student's ideas be evaluated when the words and grammar in which they are expressed render them almost unintelligible? In such cases an encouragement to rewrite and referral to a writing laboratory or consultation service are especially indicated. All students can improve their writing, but a few fall so far short of acceptable standards that instructors must do what they can to help them improve.

In addition to evaluating written assignments consistently and helpfully, instructors should return them quickly. Quick turnaround aids student learning, interpersonal rapport, and objective evaluation. Grading and returning papers quickly communicates the teacher's concern about students' feelings and makes papers come in more quickly. There is no excuse for not doing this. "It takes no more time to read papers now than later, and no unsuspected abundance of free time will appear in the future" (Eble, 1976, p. 97). Teachers should make papers due when their schedules will allow enough time to grade them promptly and well. Papers should be returned before the end of the term if at all possible. Grading papers during final exams and leaving them on a chair beside the office door shows little concern for students or their writing.

Teachers can also help students with their writing by making examples of particularly good papers available for their inspection. Many students have never read an excellent paper and can benefit greatly from examining the writing style and conceptual level of their classmates' work. Students who write fine papers are invariably flattered that theirs were chosen as models and willingly allow them to be copied for students in later courses to see.

Much of the aversion that many students feel toward written assignments stems from a lack of knowledge about what goes into producing a good paper. The suggestions offered here will not make all students relish writing papers, but they can make students more likely to learn something about writing (and rewriting) as well as reach the other objectives that the instructor has for assigning written work.

Observations Outside the Classroom

Reading and writing are the two most common things that instructors ask students to do outside class. Teachers may also sometimes ask students to make informal observations of objects, people, or situations relevant to the course under study. Masterful lectures can make ideas seem vivid and real, but sometimes personal contact with the phenomena is required for complete understanding. If a picture is worth a thousand words, a good field trip is worth a thousand slides.

For subjects such as engineering, archeology, visual and performing arts, geology, ecology, and education, direct observation is essential for all students. The subject of this section is not the field experiences required in these disciplines, however, but the optional or voluntary experiences that can be included with good effect in almost every course (Fisher, 1980).

Observations can be made individually or in small groups. For example, students in behavioral science courses can be encouraged to make individual visits to situations in which people are behaving in ways relevant to the course (Runkel, 1969; Cytrynbaum and Mann, 1969). Political science students can attend precinct caucuses, and sociology students can visit working class cafes or housing projects. Students of anthropology who observe a few mornings of hearings for misdemeanor crimes at the local courthouse will learn a great deal about taking field notes as well as witnessing a wide range of human behaviors. Philosophy students can visit Right to Life and Planned Parenthood organizations; comparative religion students might attend different churches; psychology students can volunteer to tutor children with learning problems or spend time with residents of juvenile detention, mental health, or nursing home facilities. Science students can visit scientists' laboratories on campus or in nearby industrial settings. Fine arts students can attend performances and showings in the area. The possibilities are endless. Students can be informed of possibilities and encouraged to seek out relevant experiences on their own.

Why should students take the time to seek out such experiences? Frankly, most students will not—but those who do, usually identify strongly with the instructor and are excited by the subject matter. The instructor's expectation that students will make individual observations does much to stimulate such behavior, and it is reinforced by listening to students who report their observations or by suggesting that they report observations in written work. The benefits of individual observation easily justify the small amount of time it takes an instructor to mention opportunities for such observation and show interest in the experiences of those taking advantage of them.

Group observations or field trips are more structured than individual observations and are therefore less voluntary. It requires less initiative to take part in an activity the teacher has organized than to seek a personal experience. Scheduled field trips give students valuable firsthand contact with interesting events, people, or situations. An instructor should try to schedule field trips in the last half of a term when the class has developed some cohesion.

If at all possible, the teacher should accompany the class. He or she can answer questions and lead discussion about what the students see and relate the experience to course content. The trip to and from the site also gives students and instructor many opportunities to interact informally, for students to ask those personal questions they may have wondered about all term. Coming after the first exams and initial period of unrealistic expectations, this social interaction aids students' progress toward independent relationships with an authority figure. Informal contact with the instructor also motivates students to work harder on remaining papers or exams. Group observations improve interpersonal relationships and raise morale in addition to giving students firsthand experience with examples of course content.

If these activities are so positive, why not require them of everyone or give credit to participants? Much of the value of optional activities comes from the voluntary nature of students' participation. Requiring a field trip denies students their independence and the chance to see themselves as seeking learning on their own. Also, field trips are too likely to conflict with some students' time commitments to justify requiring them. Encouraging students to learn on their own and giving them attention when they do is fine, but using the carrot and stick contingencies of grades is unwarrantable for optional experiences of the kind discussed here.

Motivating Students to Work Outside the Classroom

The best college courses and teachers so involve students that they learn as much as they can and think about the subject outside the classroom. Students eagerly read assignments and tackle independent writing tasks. They see the relevance of the subject to the real world and seek opportunities to apply what they have learned. Classroom instructors who are excited by their subject, caught up in the fascination of what they teach, foster student enthusiasm for the subject by personal example. Teacher enthusiasm infects lectures and discussion and can be spread to students' work outside class.

The next chapter makes the logical progression from the making of assignments to their evaluation. General assessment issues and specific methods of testing and grading are discussed.

CHAPTER 9

᠙᠋᠔᠙᠋᠔᠙᠋᠔᠙᠋᠔᠙᠋᠔᠙᠋᠔᠙᠋᠔᠙᠋᠔᠙᠋᠔᠙᠋᠔᠙᠋᠔᠙᠋᠔

Evaluating Student Performance: Testing and Grading

A basic source of the misunderstandings which surround evaluations of student work lies in the fact that normally such evaluation has vital consequences for the one being evaluated, whereas it has no such consequences for the one who does the evaluating. The grades a student receives not only determine whether he graduates with honors or flunks out of school; they may also guide him in choosing his field of specialization, affect his plans for graduate study, and ultimately influence his choice of career. On the other hand, the grades a teacher gives do not affect his professional stature, his commitment to a field of study, or his future success as a scholar. A student may for a long time harbor a deep resentment against a teacher who grades him harshly, but were he to confront that teacher years later, the teacher might not even remember the student and would almost surely not remember the grade. Indeed, the teacher would most probably be astounded to learn the student cared so deeply about the grade.

Cahn (1978, p. 218)

For most students and many college teachers, tests and grades are an unpleasant and unavoidable reality. Most schools require instructors to assign letter grades for student work, and society, rightly or wrongly, judges as important these distinctions between high, passing, and failing performance.

All students are concerned about exams and grades. Anxious-dependent or failing students dread them, while the more independent and capable look forward to the challenge and potential success they offer. Being evaluated represents for most students a mixture of anxiety and positive anticipation.

College teachers exhibit a similar range of attitudes toward the grading responsibility. Some, especially those new to teaching, identify with their students' dread of exams, deny their evaluative role, let students grade themselves, give undemanding exams or uniformly high marks, or admonish students not to worry about exams and grades. Others enjoy evaluation and view arduous exams and stingy grading as necessary to student achievement and maturity. For everyone, exams and other evaluations introduce the possibility of cheating, which induces guilt in students who succumb to the temptation and displeasure in instructors who encounter the result. Regardless of the reason why a student earns a failing grade, the teacher usually assigns such a grade with reluctance and regret. For everyone personally associated with higher education — students, faculty and parents — evaluation is an emotionally charged topic.

In this chapter evaluation is examined on several levels. First, specific suggestions are offered for constructing and scoring multiple-choice, short-answer, and essay examinations. The suggestions are keyed to the type of learning each kind of examination promotes. They also assess the instructor time each exam requires. Procedures for assigning end-of-course grades and dealing with cheating — including ways to prevent it — are outlined as well. Because evaluation is the most critical interpersonal issue in college classrooms, suggestions are also given for maximizing the positive effects of exams (increases in confidence, motivation, and effective coping skills) and minimizing the negative ones that can interfere with performance (feelings of anxiety, unfairness, anger, and hopelessness). Before specific evaluation methods are discussed, several introductory topics need to be examined.

Evaluation in Context

Purposes of Evaluation. Examining must first be differentiated from grading (Milton, 1978). Examining or testing refers to constructing and scoring test questions (or assigning papers) to produce comparisons among different students. The specific and evaluative comments written on exams are taken very seriously by students and can have a powerful effect on student motivation for the remainder of the course. Since more than one exam is usually given during a course, early tests can motivate students to try harder, study more efficiently, or give up and withdraw emotional investment in the course. Examining has a powerful effect on the way students study and the amount they learn during a course.

Unlike examinations, grades come only at the end of a course; they indicate how well a student did on all work in the course. Even when accompanied by narrative evaluations, grades are the final evaluative message and can have little impact on prior learning: It is too late for a student to behave differently in that course by the time the grade is assigned. End-term grading is a global evaluation, not a series of reports on specific successes and failures. The thought of grades does motivate students, many of whom study all term because of the grade they hope (or fear) they will receive at the end. Although end-term grading does influence students' future course selection, it does not motivate students and aid their learning as directly as tests.

The purposes of evaluation are many. Tests are given, students say, "to see what we don't know" or "to give the teacher something on which to base a grade." Instructors believe that evaluation aids learning through feedback and motivation. Testing gives students a gauge of the scope and depth of their knowledge, much as athletes learn their strengths and weaknesses through active competition. Similarly, just as coaches learn from observing their athletes in competition, college teachers learn how effective their teaching has been from tests. A thoughtfully constructed exam can actually teach by stimulating students to think about concepts in a new way, notice new relationships, and come to different insights. Tests aid learning most by motivating students to study for them (Cahn, 1978). Though term papers can achieve objectives unattainable through exams, few things can be counted on to prompt students to really master a content area like a rigorous examination. Overall, testing is justified because it aids learning and enhances motivation as well as providing a basis for assigning grades.

Testing and Student Motivation. How can testing and grading practices be understood in terms of what we know about the psychological needs students bring to the classroom? The need to meet challenges and overcome obstacles is a basic and long-standing psychological motive. Examinations, like athletic contests or artistic competition, satisfy these needs for many students. Without unduly emphasizing the competitiveness of exams or ignoring individual differences in ability and temperament, a skillful instructor can create exams that strike a balance between meeting student needs to feel secure and meeting the need to seek challenges. Good athletic coaches do this as well, bringing out the best performance from their players while promoting maturity and personal satisfaction. (College teachers can learn much from observing skilled coaches.) Not challenging students at all on exams is as unsatisfying to them as creating unduly harsh or unfair tests.

The suggestions in this chapter are designed to produce exams that both stress and reassure students. Testing and grading are not seen as an unavoidable unpleasantness but as an experience that can be beneficial and satisfying to students and instructors alike if high standards are coupled with personal concern.

Myths Concerning Evaluation. A few myths about evaluation must be mentioned and dispelled first. The following common beliefs are *simply not true:*

1. *The quality of education that students receive is commensurate with the difficulty of earning high marks.* Colleges, academic departments, or instructors who infer that their students learn more because average grades are lower delude themselves.

Students can learn just as much in a relatively easy course as in a hard one. If high grades are accurate, they reflect greater rather than less learning. Because tough grading is so commonly endorsed, many instructors fear being reputed to offer "slides" or "gut courses." However, the quality of a college education is more a function of the quality of the faculty, the teaching, and the overall student population than of grading stringency.

2. *Hard grading and student satisfaction are inversely correlated.* Research on the relation between grading and satisfaction (Abrami and others, 1980; Howard and Maxwell, 1980) does not support this contention. Students report liking quality presentations and good rapport, not easy grades. Students like hard graders as often as easy ones, and they have been shown to seek out difficult courses rated positively over easier ones rated poorly (Coleman and McKeachie, 1981). Teachers seen as *unfair* evaluators receive low ratings, but course difficulty does not predict student satisfaction.

3. *Strict grading is necessary to motivate students to study.* Though student motivation is enhanced by testing, the evaluation need not be harsh to be effective. Like lectures, exams should be difficult enough for most students to feel challenged and few to feel overwhelmed. Fostering positive personal relationships and activating students' need for competence are more motivating than stressing them with negative evaluations.

4. *Difficult grading encourages memorization; a nonjudgmental classroom atmosphere is necessary for higher-level learning or for independent or creative thinking to occur.* Anxious-dependent students do respond to difficult exams by dwelling on details and memorization, but not all students restrict what they study and learn to this level. Evaluation difficulty does not determine educational objectives, and objectives may prescribe particular evaluation procedures but do not prescribe their level of difficulty.

It is inaccurate to equate a college teacher's grading practices with the quality of his or her teaching. A skillful instructor uses examinations in ways that motivate rather than discourage students, and this influences student achievement more than anything inherent in testing methods or standards.

Social Functions of Evaluation. Whether they like it or not, college teachers serve an important selective function for contemporary society. Powerful, well-paid, and responsible jobs are open mainly to those who successfully run the gauntlet of formal education, who through intellectual ability, persistence, and/or conformity earn baccalaureate or advanced degrees. Higher education is a prerequisite for success for most citizens in a technological society.

How do professors view their role in this social selection process? Some believe in enduring individual differences in ability and persistence, and they relish the task of identifying and encouraging students with academic talent and motivation. Their tests are difficult, distinguishing different degrees of mastery among students so that only a few receive top grades. They believe that the role of college instructors is to encourage all students to compete so as to channel those with greater talent and self-discipline to jobs requiring such qualities.

Other instructors may wish more students to have the chance to select their occupations and for all to live less competitive lives. Those with this philosophy are more likely to favor evaluation methods that reflect mastery at the recall and recognition level — the kind of knowledge easiest to acquire from effort alone — rather than more intellectually demanding objectives that tend to reveal individual differences. Mastery learning touted in the Personalized System of Instruction (Keller, 1968), for example, rewards students for attaining objectives that are reasonable for all and rewards students less according to ability than according to persistence.

The suggestions on testing and grading offered in this chapter are more consistent with the selective than with the mastery philosphy. They are designed not so much to endorse the social function grades serve as to recognize the universality of individual differences. Setting course requirements so that every student can earn an "A" denies inevitable differences in academic skill and inclination. In a mastery system students with high talent may not receive sufficient challenge, and those with less ability may not receive accurate feedback about the difficulty of future academic challenges or their likelihood of success. This chapter proposes methods of evaluation that should motivate all students to do their best.

Examination Strategies

Preparing for Examinations. Examination procedures should be determined when the course is first planned. Because students differ in their preferences for kinds of exams (most student polls are split equally between multiple-choice and essay) and because different methods fit different objectives, instructors should use a variety of testing methods. There is no reason for college teachers (or students) to put all their eggs in one basket by having only one type of exam during a semester.

Similarly, there are very few good reasons to use only a single testing session, a final exam. There are no rules about testing frequency, but one exam in an undergraduate course is surely too few, more than five too many. The number of testing sessions should be determined by the difficulty and amount of material covered, and the exams should occur at regular intervals in the term. Testing only once denies students and instructors feedback on their progress and wastes a chance to increase student motivation. A single final exam makes grading and testing synonymous. Periodic testing during a term has been shown to improve performance on final exams (Gaynor and Millham, 1976). On the other hand, too frequent testing is costly in lost class time, lost teacher time spent on grading, and loss of internal student motivation due to overemphasis on evaluation.

Before writing tests for a course, formulate the objectives for the evaluation. Use recognition multiple-choice or recall identification items if you want to see whether students learned specific concepts or names; use conceptually complex multiple-choice items or compare-and-contrast essays if you want to assess their critical thinking. Always ask yourself *what* you wish to measure by a given question or exam. Taking the exam yourself or having a colleague take it is a good way to see whether the instructions and questions are clear. In the case of essays, this practice also provides sample answers to help with scoring.

When selecting specific topics around which to write test questions, avoid both trickery and triviality. There are always important, subtle, and complex points that can be assessed on an exam, and there is no good reason to surprise students with minutiae. Making tests difficult by focusing on unimportant details encourages anxiety, gamesmanship, and a sense of unfairness. It is better to design tests that will motivate students to learn critical content than to reward them for memorizing trivia. Neither student motivation nor learning is fostered by putting surprises on exams.

Topics included on exams should be representative of the content covered. Items should be selected from all chapters, articles, or books covered. They should also vary in difficulty. Including a few relatively easy items helps to keep the less able or less prepared students from feeling devastated after an exam. Similarly, including a few difficult items will keep the most prepared students from feeling let down afterward, from thinking as they leave the room, "I sure didn't get a chance to show what I knew on that test." An exam with varied items—perhaps even a funny one or two—is more interesting for students to take and instructors to grade. Varied items also produce greater spread in distribution of total scores.

Avoid using the same examinations every time you teach a course. Students are likely to have seen old exams in test files, and repeat exams will not reflect recent changes in what you presented or emphasized. Like old lecture notes, old exams can help an instructor prepare, but exams are unlikely to be fresh and timely unless they are constructed a week or two before they are given.

There are several ways to prepare students intellectually before an exam. Share your objectives so students will not feel that they "didn't know beforehand what the prof wanted," and make copies of old exams available as concrete examples of what they can expect. Give tips on answering multiple-choice or essay test items, especially if the students are freshmen or the course is introductory. Tell students beforehand the total number of items of each type and the number of recall, analysis, or evaluation items that will appear on the test. All these techniques will help students decide what to study and help to maximize what they learn.

Like a coach speaking to the team on the night before a contest, you should also help your students prepare emotionally for a test. Speak to them as an adult ("The test will require you to know the most important concepts thoroughly, and you should review them carefully; but the test is not designed to trick you or make you fail"). Do not joke about the exam, especially with irony likely to feed their anxiety ("Don't worry about the exam; after all, nothing rides on it except your future careers"). Also avoid speaking either as a judgmental parent ("If you don't study hard, you're likely to do poorly") or as a reassuring peer ("Hey, this test isn't the most important thing in your life"). Prepare the class to take the test seriously without spending the whole night in ineffective study or needless anxiety.

Some college teachers spend the class just before an exam reviewing material and answering questions; others hold optional review sessions for the same purpose. Many students appreciate such opportunities, but others will not attend a class (or outside sessions) with that agenda. Review sessions can be frustrating when students do not have questions and waste precious class hours. Frequently only the most compliant students come to these sessions, more to avoid missing anything than to participate or contribute. Encouraging students to telephone (even at home) with last-minute questions before the exam takes much less of your time (rarely will more than 10 percent of the class call) and meets the needs of those who really are confused.

Administering Examinations. College teachers should administer tests themselves and should be available at times during the session to answer questions and offer reassurance. A test is a major interpersonal event in the life of a class, and instructors who routinely send assistants or secretaries to administer exams miss a golden opportunity to motivate and reassure students. Tell students that you will arrive early on test day to answer questions and ensure that they will have as much time as possible to work. Most students are concerned about not having enough time, and they will appreciate this consideration. Distribute exams as soon as early-arriving students are ready, then stay around to answer questions for latecomers. Students appreciate instructors who stop by frequently during exams to answer questions and keep them posted on the remaining time.

Getting students to turn in their papers can be trouble-some. Return to the classroom ten to fifteen minutes before the next class period and say, "It's time to pull your answers together. You have only five minutes or so to go." If you remain in the class-room, many students will turn in their papers, and others will make last-minute additions. Avoid coming back at the very last minute and announcing, "Time's up; give me your exams!" Though this practice is traditional in some schools (the service academies), it raises student anxiety and tempts students to ex-ceed the time limit. If one or two anxious-dependents still have not stopped when only a few minutes remain before the next class, simply invite the students waiting in the hall to come in; then your students will stop. College teachers have an important responsibility to ensure that all students are given similar time to complete exams and that they are out of the classroom before the next class is scheduled to begin. So move them along—but gently.

Evaluating Examinations. Exams should be graded and returned quickly—by the next class meeting if possible, and within one week at the latest. Prompt return of exams is appre-ciated by students anxious to know their grades and it encourages relearning or corrective learning of the material that appeared on the exam. Avoid simply giving papers to TAs for grading. Students want papers graded by their instructor, even when assis-tants help. In large classes where assistants are necessary for scoring exams, develop specific scoring criteria and model papers for your TAs and double-check selected papers to ensure that all graders adhered to similar guidelines. The professor is responsible for the way others grade his or her students' exams, and this responsibility cannot be delegated completely even when it is con-venient to do so.

Like term papers, tests should be graded blind. Blind grading of essay papers is especially important. Even when multiple-choice exams are given, it is good practice to have students use only school identification numbers.

Write detailed comments on exams to show that the papers were read carefully and to show students how they could have done better. Even short comments such as "yes," "no," "insightful," "not quite," or "good guess" tell students that their work was taken seriously. To tell each student how every discussion item could be improved would take too much time, but try to make one or two corrective comments, especially about longer essays. Specific feedback of this kind maximizes student learning from exams (McKeachie, 1978).

Instructors' written comments are powerful communications that affect subsequent motivation. Students doing unacceptable work might receive a note saying, "I'm sorry you did poorly, Laurie. Please stop by to speak with me to see if we can find a way for you to do better next time." Students who respond to this invitation usually indicate that they know they did not study enough, but some will be perplexed by their poor performance and will welcome suggestions on studying and test-taking. Personal notes are also an excellent way to reward superior work. Comments such as "Good work, Jami," or "Excellent ideas, Amy" very positively affect students who receive them. Such notes reinforce past effort and strengthen students' desire to do well in the future. Write something like "Much improved, Sarah" for students who have improved their performance by at least a letter grade. Such comments make the evaluation process more personal for instructor and students alike.

Returning Examinations. For almost all students and teachers, the return of exams is a time of anxiety. Students want to know how they did and how the instructor feels about their performance. Instructors may be fearful that students will be angry, guilty about giving low grades, or angry at students for not mastering all content. The first set of exam papers of a term is particularly emotional, reminding instructor and students of the evaluative aspect of their relationship. Novice teachers' first sets of papers can be particularly disheartening and can lead them to question both their competence and their motivation for an academic career.

How should you return exams? First, remain calm and relaxed. Emotional instructors only stimulate emotionality in students. Avoid defensiveness or apology. Be reasonable but firm in discussing the exams. Second, exhibit the distribution of scores so that students can see exactly how their performance compared with that of others. Third, ask whether students have general questions about the exam, but do *not* spend the entire class going over specific items. Offer to go over individual papers in detail outside of class. Circulate the correct answers to multiple-choice items and pass around photocopies of the best two or three discussion papers with students' names removed. Many students have an unrealistic estimate of their own knowledge and abilities as compared to those of other students; seeing samples of peers' work provides a more realistic basis for comparison. It also provides further reinforcement for the exemplary students whose papers were selected for display. Returning exams well is essential to making sure that the evaluation process accomplishes desired intellectual and interpersonal objectives.

The final stage of evaluation is often neglected by instructors. Before being filed away, exams should be critiqued and revised. College teachers can improve an exam most immediately after grading it and hearing student reactions. If the teacher waits too long, such information will be forgotten (Milton, 1978).

The preceding strategies apply to examinations of any form. In the next section various types of examinations are discussed, with suggestions for maximizing the advantages and minimizing the disadvantages of each.

Types of Examinations

The traditional classification of examinations as objective or subjective can be misleading. Multiple-choice items are thought to be objective because they can be scored easily and reliably using templates or computer scanning devices, but subjectivity is involved in item construction and in deciding which multiple-choice option is most correct. Similarly, "subjective" discussion questions can be scored rigorously using specific criteria and a point system.

A more useful distinction is between *selection* (multiple-choice) and *supply* (short-answer or essay) examinations. Research suggests that selection items are easier (Gronlund, 1982). Multiple-choice items require knowledge of specifics, and students have adapted accordingly to study details when preparing for them (Milton, 1978). However, college teachers can construct multiple-choice items that require students to think, critique, and evaluate what they know; selection items need not deal only with details.

Supply questions are more variable. Short-answer or identification items may be as specific as multiple-choice items. More commonly, in supply items students are asked to write broad, integrative summaries (essays); thus, in studying for essay exams, students focus on broader issues (Milton, 1978). The construction of items determines the level of knowledge measured more than does the item type.

Exam items of any type must be clear and unambiguous; students should have no doubt about what they mean. Imprecision and ambiguity are the greatest failings of exam items, even on mathematics exams (Crouse and Jacobson, 1975). Teachers who write clear, precise exam questions can assess what students know more accurately and fairly than those who compose tests carelessly.

True-False and Matching Exams. True-false questions and matching tasks do not work well on the college level. The cognitive complexity of college content makes constructing "never true" or "always" items exceedingly difficult. True-false items are also poor because of the large probability that students will get them correct by chance alone. Matching lists of names or concepts promotes memorization and cannot be used to assess understanding.

Multiple-Choice Exams. Multiple-choice items are derided by many college teachers, who think that they tap only memory of isolated facts. For most teachers of the humanities, the notion of a student passing a multiple-choice test without demonstrating understanding or thinking processes in writing is an educational absurdity (Highet, 1950). Yet multiple-choice exams have become a mainstay in many disciplines and schools, especially when many students must be evaluated simultaneously. Multiple-choice items certainly can assess levels of knowledge other than memorized facts. Almost all psychological tests of intelligence, academic aptitude, and achievement are multiple choice, for example. It requires some thought and practice, but a clever instructor can construct multiple-choice items that assess educational objectives at any level.

College teachers must be careful to make sure, however, that items reflect knowledge of the subject rather than general intelligence. For example, economics students asked on a multiple-choice item to compare and contrast "maximizing utility by consumers" and "maximizing profits by companies" must weigh several possible comparisons as well as know the individual concepts. Picking the most important difference may reflect their ability to make abstract generalizations or to notice subtle differences in wording more than their knowledge of the two course concepts.

Most multiple-choice tests of memory are poorly correlated with general intelligence test scores ($r = .17$). As the level of abstraction required by an item increases, when general concepts must be applied to specific situations for example, the correlation with intelligence increases ($r = .41$; McKeachie, 1978). Instructors should ask themselves, "Does figuring out the correct answer to this question depend more on reasoning ability or on full knowledge of the material?" Though more intelligent students will better understand content with comparable amounts of study, college teachers should focus exam questions on the content and not mainly on students' thinking skills. Unless they construct multiple-choice exams carefully, teachers risk measuring differences in academic aptitude rather than knowledge acquired in the course.

Multiple-choice exams are ideal for large classes that the teacher expects to teach for several terms. Experienced multiple-choice users typically put specific items on index cards (or computer disks) showing statistical data from previous use and then select items from this pool for a given exam. Many fundamental concepts will be taught without fail every semester, and these are best assessed with proven items when possible. Revising items and adding new ones to the pool is easier than writing a whole new exam and frees the instructor to grade written work.

Potentially usable multiple-choice items come from several sources. One way to create items is to ask students to write and submit them. Letting students do this has a positive interpersonal value: It shares a bit of the control of evaluation with them and may make them more sympathetic to the instructor's role in it. This practice also suggests concepts for teacher-written items. Publishers' teacher's manuals usually contain items, though they have seldom been pretested and refined. Like student items, published items may suggest concepts for which a college teacher can construct his or her own exam questions.

Experience indicates (McKeachie, 1978; Milton, 1978) that the college teacher constructing a multiple-choice examination should do the following:

1. Begin with a single concept, definition, or research finding that has been covered thoroughly in the text or in lecture. Be clear on what is to be measured with the item; students will then be more likely to understand the question and anticipate the correct answer.
2. To reduce the role of chance, include five options rather than four; the probability that a student will get an item correct from guessing alone drops from 25 percent to 20 percent when five items are used.
3. State the main stem of the item in positive language; avoid "not" and "no," which require students to sift through double negatives.
4. Place all qualifications in the part of the item before the options; keep the answer options short and clear-cut.
5. Avoid irrelevant sources of difficulty, such as uncommon vocabulary or unnecessary details.
6. For areas of opinion, qualify the stem with "according to. . . ."
7. Avoid giving clues to the correct answer; avoid "never" and "always," and make all options grammatically consistent with the stem.
8. Vary the position of the correct answer.
9. Include options of varying difficulty: one fairly obviously incorrect answer, another the opposite of the correct answer, and one or two that are only slightly different from the correct one. The correct option must clearly be the *best,* the one reflecting the fullest understanding of the concept(s) referred to in the stem.
10. Never use "all (or none) of the above" as options; such answers are easy to construct but require little student thinking or subtlety and do not discriminate well among students with differing knowledge.

Once items are written, the teacher should select as many as students will have time to answer. Students can complete between one and two items per minute; one and one half per minute is a good average.

Even if a computer will score the exam later and compute item statistics, the instructor should make a hand-scoring template to figure tentative scores for students wishing an immediate estimate of their achievement. Usually no more than about 50 percent of a class will ask for hand scoring. The teacher will need a hand-scoring system anyway if any students take the exam late or if there are too few students to justify computer scoring (less than twenty).

To be confident that a multiple-choice exam really reflects different amounts of knowledge, a college teacher must statistically evaluate the whole exam and each item after each use. Today most colleges have computer packages for scoring and analyzing multiple-choice exams. Such analysis tells how strongly each item is related to a student's total score. Instructors should inspect computer printouts for item difficulty (percentage of students answering the item correctly) and item discrimination (statistical index reflecting the differences between the number of students in the top and bottom fifths of class who passed the item). An instructor can have more confidence in the results of analyses done on classes of forty or more students. Even then, however, item analysis data must be interpreted if items are to be improved.

What are good difficulty and discrimination scores? Optimally difficult items are those that about 75 percent of the class answer correctly. Exams should contain only a few items that more than 90 percent or less than 60 percent pass. Discrimination scores are more difficult to interpret, because they can be computed differently and because it is impossible to have high discrimination scores for easy items. For items of moderate difficulty (difficulty scores between 70 percent and 85 percent), students in the top fifth of the class on total score should be much more likely to answer them correctly than students in the bottom fifth. Teachers should seek advice from those running the item analysis service at their school for appropriate cutoffs. Items of appropriate difficulty and discrimination can be saved, while an examination of less successful items may suggest how they could be improved. Over successive semesters, college teachers can compile a sizable pool of tested items from which to select in composing subsequent examinations.

The instructor should have the item analysis results handy when talking with students about their exams. Students are usually interested in knowing how many others missed an item. Also, it is easier to argue against an answer if one can show data indicating that the student was one of only a few who chose it.

Short-Answer or Identification Exams. Short-answer questions require knowledge of details as much as multiple-choice items. In such questions, students are given a concept or term and asked to define it or "tell what is important to know" about it in a few sentences. Short-answer items can also assess thinking if students are asked to compare concepts. More space is usually required for such questions than for definitions. Multiple-choice and short-answer items are similar in what they can assess.

Short-answer exams differ significantly from multiple-choice tests primarily in the amount of time they take to construct and score. Short-answer items are quick and easy to write but much more time consuming to score. Twenty identifications commonly take between ten and thirty minutes to score for each student in the class.

But identification tests have advantages as well. Unlike multiple-choice and essay exams, they are seldom disliked or seen as unfair by students. Students can express their thoughts exactly in such tests, and instructors can see directly how well they were understood. Student verbal facility does not contribute to the quality of answers as much as it does with longer essays, and instructors need not worry about having unwittingly constructed an intelligence test. There are always definite answers to short questions, so they can be scored reliably and objectively. The time required to score short answers is excessive for very large classes, but for many, short-answer exams are an ideal compromise between assembly-line multiple-choice exams and literary-free-for-all essays.

How should short-answer exams be constructed and scored? As with any item, the teacher should begin with a specific purpose for the question. He or she should decide how much space to allow for each answer and arrange the items accordingly. Allow students between four and five minutes for each item. For scoring, the teacher should write the best answer possible based on the information supplied by the course. (Having a colleague or more advanced student take the exam also helps.) He or she should then decide how many points to give to each item and how many of the specific facts or ideas in the exemplary answers will be required to earn full or partial credit.

Before scoring any items, the instructor should read through five to ten questions to see if he or she has accurately anticipated most of the ideas students are including and to revise scoring criteria if indicated. He or she should not attempt to score all answers on each paper before going on to the next one; items can be scored more consistently if one does them one item or one page at a time. If an answer is especially good, much better than required to earn full credit, the instructor might consider giving extra credit (one-half point or so). Writing "good" or "excellent" beside the answer also reinforces students who went well beyond what was expected.

When all papers have been scored, the teacher can simply add up the points (or compute percentages) and plot the distribution, deciding which groups of scores to convert to which grades. If the class has few students and the teacher wants to check scoring, he or she can look at each item twice, keeping a record of the initial marks separately. Team teachers frequently score exams in this way to ensure agreement on the final grades awarded. Though less objective than multiple-choice exams, identification exams can be scored with acceptable reliability. The teacher should make the scoring criteria available to students (along with copies of superior papers) to provide detailed feedback about the way questions were supposed to be answered.

Though they take more time overall than multiple-choice items, identification or short-answer items are ideal when a class is small. Many college teachers include both multiple-choice and short-answer items on an exam in an attempt to satisfy students' differing preferences and capitalize on the merits of both formats. Multiple-choice and short-answer items are more similar to each other than to the final type to be discussed: the integrative essay.

Essay Exams. Examinations consisting of broad, integrative essays or discussion questions are common in the humanities and in much coursework at the graduate level. In long essays students can display detailed knowledge as well as reveal their understanding of overall contextual issues. Essay exam questions are particularly apt for evaluating students' abilities to think critically, independently, and originally. For integrating concepts and comparing theories, essays easily surpass multiple-choice and short-answer questions. Essays are ideal for measuring higher-level analysis, synthesis, or evaluation and for increasing student writing skill.

Essays are difficult to grade reliably and objectively, however. Even in a class of ten students, the range of ideas in answers to a broad discussion question will be large. Differences in how clearly, correctly, and expressively students communicate their ideas will also influence the way their knowledge of content and ideas is evaluated. Even handwriting can influence the grade an essay exam receives. In small classes, preserving student anonymity is difficult. Essay exams take considerably more time to grade than multiple-choice exams, though not necessarily longer than identification exams. The most troublesome drawback of essays is unreliable grading resulting from teacher fatigue, lack of concentration, or other subjective factors.

A one-hour exam of three essay questions will take at least as long to grade as a ten to fifteen page term paper—fifteen to forty-five minutes per student. Because all students write about the same questions, maintaining concentration when reading essay exams is more difficult than when reading term papers on variable topics. Though essays seem much fairer to many students than less personal multiple-choice questions, some will be graded unfairly if the instructor allows his or her concentration to fade.

To minimize the liabilities of essay exams, instructors should do the following (based in part on McKeachie, 1978, and Milton, 1978):

1. Focus essay questions by specifying parameters so students will be less tempted to "bullshit" ("Discuss the economic reasons why United States government leaders feared expanding Japanese power in the Pacific between 1935 and 1939" rather

than "Why did America fear the Japanese expansion of influence in the Pacific?"); ask for critical evaluation with supporting evidence rather than personal feelings.

2. Limit the space available by providing paper for the essay
    questions; asking students to use blue books encourages them
    to fill up the books with unimportant verbiage.

3. Beware of giving take-home essay exams; some students will
    spend an inordinate amount of time on them, and most will
    not study (and learn) as much in preparation. The teacher
    should tell students the general topics of the questions ahead
    of time and have them write answers in class ("We have dis-
    cussed five theories of human learning in this section. I will
    ask you to compare and contrast two of them on the exam").

4. Before scoring, read all answers to the first question in a pre-
    liminary way, noting the overall quality and deciding which
    grades to give the best and worst papers; select a model paper
    or two at each grade for later comparison.

5. Read papers for detail in groups of five to ten at a sitting;
    underline key phrases or words to maintain concentration;
    refer frequently to the model papers when deciding which
    specific grade to assign; take frequent breaks or time reading
    to keep attention on each paper.

6. Go through all students' answers to each question before
    moving to the next question.

7. Write specific comments throughout as well as an overall
    evaluation of each question, complimenting the student for
    what he or she did well and showing how the answer could be
    improved.

Essay exams have advantages and disadvantages. Constructing and scoring them as advocated here ensures that students
will demonstrate their best thinking on essay tests and that the
instructor will be able to give each one the same concentrated
attention.

Oral Exams. Though students can also answer detailed and
broad, integrative questions orally, such exams are extremely rare
at the undergraduate level. They have the liability that students
cannot revise their responses, and the instructor has nothing to

refer back to when grading, unless the answer is taped. However, an oral exam is sometimes necessary when a physical disability prevents a student from writing. Also, students bound for graduate or law school might find taking an oral exam useful preparation.

Selecting Types of Exams. College teachers base their choice of certain types of exams on personal preferences, philosophical beliefs, time available, and habit. It is far better to pick the testing format that best assesses the desired educational objectives. Most instructors have varied objectives and use several different testing methods: multiple-choice or short-answer for detail and essays for comprehension and thinking. Practical considerations such as class size and availability of test-scoring service or teaching assistants will also influence the choice of testing format, but these should be secondary.

Grading

College grades deserve neither the criticism nor the adulation given them. Receiving high grades does not assure a good education, nor does it necessarily interfere with one. Americans are ambivalent about grades and grading practices because they bring into focus the clash between egalitarian ideals and the reality of different intellectual abilities and opportunities. No doubt some college teachers abuse their power to assign grades; the final section in this chapter lists several common abuses. Some students also abuse grading in a sense, focusing so narrowly on grades that they learn neither content nor the importance of meeting challenges and handling frustration without cheating. College teachers should strive to take grading seriously but should also remember that it is of less consequence than what students learn. "And only by demonstrating that grading is not always necessary and that other kinds of feedback and evaluation are both possible and useful can one honestly minimize the importance of grades" (Eble, 1976, p. 117).

The following suggestions will keep grading in perspective for students and instructors. How a teacher chooses to combine scores on exams and papers over a semester reveals his or her attitudes about effort, success, and failure. For example, weighting final examinations as more than 50 percent of the total grade encourages students to cram at the end rather than work all during a course. Even if they have studied all along, this practice forces them to stake their fate on one throw of the dice. Allowing students to drop their lowest grade is popular, but this practice may encourage them to be irresponsible. College teachers who base final grades on how hard the student appears to have worked or on relative improvement value effort more than performance. Grading policies should be determined thoughtfully to be certain that they are consistent with the instructor's philosophical beliefs about ability, effort, and the motivational role of evaluative feedback.

The following general suggestions on assigning final grades have seemed reasonable and useful to many teachers:

1. Let students know all during the term how they are doing. Giving points to be accumulated after each exam or paper without indicating what letter grade has been earned does not give students a firm idea of the grade they are likely to receive at the end of the course, and assigning grades only on the final point distribution can produce unexpected results for individual students. The simplest way to help students predict their grades and thereby to encourage their studying is to assign a letter grade (or numerical equivalent) for each exam and average them at the end.

2. Construct a system for combining exam and paper scores that rewards effort all along, not just at the end. Describe the system to students at the beginning of the course. Students will learn and remember more if they apply themselves steadily rather than sprinting at the end. The weights given to different assignments help to determine appropriate levels of effort for each one.

3. If a student does extremely poorly on an initial exam, it may be mathematically impossible for him or her to achieve an acceptable grade of "C," even with significant improvement. Personally encourage such a student to do well on subsequent exams, and be generous when averaging that initial score with later, higher ones. Do not tell the student that you will ignore the low score, only that you will average in a higher grade if he or she improves subsequently.

4. When computing final grades, perform each calculation twice and consider all marginal cases together, including subjective factors such as class attendance, participation, and improvement over the semester. No evaluation procedures are precise enough to be used automatically. For borderline grades, college teachers must show wisdom in assigning grades that are fair to the individual students and the rest of the class.

5. Most grades are distributed somewhat normally, but never force grades to fit quotas or theoretical expectations. Administrators who declare that "no more than 15 percent of a class should receive 'A's'" have a poor method for curbing grade inflation.

6. If posting grades is traditional at your school, post them in a way that protects student identities.

7. Do not change a grade once it is turned in unless you were clearly in error. Once students have successfully begged a grade change after the fact, this can become a habitual way of handling academic pressure. Offer to write a letter explaining why a student earned a certain grade, but resist the temptation to rescue the student by changing in a stroke a grade that he or she spent an entire semester earning. Some instructors announce at the beginning of courses that students who, for whatever reason, "need" a certain grade in a course should let them know then rather than at the end when it is too late to help.

Above all, college teachers should remember the importance of grades to students and treat grades seriously but without undue anxiety. "Giving" a student a grade significantly higher than he or she deserves may provide momentary pleasure or relief to the student but is unlikely to engender respect for educational institutions or to help him or her accept responsibility or appreciate learning. The lessons students learn about responsibility and evaluation are important to their success as adults. Since the adult world is often less fair and predictable than school, college teachers have an obligation to teach students to take responsibility for themselves.

Cheating

"The wise teacher takes ordinary precautions against cheating, but equally important, uses the kinds of tests, assignments, and teaching practices that provide few rationalizations for cheating" (Eble, 1976, p. 121).

Though cheating among college students cannot be justified or condoned, the motivations that lead to it are too universal and understandable to allow instructors to treat perpetrators harshly. A teacher should not view cheating in simple terms of right-wrong, honorable-dishonorable; almost anyone is capable of cheating, given opportunity and sufficient motivation. Even the habitual offender is more likely to cheat in some courses than in others. Experienced teachers know that it is better to prevent cheating than to try to catch students in the act.

How can cheating be prevented? Students are far less likely to cheat if they are excited by a subject and if they have a personal relationship with the instructor. Cheating is most common in impersonal, adversarial relationships in which "beating the system" is expected. In a hospitable classroom students are less likely to want to cheat or to give in to the temptation.

Specifically, students are less likely to cheat if these things are true:

1. Students know why exams are being given because the instructor has shared objectives with them.
2. Students know and like the college teacher as a person and believe that he or she knows and likes them as well.
3. Students are excited by the material and internally motivated to learn it.
4. Students believe that they will be graded fairly and will receive detailed feedback on their work.
5. Students know it will be hard to cheat.

These preventive suggestions apply to plagiarism as well as to in-class examinations, but plagiarism is more difficult to identify than cheating on exams. The best prevention for this kind of cheating is detailed instructions on the sources that can be used for papers and the way they must be referenced. Some students deliberately misrepresent the sources of their work, but many more plagiarize unwittingly out of ignorance or inexperience with different instructor policies. On any work students do outside class, the instructor should be exceedingly certain that they understand what material they can and cannot use. Plagiarism is a difficult issue even for professional and scholarly writers. College teachers can make this issue easier for students to understand by specifying the rules under which they should work.

Every college teacher will eventually encounter what appears to be a clear instance of cheating. What should you do if this happens to you? Confront the student only if the offense is flagrant (notes on the lap during an exam, paragraphs in a paper lifted from books with no reference notation), if you are so sure that cheating occurred that you can risk damaging irreparably your relationship with the student by mentioning your suspicions. When confronting a student, adopt an air of concern about the reason for the cheating rather than of punishment or criticism. If possible, discuss cheating in private. The student will feel unhappy enough about being caught; there is no need to add shame to his or her misery. Indicate the seriousness of the offense and try to get the student to participate in deciding what to do about it. Students who admit cheating and turn themselves in to the honor council or whatever other administrative body is applicable are better treated and learn a greater lesson than those turned in by instructors. Speak with the student first and the authorities last. However, be sure to follow your school's procedures; do not take justice into your own hands — even with the student's complicity — and arrange a private sentence such as a lower grade or an "F." This may seem kinder than official proceedings, but it can teach students to disregard established laws and procedures.

A List of "Never's"

Though teaching by negative example is risky, it is instructive to conclude this chapter with some illustrations of extremely poor testing and grading practices that have actually occurred. The following list has been adapted and expanded from those offered by McKeachie (1978, pages 183–184).

1. Never announce that one type of exam will be given, change your mind, and distribute something different.
2. Never spend the first fifteen minutes of a one-hour exam making oral changes in the printed questions or instructions.
3. Never include two right answers on multiple-choice items.
4. Never fail to finish reading essays and cover up your failure by making a brief comment on the last page of each paper to make it appear to have been read.
5. Never give everyone the same grade on essays whether you have read them or not.
6. Never decide after the first exam (or paper) which students are "A" students, "B" students, or "C" students and sort subsequent work into appropriate piles before reading it to verify that initial impression.
7. Never fail to give an indication during a course of the grade that a student is likely to receive.
8. When a student asks about a grade, never say that he or she actually earned a grade higher than the one given but that the grade was lowered because the supervisor's, the department's, or the school's guidelines indicated that there were too many "A's," "B's," or whatever.
9. Never tell students that grade distribution was really quite arbitrary and that you could have just as easily called the "C's" "B's" or the "B's" "A's."
10. Never give a student suspected of cheating a lower grade or an "F" without telling the student or the honor council.

The final chapter of this book takes another look at the question put forth in Chapter One: What are the essential ingredients of outstanding college teaching? It gives special attention to these secondary questions: To what extent is virtuoso classroom skill the result of talent or supportive environment? How can teaching excellence be evaluated and fostered? and, finally, given the emphasis on research productivity, why should any college teacher make the effort to hone his or her teaching skills to the finest quality?

CHAPTER 10

෧෬ඁ෬ඁ෬ඁ෬ඁ෬ඁ෬ඁ෬ඁ෬ඁ෬ඁ෬ඁ෬ඁ෬ඁ෬ඁ෬ඁ෬ඁ

The Art, Craft,
and Techniques
of Masterful Teaching

> We have classified teacher prototypes in two major
> categories. The first includes those teaching modes
> in which inquiry on the part of the student is not
> required or encouraged for the successful completion
> of the learning tasks set by the professor. We call
> these teaching styles the *didactic modes*. The other
> category includes those teaching modes in which
> inquiry on the part of the student *is* required if he is
> to complete successfully the tasks set by the teacher.
> We call these teaching styles the *evocative modes*.
> Those teachers who achieve excellence in the didac-
> tic modes we shall call craftsmen; those teachers who
> achieve excellence in the evocative modes we shall
> call artists. *Axelrod (1973, pp. 9–10)*

As Joseph Axelrod suggests, excellent college teachers differ in
their styles and intellectual values. Even the evocative teachers he
studied differed considerably: Some emphasized their subject ("I
teach what I know"), some focused on themselves ("I teach what I
am: an educated person"), and others were student-centered ("I
train minds" or "I work with students as persons"). In the obser-

vations and interviews that generated the model and teaching suggestions offered in this book, considerable variation was also observed. Some professors were animated and enthusiastic, others intense and aloof; but all had presence when working before groups of students. Compared to thoroughly competent instructors, the exceptionally skilled are masters of classrooms as either dramatic or interpersonal arenas.

This final chapter returns to the seminal question, "What constitutes masterful college teaching?" A number of styles of outstanding teaching presented in the two-dimensional model in Table 3 could serve as goals for college teachers. The specific techniques for achieving teaching excellence presented in this book are consistent with that model and follow from the view of classrooms as dramatic and interpersonal arenas, discussed in Chapters Two and Four. Of concern here are several related questions: (1) Does outstanding instruction result more from individual talent or from a supportive academic environment? (2) How can college teaching best be evaluated to reflect the full range of teaching effectiveness? (3) How can graduate instructors and junior faculty be taught to teach well? (4) Given the rewards and requirements for survival in academia, why should any instructor attempt to strive for excellence in the classroom, especially in teaching undergraduates?

Talent or Effort?

To what extent are masterful teachers born or made? This question underlies every discussion of college teaching. It is difficult to answer confidently; there is evidence to support either argument.

A student's performance in a course is a function of both individual ability and the motivating effects of classroom climate. College teachers' effectiveness is also a function of both personal and environmental characteristics. Some are more naturally skilled than others, but conditions affect the way any instructor's skill is applied. The key issue is, of course, the *relative* contribution of individual skill and institutional support to the quality of teaching.

When considering individual skills, innate talent for teaching comes to mind first. An instructor's intelligence and academic preparation also are essential to good teaching; dull or shallow college teachers are not likely to be effective. Within a given faculty, the most effective in the classroom will not necessarily be the brightest or most outstanding as researchers, however. Other skills and personal qualities most distinguish the adequate from the outstanding classroom artists or craftsmen.

Foremost among personal characteristics contributing to teaching of the highest quality is an intelligent, clear, and thorough understanding of content. But the ability to present ideas dramatically is also required. Some individuals are initially more comfortable in front of groups and more able to give fresh and involving presentations. As with artistic and athletic talent, speaking talent determines how easily and quickly an individual learns to lecture and his or her ultimate proficiency. An eloquent speaker is more likely to become a master instructor than a fearful, stiff, and halting one. Regardless of degree of talent, however, no person will learn the art of lecturing without practice; and most who have no gift can learn to speak adequately.

Another quality important in teaching is the ability to explain abstract concepts clearly and simply. Natural ability is less evident here, though some individuals are better able than others to explain ideas easily to the uninitiated. Whether this results from high empathy, an ability to focus on fundamental assumptions, or a facility for thinking of creative or concrete examples quickly is uncertain. Almost any instructor can develop sufficient clarity to be a good college teacher by seeking and using student feedback.

Similarly, some instructors are naturally more sensitive and insightful than other people. Reading the meaning of interpersonal communications and empathizing with the varieties of human experience is second nature to some individuals. People of this type who become college teachers are more naturally comfortable with students than are other teachers who are less socially skilled generally, find it difficult to understand or like undergraduates, and remain distant despite attempts to promote positive relationships. Any instructor can increase his or her knowledge of classroom dynamics and learn to create a pleasant and work-conducive atmosphere, however. With effort and support from others, most new college teachers eventually overcome any initial discomfort or difficulty with the interpersonal requirements of teaching.

Talent clearly plays a role in determining how easily instructors succeed in the classroom. But persistent effort can offset low or moderate initial performance and is required for anyone to develop his or her ability to the fullest. It has been highly gratifying to see graduate instructors following the lessons presented here improve their student ratings from well below to well above departmental averages over successive semesters. These favorable results were more often due to effort than to innate talent.

A fair question to ask is, "After applying the lessons in this book, could any college instructor attain the highest levels of teaching proficiency?" Probably not. Considerable experience over several years is surely required to become one of the masterful types described in the first chapter. In addition, some flair for spontaneous oral exposition, creative examples and pedagogical approaches, intuitive empathic sense, and ability to interpret the subtle messages of students is likely to be necessary as well.

There can be no denying that individual qualities contribute to ultimate teaching skill, but whether faculty settle for being merely competent or strive to become outstanding classroom instructors is significantly affected by the environment in which they labor. We now turn to the characteristics of the academic culture that encourage or discourage outstanding teaching.

Supportive Teaching Environments

It must often seem to faculty that, by excessive emphasis on research and committee work, colleges and universities are subtly designed to promote *poor* classroom instruction. "I could be a much better teacher if only I had the time" is a common sentiment. Is the absence of other demands characteristic of a supportive teaching environment?

Not necessarily. Faculty can be overworked, but they rarely are. More commonly, they *feel* overwhelmed by the variety of things expected of them — publishing good work, becoming nation-ally conspicuous, teaching students, serving on committees, supervising individual research projects. This is inherent in the job: College teaching offers tremendous freedom to structure time and channel energy, and it requires commensurate levels of inter-nal motivation, personal organization, and self-discipline. Because classroom teaching is the most structured demand placed on college teachers, it is not surprising that many new faculty have difficulty in deciding how much energy to invest in the immediate demands of teaching and how much to direct toward the more intangible, distant goals of scholarship. Graduate instructors suffer from similar conflicts between their own studies and their teaching responsibilities. It is not work load that most creates discomfort among college instructors but the necessity of deciding how to spend time. The freedom of college teaching cre-ates more anxiety than its demands.

"Not enough time" can become a convenient rationaliza-tion for not becoming a better teacher or scholar. Some new instructors who are anxious about their teaching (especially if it is not initially easy or satisfying) denigrate its importance: "Why should I break my neck for the students? They don't give me tenure!" Others throw themselves into teaching to avoid the pres-sure to conduct important research or bring in a big grant. They can then explain their failure to complete dissertations, produce publications, or obtain tenure as a result of their choice to pursue teaching excellence. Such "champions of good teaching" often fail to notice that some colleagues *can* balance the competing demands on their time and do well at both teaching and scholarship.

Almost every teaching culture gives lip service to the importance of classroom instruction. Information sent to pros-pective students, parents, and alumni or released to the press (especially near budget time for public institutions) commonly stresses the value that the institution places on quality teaching. Speeches by deans and departmental chairpersons may also con-tain ritualistic homage to this basic academic duty. Informal, implicit messages and the actual behavior of other faculty tell a novice more accurately how much classroom teaching is valued in a given institution, however.

What characteristics of an academic community support excellent classroom teaching? First, teaching effectiveness of all faculty in an institution that values teaching is routinely assessed, and such information is used in personnel decisions about junior faculty. At such schools, teaching effectiveness may not be the primary factor in tenure decisions, but it is entered into the equation. Schools that grant tenure to outstanding researchers without polling students about their teaching give a clear message that the quality of teaching is not valued there. Similarly, when poor instructors are continued, reappointed, or promoted, it is clear to all members of the faculty that failure in the classroom will not affect professional survival. Universities and research colleges should not tenure excellent instructors who are unproductive scholars, but they should select and reward those who excel in both areas. A university's national reputation is a function of its graduate programs but its financial survival comes from its undergraduate alumni who remember most the quality of instruction they received.

The faculty's attitudes toward students and classroom performance also reflect a supportive teaching environment or the lack of it. Attitudes are communicated in informal conversation and jokes during faculty meetings as well as in official memoranda. A new instructor hearing colleagues refer to "immature," "lazy," "stupid," "untrustworthy," or "inconsiderate" students risks becoming socialized into a culture that does not value students or have rapport with them. If colleagues never comment on the process of teaching except to complain, an instructor runs the risk of adopting the beliefs that there is nothing important to learn about teaching, that one need not strive to improve as a teacher during one's career, that it does not matter how well one teaches, or that teaching is a necessary evil associated with an academic appointment. Departments or schools in which faculty discuss teaching methods they have tried and speak positively about students are much more likely to motivate new instructors to take the classroom seriously.

Supportive teaching environments also recognize high-level teaching. Teaching awards are a common method of giving public recognition, but they are too scarce to go to everyone who deserves them. Their usefulness is further limited by the tendency for political considerations to affect the choice of award recipients. Teaching skills may be recognized more effectively by letters from departmental heads or deans to instructors receiving particularly high teaching evaluations from students. Inviting those receiving poor ratings to seek consultation about their teaching is also advisable.

Whether or not it actively rewards outstanding instructors, a supportive culture at least does not punish individuals for successful classroom performance. College teachers are vulnerable to the same petty jealousies as anyone else, and in some settings junior faculty fear being too successful or popular with students. Even if a teaching award is not a kiss of death for an untenured faculty member, as the lore at some institutions suggests, college teachers risk a reputation as an unintellectual "prostitute" or "clown" among some colleagues if students seek out their classes or publicly praise their teaching. In supportive environments, however, outstanding teachers are not criticized for their popularity with students or their high teaching ratings.

Teachers who excel in the classroom for personal reasons are the most likely to be happy teaching over a number of years. Those who are motivated primarily by the hope of winning teaching awards are certain to be dissatisfied in the long run. Still, more instructors will choose to apply their energies to developing outstanding classroom skills in a supportive than in a punitive environment.

Evaluating Teaching Effectiveness

"The truth is that one cannot adequately evaluate a teacher until years after one has sat in his classroom. Proper evaluation can perhaps only be made after the spell of the powerful teacher has worn off, in the former student's maturity, when in tranquility he can recollect influence. Influence is subtle, sometimes accidental, often mysterious. It cannot generally be analyzed on a computer form in the last ten minutes of the last class of a course" (Epstein, 1981, p. xiii).

There is both wisdom and fallacy in Epstein's position on

teacher evaluation. College teaching is most often evaluated at the easiest time, at the end of a course when impressions are fresh and the students available. Though the long-term significance of particular instructors and courses in a student's life is, as Epstein says, best evaluated in maturity, his contention that ratings given while "under a teacher's spell" will differ substantially from those made later has not been supported by empirical research (see Chapter One). Epstein also assumes that people can accurately identify which of their adult qualities resulted from various earlier influences. To assess the clarity and interest of a college teacher's presentations and his or her short-term inspirational or motivational impact on students, evaluations should be made at the end of the term.

When to evaluate teaching is relatively clear. *How* to measure effectiveness and how to use the evaluations are more troublesome issues. Student ratings of instruction are the most common method of teacher evaluation and the focus of much of the controversy surrounding it. Social science faculties are generally most sympathetic to rating-scale questionnaires because this evaluation method is common in their discipline. Interestingly, rating scales commonly draw fire both from humanities faculty, who feel that they reduce teachers to numbers, and from natural science faculty, who view the application of measurement theory to people as a bastardization of scientific methodology. What both groups fail to appreciate is that students' ratings must be interpreted in order to be helpful and that such ratings, when properly understood, can be considerably more objective than any alternatives. Common alternatives are unsolicited praise or criticism, interviews with selected students, or one-time visits by other faculty. Each of these is vulnerable to distortion due to sampling. Giving well-scaled rating forms to most, if not all, students is much more objective than these options.

To be sure, teacher evaluation should include methods other than multiple-choice ratings: narrative descriptions by students, observations by faculty colleagues, or interviews with randomly selected students. Such procedures are time-consuming and are unlikely to be used widely, however, so student questionnaires are a good compromise between the ideal and the possible.

Whether questionnaires provide statistical information, written descriptions, or both, college teachers must interpret them wisely in order to improve. This section deals with ways that instructors can use student ratings to improve teaching. Specific objectives for asking students to evaluate teaching are discussed first, followed by reasons why some teachers object to ratings. After this general discussion, specific suggestions on using student ratings are offered. The broader topics of faculty research evaluation and faculty development are not addressed (see Carnegie Foundation for the Advancement of Teaching, 1975; Eble, 1972, 1983; Group for Human Development of Higher Education, 1974).

The primary purpose for gathering student ratings is to improve the instructor's future performance. Specific feedback is like specific comments on student papers: It guides future work. Overall ratings of teacher performance are like student grades: They reinforce instructors for a job well done and allow comparisons with others. As with students, the more specific the feedback, the more likely it is to guide future changes. Overall grades in teaching are most useful for their motivational value for instructors and their record-keeping function for administrators.

Students are also asked to grade instructors because it improves student morale. College teachers evaluate students all semester, and most instructors consider it fair to turn the tables and allow students to return the compliment (or lack of it). Sharing power in this way also leads students to think seriously about the education they are receiving. Teacher evaluation acknowledges students as important participants in the school's instructional program and in their own education.

If student evaluations were employed only for these first two purposes, their use would be much less controversial. When student ratings are made public, however, they are opposed by many instructors. For example, student organizations sometimes administer course and instructor evaluation programs that result in published guides to aid in student course selection. These guides have been shown to influence the courses and instructors that students select (Coleman and McKeachie, 1981). Unsurprisingly, college teachers who receive low ratings uniformly disapprove of such guides, but even some highly rated individuals see this use of student ratings as inappropriate. Similarly, using student ratings to compare departments on teaching effectiveness creates controversy. Even private use of course evaluation data by school officials to make informal comparisons is opposed by some. Other faculty members support comparisons based on student ratings (Gross and Small, 1979), arguing that systematically collected data are preferable to rumor alone.

A variety of other uses and reasons are associated with faculty opposition to student ratings of teaching. Inclusion in faculty evaluation procedures arouses the most opposition. Some professors defend student ratings in personnel decisions, but others believe that the use of student opinion in this way threatens faculty freedom and academic excellence. Other instructors oppose ratings for personal reasons. For those who fear any evaluation, student ratings will certainly arouse fear and anger. Some students do not take criticism well, and neither do some college teachers. Others dislike ratings because they remind them of what they already know but wish to deny: They are ineffective in the classroom. Still other professors dislike sharing power with students, and ratings reduce a little the status difference between them and their students. Some teachers oppose ratings because they assume that their use leads to pandering to student interests or being undemanding in exchange for high ratings. Finally, some college teachers oppose student ratings because they assume that the ratings reflect the way their research or scholarly expertise is evaluated. Though the last two reasons have not been supported by empirical research (see Chapter One), many faculty members cling to these beliefs.

In responding to colleagues who object to student evaluations, one should discern first which use of them is felt to be objectionable. There can be little argument against providing instructors with feedback on teaching. Any college teacher not interested in learning how satisfied his or her students were, especially if specific suggestions for improvement are included, is thin-skinned, even arrogant. Publication of evaluation data and weighing them heavily in personnel decisions, though supported by many, are more understandably opposed.

Using Student Ratings of Instruction

The first and most critical issue is whether a college teacher chooses to participate freely in the use of student ratings. Ideally, no instructor should be pressured to use student evaluations. Those who seek feedback on their own will most value and use it constructively. Unfortunately, the consequences of completely voluntary participation is that the college teachers most in need of improvement are unlikely to take part. Voluntary participation also produces distorted norms (Howard and Bray, 1979) because only the better teachers may be included.

If student evaluation data are seen only by faculty, things are simple. Instructors can be encouraged to gather some kind of evaluation data periodically and allowed some choice of methods (rating forms, narrative descriptions from students, inviting a colleague to observe a class). Packets of forms can even be sent to them at the end of each term and private consultation provided for anyone desiring help in interpreting data and improving. If faculty are involved in the decision to encourage voluntary self-evaluation and this is all that is done, there is likely to be little objection (Thorne, 1980).

Teachers should be educated about the advantages of student evaluations, especially about what can be gained from reviewing their teaching evaluations with an experienced instructor. Feedback from students by itself is not as likely to lead to improvement as feedback interpreted by an experienced guide who can show an instructor how to improve. Providing consultation will make it less likely that ratings will simply be glanced at and tossed in the trash (McKeachie, 1978). Instructors object less to student evaluations if their purpose is self-evaluation, not supervision, but they get more out of them if they discuss them with someone else. Given the importance of voluntary participation by tenured staff, educating them about the advantages of using teacher consultation is the only option (Cohen, 1980; McKeachie and others, 1980).

A great deal is known about the technical process of constructing student rating forms. We also know that evaluation data that are specific as well as global are more likely to be received well and used. Little is known, however, about the way instructors actually use data from student evaluations and how they can be helped to use the information in them to improve.

Use of student ratings *can* be required from graduate instructors and junior faculty. Novices most clearly need the fine tuning that evaluation can supply, and schools are responsible for ensuring that the performance of new faculty is adequate. Graduate instructors and recently hired staff should be involved as much as possible in deciding the kinds of data collected. Not only does letting them propose alternative questions or supplemental data increase their sense of control—just as students' morale is increased when they are asked to make some decisions about class proceedings—it also allows for better, more individualized evaluations. Even when college teachers are required to submit student evaluations as part of supervision or personnel review, it should be stressed that the *primary* purpose of the evaluations is to aid attempts at self-improvement.

A number of instructor evaluation forms have been developed and studied. In spite of much research, no single rating scale has been found to be clearly superior. For information on available forms see Benton's review (1982) or contact the Educational Testing Service, which distributes and scores a well-researched student rating scale.*

When considering which scale to use, an instructor should look for the presence of specific as well as general items. A few items will suffice for general comparisons ("On a 1–7 scale, what was the overall quality of this instructor's classroom effectiveness?") but ten to fifteen items will be needed to provide feedback on specific instructor behaviors ("How clear was the organization of the instructor's lectures?"). To be most useful, a standard scale of pretested items should be used with a number of classes in a given school to obtain stable norms for comparison. If enough data are available, norms can allow instructors to compare their ratings to those received by other members of their department, academic division, and experience cohort (graduate instructors, first year or tenured faculty).

*Information about the Student Instructional Report (S.I.R.) can be obtained from Educational Testing Service, Princeton, N.J. 08541.

The most useful rating forms ask students to complete one or two open-ended questions in addition to rating the instructors quantitatively. For example, students might be asked to indicate what they would tell another student about the course or instructor, how the course or teaching could be improved, and what the best and worst features of the course were. Many college teachers find students' replies to these questions more helpful than summary statistics from multiple-choice items. Each type of rating has advantages, and both should be used.

Administering a centralized program of student evaluations of teaching is a large responsibility. Whoever handles it (Dean's office, computer center, instructional support office, student government) should routinely check to make sure that data are computed accurately. Data should also be processed quickly and faculty given feedback within a few weeks after the end of the courses. The way student evaluations of teaching are conducted and the way the data are used most determine whether such evaluations will promote improved classroom effectiveness, be seen as infringing on academic freedom, or be ignored. Student evaluations of teachers are like teacher evaluations of students: If made with respect and sensitivity, they can benefit both motivation and performance.

Training College Instructors

College instructors are rarely taught to teach (Merenda, 1974). Meeting Ph.D. requirements has been counted as sufficient qualification to teach others, and it is true that many instructors have developed excellent skills on the job, without formal training or consultation, during their first few courses. Many others, however, came to dislike classroom instruction or never developed the competence they might have achieved with appropriate instruction and support. Graduate schools are not likely to select as students those persons with the greatest aptitude and interest in teaching, as some have advocated (Eble, 1976), but more schools now provide explicit teacher training than in the past. The quality of college instruction is most likely to be improved if training is offered to or required of those who are most motivated to acquire the skills: graduate instructors and junior faculty.

A common approach to training college teachers is to offer consultation rather than formal courses. Such programs have been shown to raise the student evaluations that participants received (Carroll, 1977; Erickson and Erickson, 1979). In most programs, however, the supervision of instruction is unsystematic and depends heavily on the preferences of supervisors (Koen and Erickson, 1967).

Workshops and formal courses for college teachers have also been shown to increase teaching effectiveness (Grasha, 1978; Justice, 1983; Lattal, 1978; Levinson-Rose and Menges, 1981). Such courses are usually offered by faculty development or instructional support centers rather than by individual departments, although a seminar for training sociology graduate instructors has been reported (Goldsmid and Wilson, 1980).

Offering interested graduate students a practicum involving a combination of formal coursework and supervised teaching would improve the quality of college teaching more than the traditional practice of turning them loose on undergraduates. Such a program should contain both preparatory experiences and consultation during the initial semesters of teaching. An easily administered preparatory experience is a teaching apprenticeship in which an accomplished instructor teaches the same course that the graduate instructor will later be teaching. This should be an individual tutorial in college teaching rather than the traditional system in which the TA merely helps with grading and minor tasks. The apprentice would be expected to help plan the course, attend all classes, and meet regularly with the professor to discuss such matters as the reason why topics were presented as they were or the way that the instructor handled a particular student. A teaching apprenticeship gives novices close-range experience with the course that they will be teaching in the future.

A seminar in college teaching offered before graduate students begin teaching is a more effective use of faculty time than the apprenticeship model, though it does require considerably more organization. Students can meet regularly to discuss readings on college teaching and practice the skills described in this volume. Small groups are ideal settings for gaining experience in giving short lectures and leading discussion. Going over video-tapes of practice sessions with the instructor in private augments what students can learn in class. Group discussion is useful for helping students examine their attitudes about teaching, learning, and the social functions of grading. A seminar group can also benefit from two or three follow-up meetings after its members have begun to teach.

Regardless of the kind and amount of preparation given, instructors will need regular supportive consultation during their first semester in the classroom. Novices will have questions to ask, emotions to vent, and positive and negative experiences to relate. Receiving regular consultation also helps them take their teaching seriously. A semester's teaching consultation should include at least two classroom observations with short feedback sessions immediately afterward. Encouraging students to videotape a class is also useful once they are well into their course, but it is not an adequate substitute for having the consultant pay a visit. A comprehensive program of teacher training involving preparatory and consultative experiences can go far to prevent ineffective college teaching and to start those with talent and determination on the road to excellence.

Why Strive for Excellence in the Classroom?

Harold McCurdy, one of my graduate professors, asked us at an initial class meeting to write down why we had decided to study psychology. Most students took the bait of this juicy question and filled up several pages with reasons that we thought were likely to impress our professor. One student in the front row, however, was conspicuous in the small amount he wrote—only a single sentence or so—before he put down his pencil. When we had handed in our papers, Professor McCurdy turned immediately to that short paper and read it aloud. All the student had said was, "So I'll have something to teach."

Few college teachers choose their academic disciplines only to have something to teach. Sooner or later, every instructor is likely to question whether it is worth the time and energy required to be a really effective classroom teacher. It is appropriate to conclude this book by addressing that question: Why should a college teacher strive to teach well?

First there are the negative reasons, those that do not provide sufficient justification. Instructors should *not* attempt to become outstanding classroom teachers as a way of making tenure. Moving company records contain the names of numerous assistant professors who avoided their research and put their energies into teaching, hoping success in the classroom would win the day. Assistant professors at most schools must become minimally competent teachers in order to be promoted, but outstanding teaching will not offset a poor publication record. A better way to attain tenure would be to avoid being a poor teacher and do all you can to excel in scholarship.

Once a professor has tenure, should he or she try to become a master of teaching in order to gain recognition from colleagues? Probably not; the small amount of recognition offered is not in proportion to the effort required. Administrative service and scholarly productivity are more the coin of the academic realm than is teaching excellence.

Why, then, should college teachers bother? In part, college teachers should seek excellence in the classroom in order to attract the best students to their field. Students' choice of major and career can be influenced greatly by an early encounter with an outstanding professor. Exciting and intellectually imaginative introductory courses can help to attract the top talent to that department. Introductory courses taught by graduate students or uninspired faculty are less likely to draw in the best students for subsequent coursework.

In his memoir of the teaching of Frederick Teggart, Robert Nisbet (1981) notes, "At Berkeley in the early 1930s . . . undergraduate teaching was taken seriously. No matter how illustrious one might be as scholar or scientist, the reputation for giving a good course, above all for being a stimulating lecturer, meant a great deal to the faculty and therefore to the students. . . . Even, and especially, the introductory courses were taught by mature, often distinguished, scholars and scientists" (p. 69). Students were relatively scarce during the Depression, and introductory courses were the battleground over which departments competed for the best.

There is always a scarcity of exceptionally talented students, and faculty members should recognize that superior classroom instruction is one way of investing in the future of their disciplines. With undergraduate enrollments shrinking because of economic and population downturns, instructors should appreciate that classroom virtuosity is one way of maintaining adequate enrollments as well.

Instructors should also aim for excellent classroom teaching because it is more rewarding to try to do anything well than to accept mediocrity. College teachers generally have high needs to achieve, to excel at whatever they undertake; otherwise they would not have made it through so much schooling. The classroom is a legitimate arena for satisfying those needs, though the prestige and monetary rewards are insubstantial compared to those of publishing, consulting, or administration. Faculty members should include undergraduate teaching excellence among the outlets they use to satisfy their needs for achievement. If instructors do not try to do their best at teaching, they are likely to find it drudgery.

The best reason for taking classroom teaching seriously, however, is that the kinds of college teaching held up as models in this book are highly rewarding personally. Developing one's abilities to captivate a student audience for an hour or more, to stimulate them intellectually and move them emotionally, to instill in them a love for one's subject and a desire to learn more about it, to motivate them to work on their own, to watch them wrestle with philosophical and methodological dilemmas during discussion, and to see them mature in their wisdom, is highly satisfying.

Learning to understand students well, to relate effectively to them, and to help them grow into mature and responsible adults is equally satisfying. It is more meaningful (and more fun) to teach persons we genuinely respect and care for than those we barely notice or see as hostile and lazy. Some teachers more easily view their students positively than others, but any teacher can cultivate a positive attitude and thus open the door to a number of personal satisfactions.

In this chapter I have tried to weigh the relative contributions of individual and environmental factors leading to outstanding college teaching. Teaching among colleagues who value excellence in the classroom is surely more rewarding than teaching in a school where no one cares about classroom performance or criticises those sought after by students. However, environment alone cannot inspire college teachers to expend the effort required to become exceptional classroom instructors. My interviews convinced me that *ultimately* every great teacher decided to work at mastering this art for the very personal reason that being a virtuoso in the classroom is so inherently rewarding.

References

Abbott, R. D., and Perkins, D. "Development and Construct Validation of a Set of Student Rating-of-Instruction Items." *Educational and Psychological Measurement,* 1978, *38,* 1069–1075.

Abrami, P. C., and others. "Do Teacher Standards for Assigning Grades Affect Student Evaluations of Instructors?" *Journal of Educational Psychology,* 1980, *72,* 107–118.

Alcock, J. *Animal Behavior: An Evolutionary Approach.* (2nd ed.) Sunderland, Mass.: Sinauer Associates, 1979.

Aleamoni, L. M. "Development and Factorial Validation of the Arizona Course/Instructor Evaluation Questionnaire." *Educational and Psychological Measurement,* 1978, *38,* 1063–1067.

Altman, I., and Taylor, D. A. *Social Penetration: The Development of Interpersonal Relationships.* New York: Holt Rinehart and Winston, 1973.

Axelrod, J. *The University Teacher as Artist.* San Francisco: Jossey-Bass, 1973.

Bales, R. F. *Interaction Process Analysis: A Method for the Study of Small Groups.* Reading, Mass.: Addison-Wesley, 1950.

Bales, R. F., and Slater, P. E. "Role Differentiation in Small Decision-Making Groups." In T. Parsons and others (Eds.), *Family, Socialization and Interaction Process.* Glencoe, Ill.: Free Press, 1955.

Ballard, M., Rearden, J., and Nelson, L. "Student and Peer Rating of Faculty." *Teaching of Psychology,* 1976, *3,* 88–90.

Bandler, R., and Grinder, J. *The Structure of Magic I: A Book About*

Language and Therapy. Palo Alto, Calif.: Science & Behavior Books, 1975.

Barnes-McConnell, P. W. "Leading Discussions." In O. Milton and others, *On College Teaching: A Guide to Contemporary Practices.* San Francisco: Jossey-Bass, 1978.

Barry, R. "Clarifying Objectives." In O. Milton and others, *On College Teaching: A Guide to Contemporary Practices.* San Francisco: Jossey-Bass, 1978.

Benton, S. E. *Rating College Teaching: Criterion Validity Studies of Student Evaluation-of-Instruction Instruments.* AAHE/ERIC/Higher Education Research Report No. 1, 1982.

Bloom, B. S. (Ed.). *Taxonomy of Educational Objectives: Cognitive Domain.* New York: Longmans, Green, 1956.

Bloom, B. S., Madaus, G. F., and Hastings, J. T. *Evaluation to Improve Learning.* New York: McGraw-Hill, 1981.

Bowman, J. S. "Lecture-Discussion Format Revisited." *Improving College and University Teaching,* 1979, *27,* 25–27.

Braskamp, L. A., Caulley, D., and Costin, F. "Student Ratings and Instructor Self-Ratings and Their Relationship to Student Achievement." *American Educational Research Journal,* 1979, *16,* 295–306.

Braskamp, L. A., Ory, J. C., and Pieper, D. M. "Student Written Comments: Dimensions of Instructional Quality." *Journal of Educational Psychology,* 1981, *73,* 65–70.

Bronowski, J. *The Ascent of Man.* Boston: Little, Brown, 1974.

Brownfield, C. *Humanizing College Learning: A Taste of Hemlock.* New York: Exposition Press, 1973.

Bugelski, B. R. *The Psychology of Learning Applied to Teaching.* Indianapolis: Bobbs-Merrill, 1964.

Cahn, S. M. "The Uses and Abuses of Grades and Examinations." In S. M. Cahn (Ed.), *Scholars Who Teach: The Art of College Teaching.* Chicago: Nelson-Hall, 1978.

Carnegie Foundation for the Advancement of Teaching. *More Than Survival: Prospects for Higher Education in a Period of Uncertainty.* San Francisco: Jossey-Bass, 1975.

Carroll, J. G. "Assessing the Effectiveness of a Training Program for the University Teaching Assistant." *Teaching of Psychology,* 1977, *4,* 135–138.

Cartwright, D., and Zander, A. *Group Dynamics: Research and Theory.* (2nd ed.) New York: Harper & Row, 1960.

Cermak, L. S. *How to Improve Your Memory.* New York: Norton, 1976.

Chandler, T. A. "The Questionable Status of Student Evaluations of Teaching." *Teaching of Psychology,* 1978, *5,* 150–152.

Cohen, P. A. "Effectiveness of Student-Rating Feedback for Improving College Instruction: A Meta-Analysis of Findings." *Research in Higher Education,* 1980, *13,* 321–341.

Cohen, P. A. "Student Ratings of Instruction and Student Achievement: A Meta-Analysis of Multisection Validity Studies." *Review of Educational Research,* 1981, *51,* 281–309.

Coleman, J., and McKeachie, W. J. "Effects of Instructor/Course Evaluations on Student Course Selection." *Journal of Educational Psychology,* 1981, *73,* 224–226.

Costin, F. "Do Student Ratings of College Teachers Predict Student Achievement?" *Teaching of Psychology,* 1978, *5,* 86–88.

Cronbach, L. J. *Essentials of Psychological Testing.* (3rd ed.) New York: Harper & Row, 1970.

Crouse, R., and Jacobson, C. "Testing in Mathematics—What Are We Really Measuring? *Mathematics Teacher,* 1975, *68,* 564–570.

Cytrynbaum, S., and Mann, R. D. "Community as Campus: Project Outreach." In P. Runkel, R. Harrison, and M. Runkel (Eds.), *The Changing College Classroom.* San Francisco: Jossey-Bass, 1969.

Eble, K. E. *Professors as Teachers.* San Francisco: Jossey-Bass, 1972.

Eble, K. E. *The Craft of Teaching: A Guide to Mastering the Professor's Art.* San Francisco: Jossey-Bass, 1976.

Eble, K. E. *The Aims of College Teaching.* San Francisco: Jossey-Bass, 1983.

Epstein, J. *Masters: Portraits of Great Teachers.* New York: Basic Books, 1981.

Erickson, G. R., and Erickson, B. L. "Improving College Teaching: An Evaluation of a Teaching Consultation Procedure." *Journal of Higher Education,* 1979, *50,* 670–683.

Feldman, K. A. "The Superior College Teacher from the Students' View." *Research in Higher Education,* 1976, *5,* 243–288.

Firth, M. "Impact of Work Experience on the Validity of Student Evaluations of Teaching Effectiveness." *Journal of Educational Psychology,* 1979, *71,* 726–730.

Fisher, H. "Experimental Methods." In J. Radford and D. Rose (Eds.), *The Teaching of Psychology: Method, Content, and Context.* New York: Wiley, 1980.

Freedman, R. D., Stumpf, S. A., and Aquano, J. C. "Validity of the Course-Faculty Instrument (CFI): Intrinsic and Extrinsic Variables." *Educational and Psychological Measurement,* 1979, *39,* 153–158.

Frey, P. W. "A Two-Dimensional Analysis of Student Ratings of Instruction." *Research in Higher Education,* 1978, *9,* 69–91.

Gaynor, J., and Millham, J. "Student Performance and Evaluation Under Variant Teaching and Testing Methods in a Large College Course." *Journal of Educational Psychology,* 1976, *68,* 312–317.

Gibbard, G., Hartman, J., and Mann, R. (Eds.) *Analysis of Groups: Contributions to Theory, Research, and Practice.* San Francisco: Jossey-Bass, 1973.

Gmelch, W. H., and Glasman, N. S. "Student Perceptions of Their Qualifications to Evaluate College Teaching." *College Student Journal,* 1978, *12,* 398–411.

Goldsmid, C. A., and Wilson, E. K. *Passing on Sociology: The Teaching of a Discipline.* Belmont, Calif.: Wadsworth, 1980.

Grasha, A. F. "The Teaching of Teaching: A Seminar on College Teaching." *Teaching of Psychology,* 1978, *5,* 21–23.

Gronlund, N. E. *Constructing Achievement Tests.* (3rd ed.) Englewood Cliffs, N.J.: Prentice-Hall, 1982.

Gross, R. B., and Small, A. C. "A Survey of Faculty Opinions About Student Evaluations of Instructors." *Teaching of Psychology,* 1979, *6,* 216–219.

Group for Human Development in Higher Education. *Faculty Development in a Time of Retrenchment.* New Rochelle, N.Y.: Change Magazine Press, 1974.

Guilford, J. P. *Intelligence, Creativity, and Their Educational Implications.* San Diego, Calif.: R. R. Knapp, 1968.

Harris, R. J. "The Teacher as Actor." *Teaching of Psychology,* 1977, *4,* 185–187.

Harrison, R. "Classroom Innovation: A Design Primer." In P. Runkel, R. Harrison, and M. Runkel (Eds.), *The Changing College Classroom.* San Francisco: Jossey-Bass, 1969.

Hettich, P. "The Journal: An Autobiographical Approach to Learning." *Teaching of Psychology,* 1976, *3,* 60–63.

Highet, G. *The Art of Teaching.* New York: Knopf, 1950.

Hoffman, C. D. "Students Learn More from Better Teachers." *Teaching of Psychology,* 1979, *6,* 186.

Hoffman, R. G. "Variables Affecting University Student Ratings of Instructor Behavior." *American Educational Research Journal,* 1978, *15,* 287–299.

Howard, G. S., and Bray, J. H. "Use of Norm Groups to Adjust Student Ratings of Instruction: A Warning." *Journal of Educational Psychology,* 1979, *71,* 58–73.

Howard, G. S., and Maxwell, S. E. "Correlation Between Student Satisfaction and Grades: A Case of Mistaken Causation." *Journal of Educational Psychology,* 1980, *72,* 810–820.

Howe, M. J. A. "Conventional Methods." In J. Radford and D. Rose (Eds.), *The Teaching of Psychology: Method, Content, and Context.* New York: Wiley, 1980.

Jones, E. E., and others. *Attribution: Perceiving the Causes of Behavior.* Morristown, N.J.: General Learning Press, 1972.

Justice, E. "Evidence for the Effectiveness of Graduate Teacher Training." Paper presented at the 28th annual meeting of the Southeastern Psychological Association, Atlanta, 1983.

Kaplan, R. M. "Reflections on the Dr. Fox Paradigm." *Journal of Medical Education,* 1974, *49,* 310–312.

Keaveny, T. J., and McGann, A. F. "Behavioral Dimensions Associated with Students' Global Ratings of College Professors." *Research in Higher Education,* 1978, *9,* 333–345.

Keller, F. S. "Goodbye, Teacher..." *Journal of Applied Behavior Analysis,* 1968, *1,* 79–89.

Kinichi, A. J., and Schriesheim, C. A. "Teachers as Leaders: A Moderator Variable Approach." *Journal of Educational Psychology,* 1978, *70,* 928–935.

Koen, F. M., and Erickson, S. C. *An Analysis of the Specific Features Which Characterize the More Successful Programs for the Recruitment and Training of College Teachers.* Ann Arbor: Center for

Research on Learning and Teaching, University of Michigan, 1967.

Kolstoe, O. P. *College Professoring: Or, Through Academia with Gun and Camera.* Carbondale: Southern Illinois University Press, 1975.

Korth, B. "Relationship of Extraneous Variables to Student Ratings of Instructors." *Journal of Educational Measurement,* 1979, *16,* 27–37.

Kroman, N. "Student Evaluation of Professors: Critique and Proposal." *Journal of Educational Thought,* 1978, *12,* 205–210.

Kulik, J. A., Kulik, C. C., and Cohen, P. A. "A Meta-Analysis of Outcome Studies of Keller's Personalized System of Instruction." *American Psychologist,* 1979, *34,* 307–318.

Kyle, B. "In Defense of the Lecture." *Improving College and University Teaching,* 1972, *20,* 325.

Lahr, J. *Astonish Me: Adventures in Contemporary Theater.* New York: Viking Press, 1973.

Lattal, K. A. "Workshop for New Graduate Student Teachers of Undergraduate Psychology Courses." *Teaching of Psychology,* 1978, *5,* 208–209.

Levinson-Rose, J., and Menges, R. "Improving College Teaching: A Critical Review of Research." *Review of Educational Research,* 1981, *51,* 403–434.

Linklater, K. *Freeing the Natural Voice.* New York: Drama Book Specialists, 1976.

McConnell, J. V. "Confessions of a Textbook Writer." *American Psychologist,* 1978, *33,* 159–169.

Machlin, E. *Speech for the Stage.* New York: Theater Arts Books, 1966.

Machlup, F. "Poor Learning from Good Teachers." *Academe: Bulletin of the AAUP,* 1979, *65,* 376–380.

McKeachie, W. J. *Teaching Tips: A Guidebook for the Beginning College Teacher.* (7th ed.) Lexington, Mass.: Heath, 1978.

McKeachie W. J., and others. "Using Student Ratings and Consultation to Improve Instruction." *British Journal of Educational Psychology,* 1980, *50,* 168–174.

Mann, R. D., and others. *The College Classroom: Conflict, Change, and Learning.* New York: Wiley, 1970.

Mannan, G., and Traicoff, E. M. "Evaluation of an Ideal University Teacher." *Improving College and University Teaching,* 1976, *24,* 98–101.

Marg, E. "How to Sacrifice Academic Quality." *Improving College and University Teaching,* 1979, *27,* 54–56.

Marques, T. E., Lane, D. M., and Dorfman, P. W. "Toward the Development of a System for Instructional Evaluation: Is There Consensus Regarding What Constitutes Effective Teaching?" *Journal of Educational Psychology,* 1979, *71,* 840–849.

Marsh, H. W. "The Influence of Student, Course, and Instructor Characteristics in Evaluations of University Teaching." *American Educational Research Journal,* 1980, *17,* 219–237.

Marsh, H. W., and Overall, J. U. "Long-Term Stability of Students' Evaluations: A Note on Feldman's 'Consistency and Variability Among College Students in Rating Their Teachers and Courses.'" *Research in Higher Education,* 1979, *10,* 139–147.

Marsh, H. W., and Overall, J. U. "The Relative Influence of Course Level, Course Type, and Instructor on Students' Evaluations of College Teaching." *American Educational Research Journal,* 1981, *18,* 103–112.

Marsh, H. W., Overall, J. U., and Kesler, S. P. "Validity of Student Evaluations of Instructional Effectiveness: A Comparison of Faculty Self-Evaluations and Evaluations by Their Students." *Journal of Educational Psychology,* 1979, *71,* 149–160.

Martin, B. "Parent-Child Relations." In F. D. Horowitz (Ed.), *Review of Child Development Research.* Vol. 4. Chicago: University of Chicago Press, 1975.

Meier, R. S., and Feldhusen, J. F. "Another Look at Dr. Fox: Effect of Stated Purpose for Evaluation, Lecturer Expressiveness, and Density of Lecture Content on Student Ratings." *Journal of Educational Psychology,* 1979, *71,* 339–345.

Meredith, G. M. "Impact of Lecture Size on Student-Based Ratings of Instruction." *Psychological Reports,* 1980, *46,* 21–22.

Merenda, P. F. "Current Status of Graduate Education in Psychology." *American Psychologist,* 1974, *29,* 627–631.

Milton, O. "Classroom Testing." In O. Milton and others, *On College Teaching: A Guide to Contemporary Practices.* San Francisco: Jossey-Bass, 1978.

Moody, R. "Student Achievement and Student Evaluations of Teaching in Spanish." *Modern Language Journal*, 1976, *60*, 454–463.

Naftulin, D. H., Ware, J. E., Jr., and Donnelly, F. A. "The Dr. Fox Lecture: A Paradigm of Educational Seduction." *Journal of Medical Education*, 1973, *48*, 630–635.

Nisbet, R. "Teggart of Berkeley." In J. Epstein (Ed.), *Masters: Portraits of Great Teachers*. New York: Basic Books, 1981.

Oettinger, A. G. *Run, Computer, Run: The Mythology of Educational Innovation*. Cambridge, Mass.: Harvard University Press, 1969.

Overall, J. U., and Marsh, H. W. "Students' Evaluations of Instruction: A Longitudinal Study of Their Stability." *Journal of Educational Psychology*, 1980, *72*, 321–325.

Palmer, J., Carliner, G., and Romer, T. "Leniency, Learning, and Evaluations." *Journal of Educational Psychology*, 1978, *70*, 855–863.

Perry, R. P., Abrami, P. C., and Leventhal, L. "Educational Seduction: The Effect of Instructor Expressiveness and Lecture Content on Student Ratings of Achievement." *Journal of Educational Psychology*, 1979, *71*, 107–116.

Peterson, C., and Cooper, S. "Teacher Evaluation by Graded and Ungraded Students." *Journal of Educational Psychology*, 1980, *72*, 682–685.

Raskin, B. L., and Plante, P. R. "The Student Devaluation of Teachers." *Academe*, 1979, *65*, 381–383.

Reardon, M., and Waters, L. K. "Leniency and Halo in Student Ratings of College Instructors: A Comparison of Three Ratings Procedures with Implications for Scale Validity." *Educational and Psychological Measurement*, 1979, *39*, 159–162.

Rockart, J. F., and Morton, M. S. S. *Computers and the Learning Process in Higher Education*. New York: McGraw-Hill, 1975.

Runkel, P. J. "The Campus as Laboratory." In P. Runkel, R. Harrison, and M. Runkel (Eds.), *The Changing College Classroom*. San Francisco: Jossey-Bass, 1969.

Ryan, J., and others. "Student Evaluation: The Faculty Responds." *Research in Higher Education*, 1980, *12*, 317–333.

Sale, K. *Human Scale*. New York: Coward, McCann & Geoghegan, 1980.

Satterfield, J. "Lecturing." In O. Milton and others, *On College Teaching: A Guide to Contemporary Practices.* San Francisco: Jossey-Bass, 1978.

Scarr, S. *Race, Social Class, and Individual Differences in I.Q.* Hillsdale, N.J.: Lawrence Erlbaum Associates, 1981.

Shaffer, J. B., and Galinsky, M. D. *Models of Group Therapy and Sensitivity Training.* Englewood Cliffs, N.J.: Prentice-Hall, 1974.

Sherman, J. G., Ruskin, R. S., and Semb, G. B. (Eds.) *The Personalized System of Instruction: 48 Seminal Papers.* Lawrence, Kans.: TRI Publications, 1983.

Stevens, L. A. *The Ill-Spoken Word: The Decline of Speech in America.* New York: McGraw-Hill, 1966.

Strupp, H. H. "Success and Failure in Time-Limited Psychotherapy: With Special Reference to the Performance of a Lay Counselor." *Archives of General Psychiatry,* 1980, *37,* 831–841.

Tennyson, R. D., Boutwell, R. C., and Frey, S. "Student Preferences for Faculty Teaching Styles." *Improving College and University Teaching,* 1978, *26,* 194–197.

Thompson, R. "Legitimate Lecturing." *Improving College and University Teaching,* 1974, *22,* 163–164.

Thorne, G. L. "Student Ratings of Instructors: From Scores to Administrative Decisions." *Journal of Higher Education,* 1980, *51,* 207–214.

Uranowitz, S. W., and Doyle, K. O. "Being Liked and Teaching: The Effects and Bases of Personal Likability in College Instruction." *Research in Higher Education,* 1978, *9,* 15–41.

Wales, C. E., and Stager, R. A. *Guided Design, Part I.* Morgantown: West Virginia University Press, 1976.

Watzlawick, P., Beavin, J. H., and Jackson, D. D. *Pragmatics of Human Communication: A Study of Interactional Patterns, Pathologies, and Paradoxes.* New York: Norton, 1967.

White, R. W. *Ego and Reality in Psychoanalytic Theory: A Proposal Regarding Independent Ego Energies.* New York: International Universities Press, 1963.

Williams, R. G., and Ware, J. E. "An Extended Visit with Dr. Fox: Validity of Student Satisfaction with Instruction Ratings After Repeated Exposures to a Lecturer." *American Educational Research Journal,* 1977, *14,* 449–457.

Williamson, D. A., Sewell, W. R., and McCoy, J. F. "Various Combinations of Traditional Instruction and Personalized Instruction." *Journal of Experimental Education,* 1976, *45* (2), 19–22.

Index

239

and examinations, 190–204; and grading, 204–206; myths about, 187–189; nevers for, 208–209; purposes of, 186–187; quickness of, 180, 193; social functions of, 189–190; of writing assignments, 176–180

Examinations: administering, 192–193; analysis of strategies for, 190–195; blind grading of, 193; comments on, 193–194; critiques and revisions of, 195; essay, 201–203; evaluating, 193–194; grading distinct from, 186; guidelines on, 198, 202–203; and motivation, 187; multiple-choice, 196–200; oral, 203–204; preparing for, 190–192; returning, 194–195; selecting types of, 204; short-answer or identification, 200–201; true-false and matching, 196; types of, 195–204

Eye contact, in engaging students, 89–90

F

Feldhusen, J. F., 12, 235
Feldman, K. A., 9, 231
Firth, M., 8, 232
Fisher, H., 181, 232
Flip-charts, for lectures, 112
Freedman, R. D., 7, 232
Frey, P. W., 7, 232
Frey, S., 9, 237

G

Galinsky, D., xiii
Galinsky, M. D., 15, 40, 237
Gauss, C., 4
Gaynor, J., 190, 232
Georgetown University, and Personalized System of Instruction, 160
Gesture and movement, in speaking skills, 84–86
Gibbard, G., 35, 232
Glasman, N. S., 6, 232
Gmelch, W. H., 6, 232
Goldsmid, C. A., 223, 232
Grading: blind, 177, 193; and evalu-

ation, 204–206; examination distinct from, 186; guidelines for, 205–206

Grasha, A. F., 223, 232
Grinder, J., 52, 229–230
Gronlund, N. E., 195, 232
Gross, R. B., 219, 232
Group for Human Development in Higher Education, 218, 232
Guilford, J. P., 3, 232

H

Handouts, for lectures, 110–111
Harris, R. J., 86, 232
Harrison, R., 105, 233
Hartman, J., 35, 232
Harvard University, master teachers at, 4
Hastings, J. T., 10, 230
Hettich, P., 171, 233
Highet, G., 11, 71, 96, 103, 106, 107, 108, 109, 146, 196, 233
Hoffman, C. D., 8, 233
Hoffman, R. G., 7, 233
Hopkins, M., xii
Howard, G. S., 7, 188, 220, 233
Howe, M. J. A., 96, 110, 111, 233

I

Inflection, and speaking skills, 76
Intellectual excitement: in lectures, 116–118; in teaching model, 10–12, 13–14
Interpersonal rapport: analysis of emotional impact on, 23–44; attitudes influencing, 24–27; background on, 23–24; changes predictable in, 40–44; as controversial, 16; and discussions, 124–125; interactive effect in, 25; in teaching model, 12, 15–19
Interpersonal skills: analysis of developing, 45–71; background on, 45–46; and ethics, 68–70; and feedback from students, 50–52; and indirect leadership, 52–54; in individual meetings with students, 65–68; and individual treatment for students,

DATE DUE

DEMCO 38-297